The Pope and the Economist

The Pope and the Economist

Human Action in the Thought of John Paul II and Ludwig von Mises

Jacek Gniadek, SVD

Acton Institute

The Pope and the Economist: Human Action in the Thought of John Paul II and Ludwig von Mises

The present volume is a translated and revised version of a book previously published in Poland: *Dwaj ludzie z Galicji. Koncepcja osoby ludzkiej według Ludwiga von Misesa i Karola Wojtyły* (Warsaw: Fijorr, 2011). Translated by Jan Kłos and published with permission.

ISBN 979-8-218-21324-4 (paperback)
ISBN 978-1-880-59573-2 (ebook)

ACTONINSTITUTE

98 E. Fulton
Grand Rapids, Michigan 49503
616.454.3080
www.acton.org

Interior composition by Judy Schafer
Cover design by Cantelon Design

Printed in the United States of America

To my parents, who instilled in me respect for private property in the socialist times of the Polish People's Republic.

* * *

"Human affairs depend in each generation on the free decisions of those concerned. If this freedom were to be taken away, as a result of certain conditions or structures, then ultimately this world would not be good, since a world without freedom can by no means be a good world."

—Pope Benedict XVI, *Spe Salvi*, 2007

Contents

Preface

Why would a theologian conduct a theological and moral analysis of human action as described by Ludwig von Mises, a representative of the Austrian school of economics? What can an economist and agnostic tell the moral theologian about man?

The Church teaches that economics is the science of human action and therefore it must have the right anthropological and ethical foundations. The purpose of this work is to show that the description of human action in the economic sphere presented by Mises corresponds with the Christian concept of the person we find in modern Catholic social teaching. Such an analysis is possible because, in contrast to mainstream economics, Mises is interested in the real man in action and not in the fictitious *homo economicus.*

In his economic treatise, *Human Action,* Mises developed his own anthropological concept of man. A precondition for human activity is the desire to replace the less satisfactory state of affairs with a more satisfying one. Mises' individual is guided by his own scale of values and builds it on the basis of the goals he freely chooses. Mises also recognizes that the market is only a part of reality and human activity. All this was an encouragement for me, as a theologian and missionary, to investigate whether the concept of man in the Austrian economist's writings coincides with that of the Church. Theology and Mises speak of the man in action. Moral theology speaks of the person and his deeds, and Mises talks about the individual and her activities in the economic sphere. They use different words, but might the content behind them—defining the human person as a free, rational, and transcendent being—be the same?

I was inspired by the work and publications of the Acton Institute, in particular the idea of economic personalism, which invites us to think about economic life according to the principles of ethical personalism and free-market economics. I understood that, without reference to the laws governing human action in economics, Christian personalism would be a pure abstraction. Economic personalism proposes to synthesize personalism with an appreciation of the market economy as developed by the Austrian school of economics. This idea prompted me to use Mises' praxeology to comprehend and describe human action in the economic sphere. I believe that Catholic social teaching, which is part of moral theology, needs a comprehensive conceptual basis, without which a deeper theological and moral analysis of human action in the market would be difficult and incomplete.

The free market is not in opposition to the Catholic social teaching, and what is more, it is completely compatible with it in many matters. This was demonstrated by Thomas Woods, an American historian who studied the most important documents and encyclicals of the Catholic Church on the social issues, beginning with St. Augustine, going to the *Summa Theologiae* of St. Thomas Aquinas, and ending with the most important encyclicals, including, among others, *Rerum Novarum* (1891) of Pope Leo XIII, *Quadragesimo Anno* (1931) of Pius XI, and *Centesimus Annus* (1991) of John Paul II.[1] Woods is not a moral theologian and therefore he is more interested in the free-market mechanisms, which he analyzes from the perspective of the Austrian school of economics. As a moral theologian, I go much further and draw on the encyclical *Veritatis Splendor* (1993) of John Paul II, because my goal is to analyze the essence of the moral act from the free-market perspective. As George Weigel aptly noted, the personalism of John Paul II is deeply rooted in the philosophical assumptions of Fr. Karol Wojtyła—for whom philosophy was never an end in itself.[2] For this reason, I refer to Wojtyła's philosophical work, *The Acting Person*, and

[1] Thomas E. Woods, Jr., *The Church and the Market: A Catholic Defense of the Free Economy* (Lanham, MD: Lexington, 2005).

[2] George Weigel, *Witness to Hope: The Biography of Pope John Paul II* (New York: Harper, 1999), 177.

I perceive that the convergence of the title with Mises' economic treatise *Human Action* is not accidental. The professor of ethics, who later became pope, attempted to combine Aristotelian-Thomistic realism with modern subjectivism. He developed his own original version of personalism on the basis of Thomism and phenomenology, where the acting person is able to know the reality and value of his action as a free and rational entity. In my opinion, this way of analyzing human action perfectly complements the concept of the person, operating in the economic sphere, who bases his action on subjective choices described by the Austrian economist.

My work focuses entirely on the personalistic interpretation of human activity in the socioeconomic dimension presented by Mises. It is important to study it in the context of the depersonalization of human labor currently developing and its economic effects in a world dominated by state intervention. Human action should be based on the fundamental truth of Christian personalism, showing the inalienable dignity of every human being who, in the form of the personalist norm, demands the affirmation of every other human person for his or her own sake. To serve this purpose, I carry out an in-depth analysis of human action based on a subjective theory of values, which is the original starting point to agree on two important dimensions of human life: the moral sphere and the economic one. Bearing in mind the details of divine revelation and the doctrine of the Church—especially the social teaching of Pope John Paul II—I indicate the possibilities for practically applying this theory in the lives of Christians, especially in social policy.

I study economic goods, human work and its subjective dimension, and the value of money and its socio-moral significance in the axiological context. The originality of my work lies in the fact that I analyze the concept of the human person according to Mises in the context of the moral experience of human existence taken holistically; that is, in the supernatural dimension. On the one hand, the subject of theological analysis is man with the whole truth of his existence, and on the other hand, God, whom he not only learns about conceptually but also by confronting his will, which is expressed in the laws of economics and moral life. This approach to the human person, included in the vortex of socioeconomic activity, allows me to understand his existential situation in the context of his relationship with God, the creator of the world and society. Consequently, this leads me to try to recognize the most valid and effective concepts of economics, which are best able to respect the rights of the person and interpersonal relationships and to satisfy the material needs of individuals and human communities.

Mises claims that man in action is guided by his own scale of values. The goals of human action are subjective and thus every human being has to designate them. I want to show that this has nothing to do with moral relativism and autonomous morality, because every man must himself discover God as the goal of his life. Economic liberalism is not only consistent with Catholic social teaching, but it is a much more ethical proposition than any kind of "third way" project.

Capitalism is often accused of concentrating on the production of goods, which can become an end in itself. Analyzing Mises' ideas, I show that the production of goods is a byproduct of human freedom. Man needs material things to achieve his goals. Following the arguments of the Austrian economist, I defend his position that the free market surpasses other economic systems not only in terms of production and distribution of material goods but above all because it gives the acting person satisfaction in achieving goals that the free person puts before himself—goals that are not merely earthly.

Mises was an agnostic, but he claims that human goals can be metaphysical and in no way does this weaken the action of the man who performs them in the economic sphere of the earthly dimension. Many opponents of Mises say that the man depicted in *Human Action* can create a subjective truth and then close himself in his immanent world. I try to show something opposite: that in his freedom man is capable of accepting objective truth that is not a figment of his imagination, getting beyond his world, and striving for the transcendent Truth. That is what the Christian does. He chooses Christ who is the Truth (John 14:6). Following Mises' line of reasoning, I am in favor of the free economy, a system in which every person is allowed to act and choose freely.

—Jacek Gniadek, SVD

1

The Rationality of Human Activity and Market Economics

Contrary to the mainstream in economics, which dominates most university economics departments today, Mises does not speculate about economics but studies and discovers how a real person acts in a world limited by scarcity. Our analysis opens with Mises' concept of person in the economic and social sphere from the point of view of the contemporary social teaching of the Church and Christian personalism. His method differs from the method used in the natural sciences, for man is not only an object but also the subject of the economic sciences. Mises views man as *homo agens*,[1] and it is from this perspective that we shall try to depict all man's essential properties.

Next we will approach the nature of human labor from the economic point of view. The principle of methodological individualism will allow us to determine the proper action of individuals who compose a community. Mises shows that all people, irrespective of racial origin, are subject to the same natural laws and dependencies of the external world. The logical mode of thinking is the basis of communication and gives us hope that we may find the most appropriate means to attain common social ends.

---

[1] L. von Mises, *Human Action: A Treaties on Economics* (Chicago: Contemporary Books, 1966), 14.

The chapter will close with an explanation of how division of labor contributes to the construction of society. We shall discuss the essence of society established on the grounds of individuals' actions, the way in which they maximize their profits in action, and why it is profitable for the development of society. We conclude with criticism of socialism and state interventionism, which cannot be harmonized with free entrepreneurship and, according to the author of *Human Action,* contradict rational human action.

THE PURPOSEFULNESS OF HUMAN ACTION

Mises claims that every human action is purposeful. Economics for him is part of a much broader science that deals with the general theory of any purposeful human action. According to Mises' fellow Austrian economist Friedrich A. von Hayek, the term "praxeological sciences," clearly defined and used by Mises, is best fitted to determine the general theory of human action.

Praxeology

Mises used praxeology to construct a general theory of economic action as opposed to the economic doctrines that prevailed in the Europe of his day. These theories rejected the idea of economic science based on the explanation of market phenomena in the categories of exact and universal laws.[2] Praxeology is a domain of scientific research that deals with any purposeful human action; its best-developed aspect is economics, or catallactics. Mises precisely defines the scope of economic problems and claims that economics deals with a price analysis of goods and services that are exchanged on the market. To accomplish this goal, the economist must begin his reasoning with an understanding of the theory of human action.

The Austrian school understands economics as a theory of human action, not a theory of decisions themselves. This stands in contrast to neoclassic economists who, as Lionel C. Robbins explains, treat economics as a science of the use of scarce resources to satisfy human needs. This approach presupposes that knowledge about goals and

---

[2] G. A. Selgin, "Praxeology and Understanding: An Analysis of the Controversy in Austrian Economics," *Review of Austrian Economics* 2, no. 1 (1988): 19.

means is possessed beforehand; therefore, it reduces the question of stewardship to the barely technical problem of allocation under the circumstances of well-known limitations.[3] Man appears here to be a caricature of the human person, one who is passively acted on by events.

Mises, instead, sees human activity as drawing conclusions from the past and making use of imagination to discover and actively shape the future. A proper conception of action contains the perception of a structure of goals and means within which allocation and stewardship take place. The most important element of action is not decision-making per se but making decisions in the course of a process.

For the Austrian economist, the subject matter of praxeology is human action rather than the psychological events that lead to it. Action is always something real. It consists in accepting something and giving up something else. The acting man chooses his goal and strives after it. Praxeology is based on a fundamental axiom according to which individual human creatures act—that is, are committed to conscious activities in order to accomplish the goals they have chosen.

Acting as the Essence of Human Nature

Mises distinguishes acting from working. Acting may be consuming or using a thing or "omitting what possibly could be done."[4] Man is always made to act by a certain kind of uneasiness. By acting, he wishes to replace a less satisfactory state of affairs with a more satisfactory one. Mises stresses that it is necessary to fulfill yet one more condition: one should be convinced that a purposeful act may lead to the removal of uneasiness and thereby to the accomplishment of the goal.

Mises claims that one cannot describe the properties of the absolute being by means of praxeological concepts. Acting can only be imputed to a being that is discontented, and "repeated action only to a being who lacks the power to remove his uneasiness once and for all at one stroke."[5] The very possibility of change contradicts the concept of absolute perfection.

---

[3] J. H. de Soto, "The Ongoing Methodenstreit of the Austrian School," *Le Journal des Économistes et des Études Humaines* 8, no. 1 (1998): 76.

[4] Mises, *Human Action*, 13. In the remainder of this first chapter, wherever no citation is provided, the quotation is taken from this work.

[5] Mises, *Human Action*, 69.

Mises is interested in human action because it evokes changes in the socioeconomic sphere. The causes of human action are not known, but the changes that result from this action are essential for man and, as such, make up the subject matter of praxeology. Action belongs to the essence of human nature and existence, for it is "his means of preserving his life and raising himself above the level of animals and plants."

Man is able to act because he is capable of discovering causal relations that undergo changes. According to Mises, "causality is a category of acting." A man who could not perceive causal relations would not be able to act. Such a world would have to be "chaos in which man would be at a loss to find any points of orientation" for his acting. We do not know the causes of some changes taking place in the universe, a fact which does not undermine the principle of causality. Philosophical, epistemological, and metaphysical questions dealing with this problem go beyond the scope of praxeology. A man who accomplishes the intended goals must know the causal relations that combine particular events, processes, or states of affairs.

Mises thinks that there are only two principles according to which man can rationally grasp reality: purposefulness and causality. Events that cannot be interpreted according to one of these principles remain incomprehensible and mysterious. Due to the limitations of the human mind, the two principles of knowledge are imperfect, but if we do not want to go beyond the sphere of reason and experience, we have to assume that people act and reach the intended goals. Praxeology that deals with such purposeful action seeks to attain ends that the acting person sets for himself and focuses on the meaning that he attaches to his actions. It does not deal, however, with the overall and objective explanation of the meaning of events nor with the sense of development in history.

Mises' Apriorism

Human action is the subject matter of two sciences: praxeology and history. Mises makes this distinction, for the subject matter of the historical sciences is the past. History contains the whole of what human action has experienced, and, in terms of its methodology, is a methodically organized record of human action—that is, a description of the phenomena that have taken place in the past. In contradistinction to the exact sciences, history is not interpreted in the light of repetitive categories. For this reason, "the study of history ... does not by itself provide any knowledge and skill"[6] to build theories or predict future tasks.

Mises rejects experience that is the subject matter of research in the natural sciences as well. These sciences also deal with past events; each experience is an experience of something that has a past. Now economics deals with real human actions, and these actions cannot be subjected to laboratory experiments. During a natural experiment one observes elements that compose a change in isolation, but human action cannot be observed within the frame of only one event while its other elements remain unchanged. For Mises, therefore, "there is no means to abstract from a historical experience any *a posteriori* theories ... concerning human conduct and policies."

Mises rejects the methods of the natural and historical sciences because praxeological knowledge has a purely formal and general character. It can be neither verified nor falsified on the basis of experience and facts. Our knowledge in economics has an *a priori* character: it precedes all empirical experience and bears the status of "apodictic certainty."[7] Despite this, Mises can be regarded as an Aristotelian, rationalist empiricist, not a Kantian apriorist.

Thinking and acting are two specific human features characteristic of all human creatures. The human mind is not a *tabula rasa*, nor does it depend entirely on external stimuli that would be supposed to shape the man. Mises affirms that our experience of cooperation with others demonstrates that all, irrespective of race, manifest the same logic of thinking and may draw from the process of thinking the same conclusions. The human mind cannot comprehend the kind of action whose categories would differ from the categories that guide our action. We all have a similar structure of thinking, which calls for an application of what Mises calls "methodological apriorism." The universal, *a priori* tools of the human mind do not serve, however,

---

[6] L. von Mises, *The Ultimate Foundation of Economic Science: An Essay on Method* (1962; repr., Indianapolis: Liberty Fund, 2006), 38, 40–41; *Human Action*, 30–31.

[7] L. von Mises, *Epistemological Problems of Economics*, translated from the German by G. Reisman (Auburn, AL: Ludwig von Mises Institute, 2003), 18.

to learn the formal structure of behavior; they only reveal a certain aspect of reality.

This means that for the author of *Human Action* logical thinking and reality are not two separate spheres. For man, logic is a means to rule over reality, because what is contradictory in theory must also be contradictory in reality. In terms of logic, the category of action results from the category of causality, since without an idea of the cause-effect relation man is not in a position to act at all.

Methodological Individualism and Methodological Singularism

Mises is an advocate of methodological individualism. All actions are always individual actions. Cooperation and social action compose only a special case of the general category of human action. The communal whole fulfills its task only through individuals; the character of its action depends on the meaning that the acting individuals confer on it. Mises writes: "For a social collective has no existence and reality outside of the individual members' actions."

Human actions may be explained and understood only in the categories of individual goals and plans. This does not mean, however, that methodological individualism contradicts the existence of social groups. An additional difficulty consists in the fact that the individual often belongs to more than one group at the same time and it is impossible treat this phenomenon from the praxeological point of view; each group should be considered as the first and basic in order to understand human action. Methodological individualism helps us to avoid this problem.

A second essential principle in Mises' praxeology is methodological singularism. Mises is interested in a single and concrete action, which a concrete individual takes in a concrete time and place. The act of decision always means a choice among various possibilities. Human life consists of an uninterrupted series of single tasks, which are not isolated from each other and which make up a chain of actions. Each action has two aspects. On one hand, it is a particle in the chain of actions extended over time and intended to accomplish long-term goals. On the other hand, it is a certain whole in relation to the actions that compose them. It does not matter for praxeology whether an action is intended to accomplish a long-term goal or one that is more immediate. What is essential is an analysis of each action in an immediate cause-effect context.

The chosen goals and means applied to accomplish a goal depend on man's individual traits. Mises is well aware that heritage and milieu have an impact on human action and only few have the gift of thinking in a new and original way. Man decides to follow traditional patterns of behavior, believing that this is the best way to safeguard his well-being. Relying on routine is itself an action that may be changed.

It is the task of praxeology and history to explain the sense and meaning of human action. For this, praxeology uses conception. Praxeological knowledge is conceptual knowledge and deals with what is necessary in human action. Reasoning is the tool of history. Such a process of thinking inevitably entails an element of subjectivity, for a historian's reasoning is always marked with his personality and reflects the state of his mind. *A priori* sciences, one of which is praxeology, tend to an unconditionally correct knowledge for all creatures endowed with a logical structure, such as the human mind.

The Question of the Causality of Human Action

Mises' main concern was the question of causality. His methodological individualism was supposed to help him in studying the causality of the relations of individual actions observed in economic phenomena. He needed a respective language, which would not impose on the object under study the student's own limitations. The concept of cause and effect presupposes the use of a means and an end, where cause and effect should be understood in the categories of the acting individual's goals and plans.

The language of mathematics is proper to describe the consequences of human action, but a mathematical description is unable to present the concepts of causality and finality. Equations and formulas used in mathematical economics allow us only to describe the "states of equilibrium and nonacting." Mathematical economics does not deny that a given cause may be found in the action of the market's participants but is unmoved by the fact, because mathematics is silent about cause and effect. Mises claims not only that syllogisms are sterile but also that they "divert the mind from the study of the real problems and distort the relations between the various phenomena."[8] The use of mathematical language makes it impossible for contemporary economists to pose essential questions. What distinguishes praxeology from logic and mathematics is that it applies the categories of time and causality to the description of human action.

The equations that describe the economy in equilibrium have no practical application. In their calculations, mathematical economists take into consideration consumers' preferences present on the market at the moment of balance. Mises shows that even contemporary preferences are well known only on the basis of the impact the current state of the market has on the price system. No one can predict what demand would be like if the price were different. The state of equilibrium described by mathematical equations is therefore a purely mental and theoretical construction, which will never come to existence in reality and is irrelevant to economic calculation. According to Mises, in order to guide the economy it is necessary to know only the next step that should be made. The future is always uncertain, and consequently, each transaction, made with a view to the future, is always and only a pure speculation.

The Category of Time

Causality contains in itself the existence of time. The concepts of change and time are inseparably interrelated. Each action is preceded by a cause and oriented to changes that take place in a temporal order, and it contains a distinction between "before," "during," and "later." Man is incapable of imagining a world with nontemporal existence and nontemporal action.

Human action, Mises continues, is always directed toward the future: "Man becomes conscious of time when he plans to convert a less satisfactory present state into a more satisfactory future state." What permits man to be aware of the categories of change and time is the will to change his own living conditions. From the praxeological point of view, "there is between the past and the future a real extended present." Action always takes place in the real present time because it uses a given moment and in this way is made real.

---

[8] R. W. Garrison, "Mises and His Method," in *The Meaning of Ludwig von Mises*, ed. J. M. Herbener (Norwell, MA: Kluwer Academic, 1993), 103–7.

The amount of time is insufficient; hence the acting man must be sparing, in a manner similar to other rare goods. This kind of economizing is of a special character because of the nature of time, which flows and cannot be repeated. Mises stresses, however, that "the economization of time is independent of the economization of economic goods and services."

The Austrian economist makes a very important observation. Two different actions of the same individual never occur at the same time. The temporal relation is ordered in the categories of "earlier" and "later." From the praxeological point of view, the simultaneous character of actions can be conceived only in relation to more than one person acting simultaneously. The actions of a single person—and it is only with such that praxeology is concerned—always "follow one another in a more or less rapid succession."

According to Mises, uncertainty is inherent in every kind of thinking about action: "If man knew the future, he would not have to choose and would not act." Man is acting, for he believes that his situation in the future may be changed by his action. There remains, however, an area of uncertainty concerning the future and the way it will develop.

Mises does not consider whether man is free to make decisions. He assumes action to be certain; there is no scientific method to explain why a given man acts in this and not in that way. The methods of the exact sciences are not able to predict the future and effects of a given human action, for our knowledge about natural phenomena is insufficient. Human action is unpredictable and refers to an unknown future. Failure or success depends on a greater or lesser ability to predict the future and adjust one's action to the actions of others. In the course of human life, therefore, there is no stability or safety.

Causality, uncertainty, and time are inseparable and necessary praxeological categories, but they do not suffice to take action. There must be fulfilled still three other conditions. The acting person must feel some dissatisfaction in the existing circumstances, be capable of imagining a more desirable situation, and believe that he has appropriate means to create the chosen state of things. From these fundamental presuppositions, characteristic of each conscious human action, Mises elicits all the main principles and relations of economics.

Goals and Means

To precisely describe the nature of human action, Mises defines two essential concepts: goals and means. Human action always entails the use of means for a goal. The effect of action is to accomplish a goal—that is, to be liberated from some present anxiety. The means is what serves the attainment of the goal. "Means are not in the given universe," Mises explains; "in this universe there exist only things." A thing becomes a means when human reason plans to employ it as a tool.

Mises assumes that each person has a right to pose his own goals; he places this right beyond the sphere of rationality or irrationality, shifting it beyond the domain of knowledge and reflection. Praxeology does not deal with the external material world. It is therefore not important what the motive is for action taken to remove felt uneasiness. The area of its interest is man, his understanding and action. Nor is praxeology's task to discern human action that would be inspired by perfect knowledge available to all people. "Means are what acting man—who is not a perfect being and makes mistakes—makes [his] means."

Man lives in a world in which there are not sufficient means to attain at once all desired goals; therefore, he is forced to coordinate his means and goals.[9] This ability to choose values and means is inherent in man and it indicates rationality of human action. Man can correlate means with goals in order to accomplish what he intended. Mises stresses that human action is not mechanic nor guided by an unconscious instinct, but it falls under a well-thought-out individual intention to accomplish certain goals using the most effective means. In a sense, the choice of means is a technical problem, but the choice of the ultimate goal is for Mises always a personal, subjective, and individual matter.

Mises depicts a man whose action is always purposeful, for he is capable of discovering causal relations. This way of understanding is true of all people, irrespective of cultural context. Human life consists of an interrupted series of interrelated events. Each man chooses such means that from his point of view best serve the attainment of

---

[9] L. von Mises, *Theory and History: An Interpretation of Social and Economic Evolution* (Indianapolis: Liberty Fund, 2005), 7.

his chosen goals in an unknown and uncertain future. The necessity to choose between goals calls for ordering those goals according to one's own scale of values. This suggests that man evaluates the costs and benefits of particular choices.

The Subjective Character of Human Choices

Mises claims that choice is the foundation of each human decision. Man does not choose only between particular material things and services; his choices concern all spheres of life. The classical theory of values was limited to the economic aspect of human aspirations and efforts to acquire goods and improve material conditions. Mises' subjectivistic theory of choice and preferences goes beyond the purely economic. Praxeology is a science that studies all kinds of human action, and economics is the best-developed part of this universal science. A proper approach to economic problems should therefore begin from an examination of the acts of choice.

Mises claims that human action presumes the replacement in the future of one state of affairs for another, more desirable, one. This change he calls a choice, and this choice presumes a comparison of at least two objects or states of things. The choice, however, does not deal with two abstract units isolated from reality. It is not a comparison of sentiments or thoughts with some goods that man could possess without a strict connection and reference to those goods that he really possesses.[10] The choice consists in comparing what we have with what we do not have yet.

The choice is therefore a basic element of human conduct. Mises reminds us that man is able to define his needs only in action. Preferences become reality in the moment of choice. Praxeology is interested only in a choice between two concrete possibilities.[11] According to Mises, the border that separates economics from non-economics runs precisely along the line that separates action from inaction. Action occurs only when there is a need to choose between two possible goals.

Man in action chooses between various possible data. Mises claims that he is directed by his own scale of values when making choices,

---

[10] D. Mahoney, "On Austrian Value Theory and Economic Calculation," Mises Institute (2005), 2, http://mises.org/journals/scholar/Mahoney5.pdf.

[11] Mises, *Epistemological Problems*, 158.

on the basis of which he satisfies first the most important need. He stresses that such a scale of values "has no independent existence apart from the actual behavior of individuals." Ethical systems usually seek to determine a scale of values according to the principles that should govern man, a fact that does not mean that in reality he thinks and acts in that way. Praxeologists, however, are aware of the fact that man's ultimate goals do not fall under an evaluation from the point of view of absolute standards. Ultimate goals are purely subjective and vary with respect to individuals. Praxeology's task is only to determine the means for the attainment of the intended goal. Praxeology remains neutral and is interested only in whether the means used by the acting person are proper to accomplish the goal.

Action, always oriented at substituting a more satisfactory state of affairs for a less satisfactory, is called an *exchange*. What brings fewer benefits is abandoned on behalf of what is preferred. The difference between the value of the paid price and the attained goal is called profit. This profit is purely subjective and composes a psychological phenomenon that cannot be measured in an objective fashion by the external observer. It may happen, however, that a concrete action triggers a less desired state than the one that has been planned. In this case, the difference between the evaluation of the result and costs is called a loss.

Usefulness in praxeology is synonymous with the meaning we ascribe to things with respect to our belief that they may remove our felt uneasiness. From the objective point of view, the useful value is a relationship between the thing and the effect that it may evoke. This approach solves the so-called "value paradox" that troubled classical economists, for they did not take into consideration that the acting man never chooses between "water" and "diamonds." The acting man is always dealing with a choice between strictly definite amounts of goods that he cannot have altogether. The economic choice is never a choice between abstract factors, because a person's preferences in action are linked with a concrete act of choice between particular means that serve to attain concrete ends.

Mises shows that man makes decisions on the basis of his subjective values. From the point of view of the individual, these decisions are always rational, for they reflect his or her best interest, although from a different point of view they could seem irrational, unreasonable, and shortsighted. The subjectivist value theory is therefore an important element of the praxeological theory of value, and its task is to study all choices and values.

According to Mises, value is what man ascribes to the final goal. He values means only because of their usefulness to attain the chosen ends. The Austrian economist stresses that a value is not something innate and does not depend on objects. Value is inherent in man and his manner of reaction to the surrounding conditions. Nor does it matter what people say about values. What counts is only acts that affect the course of human events. Value is a relationship which, from the praxeological point of view, is indispensably linked with the current choice made by acting man.

Rationality of Human Action

Mises claims that each action is of necessity always rational.[12] For this reason, the term *irrational* is not used in relation to the ultimate ends of action. The ultimate end of action is the fulfillment of some need of the agent, and no one is able to apply his own judgments of values to actions taken by another person. The terms *rational* and *irrational* serve only to describe the selected means to attain ends, and not to evaluate the end itself. Means and methods are evaluated with a view to whether they can serve to accomplish the intended goal.

Human action is intent on change, and therefore it is subject to time. Mises says that man "comes into existence, grows, becomes old, and passes away." Man has little time. He himself, as a subject of his own action, is subject to the flow of time and must use it with prudence. Time preference is therefore an indispensable categorical condition of human action. Mises claims that the acting man's goal is always to remove uneasiness in the future, but this does not concern the future in general; it concerns instead a concrete segment of time in the most proximate future. For this reason, the satisfaction of needs in the proximate future is valued more than their satisfaction at a later time. This means that the present good is valued more than the same future good.

Postponing consumption, which can take place only after satisfying current needs, and the decision to save make possible action that is oriented to future goals and are a motor force for a capital structure

[12] Mises, *Epistemological Problems*, 36.

to arise in the economy. Mises shows that there is no abstract capital in the form of accumulated labor and nature but only concrete capital goods whose character is passing. Time preference has basic significance in the establishment of prices, commodities, and services. People's time preference and their tendency to save and consume ultimately affect the level of interest rates and appear on the market in the form of interest—that is, a discount of future goods in relation to present goods.

Mises does not deal with the category of *homo economicus*, for it is a fictive conception of man. His only interest is in concrete things—for example, a real man. Householding or maximizing behavior is only one element of economics. Moreover, there is room in praxeology for the person's "clinging" to his moral beliefs, which are not understood as obstacles on the way to the choice of means that serve the attainment of personal goals, but as a part of those goals.

Mises affirms that a truly human choice calls for a decision of the whole person. This means that the social sciences must take into account each person with his individual goals and plans and not concentrate on a group of individuals as a collective. Only this approach allows us to perceive what is principal for the human creature, and this in turn will allow us to understand the nature of human behavior. The radically subjective character of goals therefore demands that the economist remain quiet about them.[13]

The Principle of Wertfreiheit

Mises believed that one might distinctly separate objective economic analysis from the scientist's personal beliefs. The principle of *Wertfreiheit*—that is, a science free from valuation—was for Mises the central pillar of his praxeological system.[14] He believed the postulate of *Wertfreiheit* could easily be fulfilled in praxeology because it is also applied in other *a priori* sciences. Mises calls praxeology an apolitical science. It is in all respects neutral, for it refers only to means and not to the choice of the ultimate goal.

---

[13] J. G. Hülsmann, *Mises: The Last Knight of Liberalism* (Auburn, AL: Ludwig von Mises Institute, 2007), 204.

[14] I. M. Kirzner, *Ludwig von Mises: The Man and His Economics* (Wilmington, DE: ISI, 2001), 90.

Mises was convinced that if studies are supposed to be scientific, they should be conducted in an impartial manner, without attributing to them any values that could affect the course of research. One should especially withdraw from political evaluations. According to Mises, economics teaches us about means that are necessary to promote values confessed by the majority of people. These means basically refer to the maintenance of free economies.

The main motor that pushed Mises toward research on economics was the survival of the human species. It is only a seeming paradox, for—as Israel M. Kirzner rightly noted—this motivation indicates only Mises' passion for trying to achieve what he understood as sound economics. In no way does it eliminate the impartial objectivity with which he conducted his research. The subjectivistic value theory explains the essence of exchange that makes up the basic element of human action. Exchange means that both parties receive goods that are more valued by them and dispose of goods that are less valued. Mises demonstrates convincingly that value is not inherent in things but is a relationship that is inseparably linked with the current choice. The value of things therefore depends on the goal that a man attributes to his action and that only he knows. The subjectivistic value theory is a good introduction into the understanding of the essence of labor, which has its source in free human action.

Labor and Its Division in the Free-Market Society

Labor for Mises has all the signs of action as a free exchange in which man seeks to replace the less satisfactory state of affairs with the more satisfactory one. To remove the felt uneasiness, the acting man orders and gradates the available means in the world according to their acquired usefulness. This is, however, a specific kind of exchange in which, in view of the fact that man has to earn money, he agrees to bear difficulties linked with his labor and gives up rest. From the point of view of catallaxis, only work conducted due to the necessity to earn is thought to be labor, and Mises calls it *extroversive* labor. Mises insists upon an essential difference between production and a creative act. In his view, artists cannot be included in the praxeological conception of labor. Art is not work, because for its creators it is not a means but a goal.

Man is constantly striving to improve his material living standards. The point of departure for this kind of action is economizing and accumulating capital goods. Mises firmly stresses that there is no artificial division between consumer goods and capital goods. This division always depends on the situation of the acting person as a subject making choices. Consumer goods may for someone be capital goods—that is, means that ensure survival for him and his employees during a time of expectation. The concept of capital is therefore the concept of economic calculation and the most important intellectual tool of actions taken in the market economy, which does not exist beyond the mind of people making plans. It is an invention of capitalists and entrepreneurs who want to gain profits and avoid losses. The concept of capital in economic systems in which there is no private ownership of the means of production—and thus no market that prices these means—is deprived of practical meaning.

Uneasiness of Labor

Mises claims that labor in the real world is associated with uneasiness. In our world, the state in which one does not have to work is more satisfactory than working. Man puts rest before work and he does this when the gain of his work is, in his opinion, less desirable than pleasure that attends on leisure. One of the benefits that the civilized man can enjoy in greater abundance than his less civilized ancestors is leisure time. The exceptional position that labor has gained in our world results from its special character. It is not only useful but also indispensable to carry out all the conceived processes and implement modes of production.

People do not spare labor as such but instead a concrete type of labor that is available. For this reason, there is never supply or demand for "labor" in general on the market but only for labor of a definite kind and character. Labor is differentiated because people are not born equal, and the skills and experience they gain in the course of their lives make the differences still greater. Mises notes that labor is rarer than the material means of production in our world, for it is needed and still lacking in each sphere of production.

The author of *Human Action* points to two sources of pleasure in labor that do not emerge in the socialist system. People find the joy of labor in the satisfaction of its completion. This joy, however, does not result from labor itself. For Mises, the most important source of joy is satisfaction that the laborer draws from the fact that his work is so well evaluated that he may thereby earn enough to maintain himself and his family. He rejoices, for in his skill and ability to work he can see a foundation for his own existence and social position and a guarantee of future economic success. The cause of joy and pride is the sense of doing something good for society, something for which people pay and which they may buy on the market. In the socialist society, the laborer will never feel such joy, for the relationship between the gain of his labor and income is not clear, and the laborer always has the sense that he has been burdened with too much work.

The only means that can make people work more intensively and better is to offer them a better wage. Joy and boredom in labor are psychological phenomena that have no influence on the individual and subjective assessment of labor or the price that is paid for it on the market.

Labor as Factor of Production and Source of Maintenance

Labor is an insufficient factor of production and, as such, it is bought and sold on the market. For a man in action, his own work is not only a factor of production but also a source of maintenance. He evaluates it with a view not only to expected profit but also to difficulties that it brings. It should be stressed that the work of other people is sold on the market as a factor of production. Man deals with the work of other people in a way similar to other insufficient material means of production. The level of wages is determined on the market in the same way as the value of other articles—that is, through the consumers' demand for goods and services.[15] Only in this meaning does Mises regard labor as a commodity.

The scale of wages is determined only by the market. For Mises one cannot speak about labor in a nonmarket context. Each entrepreneur is willing to buy any labor he needs to carry out his plans at the lowest cost. Prices must, however, be duly high to draw laborers away from competing entrepreneurs. The level of wages for each kind of labor on the market depends on its marginal productivity, which is based on

---

[15] L. von Mises, *Bureaucracy* (Grove City, PA: Libertarian Press, 1983), 39–40.

the supply of labor, the material factors of labor, and the anticipated future prices of consumer commodities.

Mises claims that the economic system of calculation is a sufficient test of the effectiveness of labor, which does not exist in the socialist system. The private entrepreneur settles the wages that his employee receives, but his power is limited and he cannot dismiss his laborers or treat them badly, for in this manner he would harm himself.[16] Striving to buy labor as cheaply as possible, the employer fulfills one of his most important social tasks.

Voluntary and Institutional Unemployment

A man seeking a job in the free-market economy may not always find an occupation that fully corresponds to his interests and his expected wages. The man who for this reason decides not to take any job remains unemployed. That fact that those who seek a job may choose to wait is, according to Mises, the only cause of unemployment. The individual who does not want to wait can always find a job, because there are always potential uses of natural resources that are not realized. It suffices only to accept a job for lower wages or to change one's occupation or place of work. Unemployment therefore does not differ from other market phenomena. Mises calls this kind of unemployment *catallactic.*

He lists three circumstances that can force people to remain unemployed. The individual who seeks a job may believe that later he will find an appropriate and well-paid job in the vicinity of his place of residence.[17] Second, the supply of workers performing some jobs is subject to seasonal vacillations. Or third, non-economic factors are decisive when one decides not to take a job that would be contrary to his religious, moral, or political beliefs. Irrespective of the causes, unemployment on the free market always remains voluntary.

---

[16] R. M. Ebeling, "A Rational Economist in an Irrational Age: Ludwig von Mises," in *The Age of Economists: From Adam Smith to Milton Friedman,* ed. R. M. Ebeling (Hillsdale, MI: Hillsdale College Press, 1999), 98; Mises, *Bureaucracy,* 40.

[17] H.-H. Hoppe, "The Misesian Case against Keynes," Mises Institute, https://mises.org/library/misesian-case-against-keynes.

The Austrian economist distinguishes between catallactic unemployment and institutional unemployment. The first is voluntary, while the second does not follow from the decisions of job-seekers but is instead an effect of the state's interference with the market. Institutional unemployment always appears when the government and labor unions seek to settle the wage level higher than the one that would be settled on the free labor market. Catallactic unemployment always has a tendency to disappear, for market wages tend toward a level at which all those willing to work would find employment and employers would hire as many employees as they need. Institutional unemployment lasts as long as the government's interference that imposes an artificially high wage level.

The Catallactic Wage Theory

Mises reminds us that the primitive man's life was a continuous struggle to survive in a condition characterized by a scarcity of natural resources. The contemporary inhabitant of capitalist countries has been liberated from this incessant struggle for the maintenance of life, for each day he earns more than he needs to survive.

From the psychological or biological point of view, it is impossible to determine a minimum of existence that would refer to everyone at every time. A considerable increase in the living standard in capitalism is a fruit of the increase of investment capital, not an effect of the natural law of the growth of humankind. It is a result of the mutual and free interaction of the forces that bring about this effect only in the capitalist economy, but this situation is not a permanent phenomenon. Each laborer has his own view of how much he should earn to maintain his social position, but the ultimate factor that determines the level of his salary is the value that others attribute to his services and endeavors.

The economic analysis of the market that is complete and satisfactory in the logical sense is based only on the catallactic theory of salaries. For this reason, Mises rejects the "iron law of wages" as one that cannot be reasonably defended, and he rejects the Marxist method of determining "the value of workforce" through "the time of labor indispensable to production"—the method that is in principle identical with that law. Mises, like his predecessor Carl Menger,[18] rejects not only the claim that the natural price of labor is the amount that enables laborers to survive but also the idea of the "social minimum" necessary to maintain the living standards time-honored by historical tradition and customs inherited from ancestors. Market wages are not based on historical or moral aspects but on existing and current relations and sequences of events within the framework of market forces. The introduction of a just price and salary would inhibit man's incessant quest to improve his material conditions and to maintain, at any cost, a concrete social order. Mises notes correctly that the social system of labor cannot be maintained if some of its participants are doomed to earn below the level that ensures survival.

"Labor is a scarce factor of production." The price that one who sells labor can receive for his services depends on the situation on the market. The amount and quality of labor that man can provide depend on his innate and acquired abilities. Man can try to show his abilities in order to sell them at the highest price in the given conditions of the market, but he cannot change his nature to better adjust himself to these conditions. Mises stresses that workers often lack adaptive skills to new conditions of labor enforced by consumers on the market, for they lack the innate talent of entrepreneurs. Therefore, one should see it as a lucky coincidence when the market offers a given person an abundant remuneration for his work.

The prices for labor are prices paid for a factor of production, and they are determined by the labor market. The level of wages depends on the final prices of the products expected at the moment of the sale and purchase of labor. Mises follows here the line of reasoning adopted by Menger. The latter claims that—as in the case of other goods—wages for labor are determined in a market-wise mode by the value attributed to it on the market.[19] Mises means here not only the work sold by the employee to his employer but also the kind of work performed when one who labors takes on himself the risk of combining his labor with production factors and the services of other people.

---

[18] C. Menger, *Principles of Economics*, trans. J. Dingwall, B. F. Hoselitz (Grove City, PA: Libertarian Press, 1994), 170–71.

[19] Menger, *Principles*, 171.

Mises notices the specific character of human labor, which is that the employee is not only a provider of production factors but also a human creature, and it is impossible to isolate him from his activity. In this case, when a job is chosen from the economic point of view, what comes into play is not only the assessment of the tedium of labor and its indirect gratification but also concrete conditions that may affect the whole life of the employee. Analyzing the market price for labor, Mises also takes into account the fact that the employee and the consumer are the same individual.

The Voluntary Character of Human Labor

Material changes in the universe result from spiritual processes. Production is not a physical, material, or external process. It is a spiritual and intellectual phenomenon, although the author of *Human Action* hastens to add that he does not refer to metaphysics, for reason belongs to the universe and nature. The essential requirement of labor is not man's manual or physical activity, nor the external forces of nature and things, but the decisions made by reason to use those forces and means to attains ends. Human reason processes human and material factors into means. Owing to reason, man produces, chooses the end, and selects means to attain it. For this reason, the claim that the economy deals with the material conditions of human existence is erroneous. Human action is a manifestation of human reason.

On the free market "the workers sell their services as other people sell their commodities.... The employer ... is simply the buyer of services which he must purchase at their market price." The market makes the worker independent of the executive decisions of the employer. The employee is a free man because the employer, under the pressure of the market price structures, treats work as a commodity and instrument that brings income. The employer pays for services, and the employee performs them to gain wages. If an agreement is reached, then the situation of an employer and employee is more profitable than the situation in which such an agreement was not reached. On the free market one may accomplish all this without resorting to force.

The Division of Labor

According to Mises, the existence of society "is the outcome of conscious and purposeful behavior." Society arises and develops not because of some law imposed from above on the individual contrary to his or her interests but because of the individuals' free actions. They collaborate in order to attain their intended ends, using higher productivity that is an effect of division of labor. People are born in an organized society, and only in this sense can we say that society is antecedent to individuals. Particular individuals live and act in society, but society is only a collection of individuals made for common effort.

Society is an intellectual and spiritual phenomenon. The fundamental impulse that caused the birth of society and civilization and made man a human creature is the fact that specialized labor in cooperation with others is more productive than the labor of isolated individuals—and human reason is capable of assenting to this truth. In a hypothetical world in which division of labor would not be able to increase productivity, society would not exist. The principle of division of labor has essentially contributed to evolutionary changes.

Mises notes the historical role of the theory of division of labor worked out by the British economists of the eighteenth and nineteenth centuries. It consisted in a total refutation of the metaphysical doctrines concerning the origin and nature of human cooperation. Social institutions are of human origin, they are governed by their own laws, and they serve human progress and the common good. Man does not have to give up his own well-being for the good of society. The role of God no longer consists in interfering in the affairs of princes and politicians but in endowing his own creations with reason and supporting them on their way to happiness.

Action is always taken by individuals. Society and the state are for all people the most important means that serve the attainment of their ends. They are created by human effort. Society cannot exist, however, if the majority is not ready to use threat or force to stop the minority from destroying the social order. According to Mises, this power should be entrusted to the government. The state is principally an institution established to ensure that citizens observe the peaceful principles of interpersonal relations. The role of the state consists exclusively in the protection of life, health, liberty, and property against coercion and aggression.[20]

Mises thinks that each form of the state is an apparatus of compulsion and violence. It is so not only in the case of a socialist state, wherein citizens are by force deprived of any control over the means of production, but also in the case of a state understood as a "night watchman." The goal of the state is always to deter behaviors dangerous for the existence of social order, and it may do it only by use of force. Liberal society cannot live without such legal institutions of coercion and violence, but the state must be constituted in such a way that the scope of its laws leaves the individual the largest possible opportunity of free action. By freedom, Mises understands the freedom of each individual to govern his own goals and plans, which permits social integration through free agreement in a society based on the division of labor and private property.

David Ricardo's theory of comparative costs proves that an increase of production under the division of labor follows when an individual or a group more efficient in all respects cooperates with less efficient individuals and groups. The benefits of the division of labor are always reciprocal. This law permits us to understand the tendencies in a gradual increase of human cooperation. People do not regard themselves as rivals in a struggle for the distribution of limited means available in nature. Each step toward a greater specialization serves all the participants of the division of labor. Having discovered this law, man understood why he was not left a recluse and he no longer has to resort to empty hypotheses about the innate desire to live in society or look for miraculous divine interventions.

---

[20] L. von Mises, *Liberalism in the Classical Tradition*, trans. R. Raico (Irvington-on-Hudson, NY: Foundation for Economic Education, 2002), 52.

The Nature of the Human Person: Social and Individual

Mises stresses that the foundation of society is private property. This basis makes it possible for the individual to develop and improve his or others' situations owing to the individual's participation in this division of labor. The distinction between owners and nonowners results from the division of labor.[21] Private property has always been regarded as a privilege of the few, an outcome that is wrong from the ethical point of view. Liberalism was the first to recognize that the social function of private property, especially the means of production, is to put goods into the hands of those who know best how to use them. Each kind of limitation, like exclusive rights or other privileges given to producers by governments, blocks the social function of property. Individuals have the right to possess and use not only ready-made goods but also the means by which goods and services can be produced for sale and common use. The amount of a person's wealth and income in society depends on his success in serving others in the system of the division of labor. This inequality is principally an element of market economics. The individual's efforts are rewarded in accord with his value deriving from his own faculties and abilities.

According to Mises, the concept of causality in the social sciences remains a fundamental principle of reasoning. Society is a product of thought and will. Its origins rest in man, not in the external world. Man is a social being not because his material needs could not be satisfied in isolation but because he has accomplished a level of reasoning and perceptive skills that would not be available to him without society. Man cannot be imagined as an isolated being, for humankind exists only as a social phenomenon.

Mises is aware that we are far from understanding the ultimate and most profound secret of life. One of the ways to enlarge our knowledge about the nature of life is an attempt to understand social organization. The division of labor finds its justification in the inequality of human abilities and the variety of the external conditions of human life. In both cases we are dealing with something that is not repeatable and

---

[21] L. von Mises, *Socialism: An Economic and Sociological Analysis* (Indianapolis: Liberty Fund, 1981), 276.

that creates the universe in its infinite and inexhaustible variety. Mises stresses that social life would not come to existence among people of equal abilities and in a world that is not geographically varied. People obviously would join their forces to cope with the tasks that are beyond the capacities of particular individuals, but such an alliance would not make a society. Such relations would only be transitory.

The personal division of labor shows that particular individuals draw benefits from their cooperation not only with people whose abilities surpass their own but also with those who are less efficient. The profit of the division of labor is thus reciprocal. The most precious fruit of labor under the division of labor is its uniting influence. Owing to labor, people treat themselves as comrades in their common struggle for the good, not as rivals in the struggle for survival. As Mises observes, the division of labor turns enemies into friends, war into peace, and individuals into society.

Owing to cooperation, not only are people able to accomplish what they would not be able to do singlehandedly; the labor that they do individually is more worthwhile. The division of labor provides opportunities for further development of individual talents. Society therefore becomes a means by which each individual seeks to accomplish his own ends.

The Individual in the Free-Market Society

Mises speaks about a single man who acts on his own and is independent of others. This perception of human action is dictated by Mises' desire to understand better the problems of social cooperation. In no way does he claim that such an isolated and self-sufficient human being has ever existed. Man appeared on earth as a social being. An isolated individual is only a fictitious mental construct created for the sake of praxeology. From the point of view of the individual, society is a means to attain his ends, and he aims to realize those ends by means of his action. His actions are the only factors that govern the market. All market phenomena are a result of the action of particular individuals and thus are in no way automatic or deterministic.

Mises is a decisive critic of the basic theorem of classical economics according to which man, as a rational creature, always tends to maximize the accomplished profits and acts exclusively by "economic" motives. The concept of *homo economicus* is in Mises' estimation a fictitious and hypothetical image of man that has no equivalent in reality.

Mises shares the view that man at any cost seeks to eliminate the probability of mistakes from his action in order not to act on the basis of ignorance and not to permit any negligence on his part. He claims, however, that man's action is not entirely governed by the highest monetary profit. Assuming this, classical economists could not create an appropriate value theory. They concentrated exclusively on the actions of entrepreneurs interested in the purchase of goods on the cheapest market and sale on the most expensive market; they did not concentrate on the consumers who are not governed exclusively by economic motives. According to Mises, classical economics for this reason failed to create a satisfactory theory of demand.

In a society based on castes, classes, and/or status, man's position was once and for all determined and he was relegated to a definite social stratum. In a free-market society, the position of each individual depends on his own action.[22]

Praxeological Meaning of the Individual's Freedom

Freedom is one of the most important concepts on which Mises builds his theory of human action. His social analysis is based on the principle of methodological individualism; that is, a belief that only the individual takes action, makes free choices, and bears complete responsibility. Freedom as a praxeological term refers to the sphere in which the acting individual is to choose between modes of action. Man is free inasmuch as he can choose his goals and the means that he uses to accomplish them.

Man cannot benefit from the peaceful cooperation that results from division of labor in society and at the same time be free to take actions that lead to the disintegration of community. In order to establish and maintain social cooperation and civilization, some measures are taken to prevent asocial actions that could squander all that man has achieved during his whole development. This function in the social system is played by government. It is thus indispensable to maintain courts, the police, and the army. Mises thinks that levying taxes for this

[22] L. von Mises, *The Anti-Capitalistic Mentality* (Grove City, PA: Libertarian Press, 1994), 9.

purpose is completely compatible with the freedom that individuals cherish in the free-market society. At the same time, he warns that each step taken by government that transcends the boundary line of its competence with regard to the protection of the free market against the aggressor leads to a totalitarian system and destruction of the free-market economy. Freedom and free action are necessary conditions for the existence of a contractual society. According to Mises, social cooperation in a system based on the private means of production implies that, within the framework of the free-market economy, the individual is not forced to obey and serve the sovereign. Obviously, this does not mean that the individual is independent of society. Any member of contractual society is also free when he serves others because in this manner he serves also himself.[23] He is only limited by the unavoidable natural phenomenon of scarcity in nature.

According to Mises, the social sciences deal with various aspects of social phenomena and processes; the individual matters for them only as a member of the group. They make a consequential mistake, for man never belongs only to one social group. Mises is aware that the market is an astoundingly complex phenomenon. He attempts to understand it by isolating key components in order to describe functions that people play in the market economy. In economic theory, the entrepreneur, capitalist, laborer, and consumer are not the living people we encounter in the real world. These are merely terms denoting ideal types and catallactic categories. The living and acting man of necessity comprises various functions. He is not only a consumer but also simultaneously an entrepreneur, capitalist, and laborer.

---

[23] L. von Mises, *Economic Policy: Thoughts for Today and Tomorrow* (Auburn, AL: Ludwig von Mises Institute, 2006), 23.

UNCERTAINTY, CHOICE, AND OTHER ELEMENTS OF THE MARKET ECONOMY

Speaking about entrepreneurs, Mises has in mind uncertainty in human action, which is linked with confronting the fact that the future is difficult to foresee. Entrepreneurship is an attribute of each human action and deals with each man, for in the face of the unpredictable future we all have to take risks. The Austrian philosopher rightly notes that risk and uncertainty bring the entrepreneur to life, and uncertainty itself follows from human choices. The true and real choice is not entirely known to the individual at the moment of decision-making, for otherwise he would not be able to compare various solutions and would not have to make a decision.

Uncertainty and true choices exist only in the free-market economy. A contradiction to the capitalist system is for Mises the evenly rotating economy in which all events are well known in advance. The evenly rotating economy is a mental construct that Mises introduces into his considerations, describing the economy at rest. In the market economy we may encounter such a state now and again, but the state of rest does not last long and the changes in the market force its participants to act.

The basic property of the evenly rotating economy is that there is no uncertainty in the future; hence the entrepreneur is redundant. In this economy, there is no room for free and creative action. Contrary to socialism, in the capitalist economic system entrepreneurs affect the course of events, and in their actions they are entirely dependent on consumers. Like every man in action, the entrepreneur is always a speculator. Mises emphasizes that each human action is rooted in time and therefore it deals with speculation. By the force of events, not only the capitalist but also laborers and consumers are speculators.

Entrepreneurs

It is "uncertainty and risk that create the need for the entrepreneur role." The entrepreneur's success or failure depends on the correct prediction of future events. The entrepreneur draws profits only from the fact that he can predict demand better than other entrepreneurs. If he fails to produce the least expensive and best goods, he suffers losses and loses the position of entrepreneur. His place is taken by those who are better at serving clients. Therefore, the entrepreneur's concrete profit or loss does not depend on the amount of physical production but exclusively on his adjustment to consumers' needs. Mises rightly notes, therefore, that if all entrepreneurs correctly predicted the future position of the market, there would be no profits or losses.

Mises calls the free market a democracy of consumers, for it is the place of daily voting by means of money for the preferred commodities and services. By buying or refraining from buying, consumers determine producers' success or failure. In like manner, they choose those entrepreneurs who have best satisfied their needs and withdraw the means of production from those who do not know how to serve them best. Their choices, moreover, may change at any moment depending on the change of their preferences.

Mises does not agree with the claim of socialists and advocates of interventionism that profit is the income that comes from labor and is accomplished at the expense of laborers. He explains that the physical effort itself is inadequate if it is not accompanied by the savings and capital the entrepreneur has accumulated beforehand. Useful commodities arise only as a result of purpose-oriented labor by the human mind. If we replaced the desire to gain profit with so-called moral motives, this would cause the system of prices to collapse and, in consequence, economic conditions would get worse, for there are no other methods to adjust production to changing conditions than the properly functioning market.

Capitalists

We should agree with Mises that what is essential for entrepreneurs is also important for capitalists. Their actions within the framework of the free-market economy are also placed in time and have a speculative character. In a purely mental construction, the capitalist on the market is the individual who lends the entrepreneur capital, in the form of money credit, that is indispensable to take entrepreneurial actions. Providing credit is possible because capitalists refrain from consuming a part of available goods.

Making loans is always related to enormous risk, for the lender must take into account that he may lose part or all of the capital he has lent. Mises rightly notes that only the capitalist who knows how to properly use his capital from the point of view of the consumer's needs is able to retain and at the same time increase his property. The capitalist achieves profit owing to the exchange of current goods for future goods, gaining from the difference in prices between the two. The lender is therefore always an entrepreneur. He can never be sure whether the investments of the borrower will bring the desired effects; therefore, he demands of the borrower a certain bonus, an "entrepreneurial component" of the market—the gross interest rate. The second element constituting the interest rate is a "price bonus," which occurs in relation to postponed payments. Only those capitalists whose operations have succeeded gain this interest.

Workers

The next catallactic category is the *worker*: one who sells his work, for which he is paid, in order to accomplish his own goal. One of the traits of human labor is its disutility. This means that in our world people prefer leisure to work. This correct observation permits us to better understand Mises' reasoning with regard to the economic function of the entrepreneur in the free-market economy.

The worker is not, however, merely a provider of the means of production for the entrepreneur but also a human creature; therefore, man cannot be isolated from his labor. What kind of work he performs is not a neutral question for the worker. Some may be surprised that people prefer certain jobs, conditions of work, or places of work to others. Mises rightly notes that people do not perceive their work only from the point of view of disutility and direct remuneration but also take into account the conditions and circumstances in which they work, analyzing whether these stand in the way of their willingness to draw pleasure from life. Workers and consumers are in principle the same individuals, and only economic reasoning divides this unity into two schemes of thinking. Background, language, education, religion, mentality, family ties, and social milieu bind the worker in such a way that he no longer chooses the place or kind of work with regard solely to the amount of remuneration.

In the free-market system, the employee sells his services in the same way as other people sell their products. The employee is not, however, dependent on his employer, for the latter is a buyer who buys at a market price the services needed to realize his plans. The price of human labor results from the same mechanism as all other prices.

Employees and employers on the free market are subject exclusively to the rule of consumers. In the free market, the employer pays for services rendered by employees, and employees work in order to earn wages. The hired employee does not owe his employer gratitude; he owes him a definite quantity of work of a definite quality.

The Sovereignty of the Consumer

Aside from the entrepreneur, capitalist, and employer, there is the consumer. Consumers occupy an especially important place in the free-market system, for the goal of all production is ultimately consumption. Mises emphasizes that in order to precisely define what kinds of goods are supposed to be produced with the use of scarce resources at the disposal of society, one must properly ascertain the consumer's preferences—a phenomenon Mises calls "consumer sovereignty." The entrepreneur cannot run his enterprise in just any manner if he does not want to go bankrupt. He must produce in accord with demand, which is based on consumers' wishes.

In buying or refraining from buying, the consumer immediately shows his preferences and wishes. Mises claims that the consumer chooses between things that bring him instant satisfaction. The consumer's preferences may be subject to criticism from the philosophical point of view, but the assessment of values is always a personal and subjective matter. The consumer chooses, however, according to what he deems best serves his goals. The consumer's expectations may be wise or stupid, moral or immoral, but this in no way changes the ancillary role of producers and thus these expectations remain amoral in the praxeological sense.

Mises recognizes the principal and often-ignored element of the free market. The free-market economy is characterized by the fact that each acting person is both a means and an end for himself, and at the same time a means for other people in their attempt to accomplish their own goals and profits. The concept of consumer sovereignty therefore does not mean tyranny and oppression on his part. Man is fully free to oppose the consumer's preferences—for instance by not selling goods or services to those toward whom he has some moral reservations—but he must be ready to give up the profit he would earn from this enterprise.

What makes it possible for the consumer—that is, each of us—to assess accurately the value of goods and services on the free market is economic calculation. Mises is aware, however, that striving after better conditions is never an inevitable process. It is always possible to return to unsatisfactory conditions, if we abandon economic calculation on which the principles of social cooperation depend. He is convinced that the method for rational economic calculation and thus the most beneficial distribution of goods is offered only by the institutions of market economics.

Irrationality of Socialist Planning and Governmental Interventionism

In his considerations on the nature and actions of the individual in the economic sphere, Mises concludes that there is no feasible alternative to the free-market economy, since the indispensable conditions for the existence and evolution of human community are freedom, property, and sound money. In his essay "Economic Calculation in the Socialist Commonwealth" (1920), he proved that socialism is not only a less efficient economic system but is literally "impossible."[24] Socialist central planning and the suppression of private property lead to the elimination of economic calculation, and this means that all economic rationality has come to an end. Interventionism is not an alternative to the free market, for it interferes with the functioning of the price system and undermines entrepreneurs' activity, as they are motivated by the possibility of profit deriving from serving clients as well as they can. Arguments on behalf of socialism and interventionism often seem enticing but, according to Mises, this appeal is due above all to the failure to understand the nature of human action and the market economy.

Mises argues that the market economy is a social institution that arose totally spontaneously and is a product of the evolutionary process. The principal task of the state should therefore be to determine the legal frameworks that enable the proper functioning of economic subjects by ensuring free competition and the determination of prices

---

[24] L. von Mises, *Economic Calculation in the Socialist Commonwealth,* translated from the German by S. Adler, (1920 [German]; 1935 [first English ed.], repr., Auburn: Ludwig von Mises Institute, 1990), 21.

by market mechanisms. Adam Smith and classical economists showed that the socioeconomic order may be introduced without central planning, but this does not mean that market relations are due to an irrational process of accidental selection. They result from a conscious and teleological tendency of each person, who strives to adjust his action as best he can to the conditions of the environment, which he cannot always change. In Mises' social theory, the characteristic trait of market society is therefore not spontaneity but purposefulness.

Market Prices

One manifestation of man's purposeful action is the price structure, which appears in the course of market processes. As a result of the processes of buying or not buying, each individual participates in the formation of market prices. The price is therefore never an isolated or unchanged object on the market, determined by an arbitrary decision of government. Instead, it expresses the significance that acting people attribute to things as they strive to remove uneasiness, and it is always a product of subjective evaluation. The structure of market prices is for the individual a point of reference that permits him to adjust his behavior to the market. What is called a price is always a relationship within an integrated system, which is a complex composite of human relations on the market.

The starting point for understanding the essence of monetary calculation is the assumption that the difference in the value assigned to the exchanged commodities is the basis for their exchange. This is contradictory to the position held from the time of Aristotle to that of Menger: that goods are exchanged only for commodities of the same value. Mises claims that people buy and sell commodities and services only because they value what they receive as a result of the exchange more highly than what they give away. Exchange therefore is not based on an objectively determined value of goods and services but depends on the comparison of usefulness by particular participants in the process of market exchange.

Money as a Means of Exchange

The means by which economic calculations are made is *money*. Mises defines money as a good for which there is the highest demand on the market. The uncertainty of tomorrow induces people to keep money so as to satisfy the most indispensable future needs that will have to be satisfied by way of exchange. Money is therefore an economic good. It cannot serve as an objective measure of the value of commodities and services, for it is valued and appraised on its own merit.

Mises was a faithful advocate of the subjectivistic value theory, which he used also in money theory. Similar to other critics of socialism, he denied the labor theory of value according to which the value of commodities is related to the labor needed in their production, emphasizing the theory's inherent contradiction and unfeasibility.[25] What makes him different from other opponents, however, is the clarity with which he presents the problem of economic calculation within the frame of a society based on the public ownership of the means of production.[26]

Mises stresses that, without a monetary medium of exchange by which the prices of all commodities may be expressed, the goods on the market would not have a common denominator that would make it possible to compare and evaluate their relative value in the categories of mutual relations. Mises has in mind above all the means of production, whose presence on the market serves the assessment of relative costs of market goods and services in an alternative combination and selection of the least expensive methods of their production. Economic calculation requires that not only goods ready for consumption but also higher-order goods (i.e., means of production) be exchangeable via the general medium of exchange. Without this aid, the human mind would be completely lost in the chaos of alternative materials and processes.

If we do not take into consideration all members of society in the process of exchange, market prices cannot contain the assessment and preference of the community as a whole as well as the broad range of information on the alternative application of goods and resources. None of these tools of economic calculation exist in a socialist society. On one hand, through nationalization of the means of production and lack of the market prices for these means, the state makes it impossible for individuals to find on their own alternative applications for those

---

[25] Mises, *Socialism*, 116.

[26] R. M. Ebeling, "Economic Calculation under Socialism: Ludwig von Mises and his Predecessors," in *The Meaning of Ludwig von Mises*, 87.

resources. On the other hand, socialist planners without a structure of prices lack a rational method for using the means of production that they have at their disposal. The socialist state, says Mises, thereby deprives itself of the only rational opportunity for an effective allocation of its resources.

Economic Calculation

The author of *Human Action* asserts that the mind of one man is unable to understand all the productive opportunities that the goods of a higher order furnish. No one has ever done it without the help of some system of economic calculation. The calculation of costs and profits is possible only when private owners of the means of production are free to exchange goods and services for money according to their individual valuation. In the market society, each has an assigned double role in determining monetary calculation—as a consumer and as a producer.

Monetary calculation is, according to Mises, a compass that enables people to move in the social system of the division of labor. The individual always calculates in order to distinguish the profitable production from the unprofitable one. Each step of entrepreneurial activity is examined by way of economic calculation. Economic calculation in monetary categories is used not only by entrepreneurs producing for consumers in the market economy but also by buyers of their products.

Mises is aware of the limitation of economic calculation, for it is not concerned with things that cannot be sold or bought for money in the course of market exchange. Honor, virtue, glory—likewise vigor and life itself—have great meaning in action as means and ends, but they do not enter the category of economic calculation.

The Austrian economist stresses that estimation of the value of products by means of money makes no sense if their price is not negotiated on the market. Prices on the market are always only historical facts that express the state of affairs that occurred in the past and has become dominant at a concrete moment of irreversibly passing time. For this reason, prices can never be used as a clear indicator for production, which is always oriented at the satisfaction of the market in the future under the impact of various economic factors.

Economic calculation is possible only in definite conditions, in which goods and services are bought and sold by way of a generally recognized medium of exchange (money). The elements of those conditions are the social system of the division of labor and the private ownership of the means of production. If these conditions change as a result of social evolution, owing to the abolition of private property, this will make rational actions impossible and the social division of labor will fall apart into components, falling to the level of a household. For Mises, it is obvious that human cooperation is made possible only in the market economy.

Mises carefully and frequently emphasizes the difference between economic calculation and knowledge that economists and planners have about the essential economic data. The economic problem consists, however, in a proper use of limited means of production that satisfies our various needs. Inability to calculate and lack of knowledge are two distinct things from the logical point of view. Responding to the criticism of socialists, who maintain that economic calculation is not infallible, Mises stresses that all future-oriented human action is always uncertain; hence entrepreneurs make mistakes in their calculations. The paradox of the actions of socialist planners, however, is that they cannot plan, for they have deprived themselves of the tools of economic calculation as a result of the nationalization of the means of production.

Cost accounting is for Mises a mental tool of human action. This tool purposefully serves the choice of the best means to improve future conditions. Therefore, it is not a purely arithmetical process that can be established and examined by an indifferent umpire on the free market. Economic calculus appears—and is meaningful—only in the context of the personal point of view of the individual who enters the orbit of the process of exchange. Mises claims that there are no objective norms by which to assess materials and people on the market. For this reason, economics for him is a science not about things and tangible material objects but about men and their actions.

Mises has demonstrated that socialism repels rational economics. In his view, the only economic system justified from the rational point of view remains the market economy. An indirect way, or a form of social cooperation based on the private ownership of the means of production but linked with governmental intervention by way of directives and prohibitions, cannot persist in the long run. The means of production therefore can be either private or public property. There are no intermediate stages between socialism and the market economy; they can both be neatly distinguished and cannot be combined.

Negative Effects of Governmental Interventionism

Each government can introduce any law on its sovereign territory, limit consumption, raise taxes, introduce restrictions, regulate and control prices. Mises, however, asks whether it will achieve its objectives by way of this policy. Such a government would create a restricted market, in which consumers would no longer control what should be produced, where, how much, and by whom. The state would demolish in this manner the laws of the market and would hamper the building of the market structure.

Each intervention of the authorities undermines the natural work of the market. In the case of government's interference with the structure of prices, the market equilibrium between demand and supply is disturbed. Introducing maximum prices, the government creates a situation in which potential purchasers cannot buy a good although they are ready to pay the price fixed by the government or even a higher price. Minimum prices create a situation in which potential sellers cannot sell their commodities, because they are unable to price them below the level determined by the authorities. Owing to governmental interference, goods and services are allocated in a new way. Prices cease to serve the segregation of the potential buyers and sellers. In this situation, the government is forced to resort to a system of rationing to avoid chaos. Mises frequently warns that distortion and imbalance introduced by price controls always lead to the expansion of governmental control over new sectors of the economy. Contrary to the initial intention of the authorities, the center, directing the whole of production and distribution, will gradually fall into the hands of the government, the effect of which will be the slow transformation of a market economy into a socialist economy.

Another effect of governmental interventionist policy is trade cycles—the economy's tendency to booms and recessions—which would not take place with commodity prices. Mises claims that the reason why there are cycles is excessive credit expansion spurred by central banks in economies in which fiduciary money is used.[27] Today credit expansion is practiced exclusively by governments, which have the final word in all matters concerning the dimensions of fiduciary credits. Credit expansion is their main tool in their struggle against the market economy.

A systematic presentation of Mises' views on the rationality and logic of human action prepares a conceptual apparatus that will be indispensable to carry out a theological-moral analysis of his conception of man from the perspective of the order of faith, which is—for obvious reasons—absent from Mises' thought. The Austrian economist discovers the world of human action and shows us that its structures and governing laws may be recognized by our reason. The cause-and-effect approach to the discovery of the laws governing human action in the economic and social sphere determines the essence of Mises' thinking. Contrary to mathematical economists, he bases the principles of economics on the foundation of immutable principles at which he arrives through intellectual reflection on the reality and nature of human action in the economic sphere.

Mises has demonstrated that praxeological laws are universal and can be discovered by way of deduction. The starting point to build an economic system is for him the axiom that people act and make free choices between alternative ways of action. A study of human action therefore must be based on the principle of methodological individualism and the theory of subjective value. Mises thereby rejects both the mathematization of economics and the idea that it should be based on the method applied in the historical sciences. Mises' coherent economic theory is a tool without which empirical data would be deprived of any sense and without which we would not be able to confer any meaning on human history.

Rationality, freedom, purposefulness, and individuality are those elements in Mises' economic system that have a profound philosophical kinship with Christian anthropology. The Church does not reject man's individualism. It is even emphasized in a special way, for the human person is always perceived in his or her inalienable

---

[27] L. von Mises, "The 'Austrian' Theory of the Trade Cycle," in *The Austrian Theory of the Trade Cycle and Other Essays*, ed. R. M. Ebeling (Auburn, AL: Ludwig von Mises Institute, 1996), 28.

uniqueness. What is not accepted is the egoistic approach to life. The foregoing analysis of the meaning of various actions taken by individuals is a good introduction to understanding how Mises perceives man as a social being, and a foundation for the discovery of the laws governing society as a whole and the grounds of the rationality of market economics.

In Mises' view we face a choice between the market economy and freedom on the one hand, and socialism and dictatorship on the other. First, the creation of a mixed economy based on state interventionism, often called the third way, is unfeasible from the rational and logical points of view. Second, sooner or later each action of this kind gradually leads to the state taking over ever larger areas of freedom, limiting human entrepreneurship and impoverishing society. He is a decisive defender of the individual against the oppression of the state, but in no case does he affirm absolute individualism. He is aware that the safest place for man is community. Each individual on the free market knows that his self-interest is best protected when he adjusts his action to the requirements of social cooperation in the frame of the division of labor.

Mises has shown that economists are wrong when they reduce the individual's action on the free market exclusively to *homo economicus.* Market phenomena are a result of the actions of particular individuals who maximize their action not because of economic calculation but because they realize their concrete intentions. Mises does not reduce the free market to anonymous forces that put the market mechanism into motion and divide people into the classes of producers and consumers. Society should be the space of freedom, where each acting person pursues his own goals while serving as a means for other people to achieve their own ends. Mises' conception of the individual as a free being, acting purposefully and fulfilling himself in society, has much in common with the Christian vision of the person. We now turn to a theological and moral analysis of that conception.

2

The Dignity of the Human Person in the Free Economy

In Mises' writings, we do not find a view of man from the perspective of faith, nor any answer to questions about man's origins or ultimate end. Moving only within the economic-social sphere, Mises acknowledges, however, that man has a central position and defends his uniqueness.

Mises maintained that the theory of human action in economics has an *a priori* character and for that reason the Austrian school of economics could not enter a fruitful dialogue with Christian philosophy. Kantian epistemology is not, however, an indispensable assumption for Misesian praxeology. Murray N. Rothbard, Mises' disciple, claimed that the fundamental axiom and additional axioms derive from the experience of reality; they have an empirical character, and the human mind does not have to impose the alleged "laws of logical structure" on the chaotic structure of reality.[1] Gabriel J. Zanotti is of the same opinion. He concludes that the main assumption of Mises' praxeology does not entail neo-Kantian epistemology and may easily

---

[1] M. N. Rothbard, "Praxeology: The Methodology of Austrian Economics," in *Economic Controversies* (Auburn, AL: Ludwig von Mises Institute, 2011), 59–79, https://mises.org/library/praxeology-methodology-austrian-economics.

function within the structure of Thomistic philosophy.[2] Mises' theory of human action is therefore a perfect supplement of Thomism and helps us better understand human behavior in real action.

In the first part of this chapter we shall present the personalist foundations of human action in the economic theory of the author of *Human Action*. Then we shall analyze the limits of human freedom, an analysis which will permit us to grasp the role of private property as an extension of the sphere of the freedom of human action. The last part of the chapter, concerning the transcendent dimension of the person in human action, will prove that the objectives of human actions in the economic-social sphere have a social dimension and are not limited to empirically verifiable reality.

THE PERSONALIST FOUNDATIONS OF HUMAN ACTION

The Church teaches that the whole of social life concentrates on the human person—the main and unique participant in this life. Each man is perceived as an image of God himself. In this image, man finds his explanation and is called to an ever more profound understanding of himself in the mystery of Christ who is the perfect image of God and in like manner reveals him to man and man to himself.[3]

The social doctrine of the Church is developed on the ground of the principle that affirms the inviolable dignity of the human person.[4] Mises calls the human person "an individual," but this does not mean that he reduces man to an element or a particle of the social body. It can be elicited from Mises' writings that to man can be attributed all basic features of the human person as a transcendent being. The individual there is an acting subject in a conscious and free relationship to the whole of reality. In Christianity, the ground of this relationship toward the whole world is God.[5] In Mises, it is reason and free will.

---

[2] G. J. Zanotti, "Misesian Praxeology and Christian Philosophy," *Journal of Markets & Morality* 1, no. 1 (Spring 1998): 60.

[3] Pontifical Council for Justice and Peace, *Compendium of the Social Doctrine of the Church* (2004), no. 105.

[4] John XXIII, Encyclical Letter *Mater et Magistra* (1961), no. 53.

[5] To be a person, according to Karl Rahner and Herbert Vorgrimler, means "self-possession of the subject as such in a conscious relation to the whole

Freedom is understood, however, only in its negative sense,[6] which results from Mises' praxeological assumptions, according to which to define the goal of human action is to go beyond the domain of economics.

The Church teaches that the law of God and the natural law determine man's way of practicing good and striving after the goal. God is the source and judge of all good.[7] There arises a question as to whether this teaching can be squared with Mises' subjectivist value theory as the ground for human cooperation and development not only in the market economy but in all spheres of action.[8]

The Earthly Reality

The majority of economists approach economic analysis from a utilitarian perspective, which is based on an anthropology that cannot be reconciled with the teaching of the Church. Economics is firmly rooted in earthly reality, in which the utility of goods plays a principal role in the understanding of the action of economic processes, but it does not have to be based on the maximization of costs in the conceptual categories of the philosophy of utilitarianism.[9] In the first part of this chapter we shall try to show that the subjectivist value theory, on which Mises builds his theory of human action, is based on natural human rights and personalist principles.

To analyze Mises' subjectivist value theory, we must understand the assumption on which he built his economic system. Mises claims that man could not understand a world in which things would not run

---

reality and to God as its infinite foundation." K. Rahner and H. Vorgrimler, *A Small Dictionary of Theology*, translated from the Polish by J. Klos (Warsaw, 1991), 307.

[6] Isaiah Berlin thought that only "negative freedom" is a true freedom, which may usually be measured by the range in which nobody can interfere in our activity. Isaiah Berlin, "Two Concepts of Liberty," in *Liberty* (Oxford: Oxford University Press, 2004), 1–54.

[7] *Catechism of the Catholic Church* (1993), no. 1955.

[8] Mises, *Human Action*, 4.

[9] P. A. Cleveland, "Connections between the Austrian School of Economics and Christian Faith: A Personalist Approach," *Journal of Markets & Morality* 6, no. 1 (Spring 2003): 663.

"according to eternal, merciless, and great laws."[10] Rational human action is therefore possible only in a world in which phenomena are in accord with the natural law that appears to us as the foundation of human existence. Mises perceives the positive factors of the natural law and emphasizes their threefold contribution to economic sciences.[11]

First, man discovers praxeological laws in the same way that he discovers other laws of nature.[12] Mises acknowledges indirectly that all natural laws, among which he includes praxeological laws, are recognized by the natural light of human reason. Man is the only creature on earth who discerns them in a conscious and free manner.[13] Human reason is for Mises a means to learn the natural order. The Church teaches that we learn the truth about the world most fully by faith, but a large part of this truth is available also to those who have at their disposal only natural mental faculties. In the encyclical letter *Fides et Ratio* John Paul II stresses that exploring truth by way of reason is not only man's task but is also the essence of his nobility.[14]

Second, Mises states that there is an order of things given by nature to which man and economist must adjust themselves, if they want to succeed.[15] In his behavior, man enjoys autonomy, but this does not mean that he does not depend on this world. He discovers certain laws that he made himself and that he must respect and observe if he wants to survive and develop. All these laws remain closely interrelated.

Third, the only available method to evaluate any action is its effect. This way of thinking brought Mises to a special kind of utilitarianism, which is based on the logic of cause-effect relations, and this is nothing new in the development of economic thought. It was already St. Thomas Aquinas and Late Scholastics who used utilitarian arguments

---

[10] Mises, *Epistemological Problems*, 211.

[11] Mises, *Theory and History*, 30; A. Chafuen, *Faith and Liberty: The Economic Thought of the Late Scholastics* (Lanham, MD: Lexington Books, 2003), 26.

[12] Mises, *Human Action*, 761.

[13] J. Majka, [*Social Philosophy*] (Wroclaw, 1982), 207–10. Throughout this book, Polish sources will be cited by their titles in English translation, in brackets.

[14] John Paul II, Encyclical Letter *Fides et Ratio*, no. 17.

[15] Mises, *Theory and History*, 44–45.

to prove the natural economic order;[16] for them the value of a commodity or service resides not so much in their objective value but in how people value them at the moment of exchange. This means that economic value is a result of individual preferences and in the final analysis is always subjective.

Our foregoing analysis has shown that Mises takes into account the natural order of the world. Understanding the cause-effect relations is always useful for man, since it permits him to discover laws that come from the eternal law.

Social Cooperation

Mises perceives society as an association of individuals who consciously establish cooperation in order to enhance their productivity and gain greater individual and communal profits. This is a rational phenomenon because, owing to reason, people can grasp profits that result from social cooperation, a cooperation that is fully realized only when people are free to know, choose, and act.

This way of understanding leads us to one of the principal features of human nature, which is, according to Aquinas, an expression of its social and dynamic character. This tendency comes from the main command of the natural law that "good is to be done." Saint Thomas claims that "the order of the precepts of the natural law is according to the order of natural inclinations."[17]

The natural inclination to develop personality in society has been described by St. Thomas as follows: "to shun ignorance, to avoid offending those among whom one has to live."[18] In his commentary on Aquinas's text, Mieczysław A. Krąpiec remarks that man must live in a social group to learn his own needs and satisfy them.[19] Man needs mutual contact and cooperation to make real the potentiality of his nature in relation to other persons. Individual good and social good are two aspects of the same object.

Mises distinguishes between social cooperation based on contracts made with respect to human freedom and relations based on hegemony

---

[16] Chafuen, *Faith and Liberty*, 80.

[17] *Summa Theologica*, I-II, q. 94, a. 2.

[18] *Summa Theologica*, I-II, q. 94, a. 2.

[19] M. A. M. Krąpiec, [*Man and the Natural Law*] (Lublin, 1999), 205ff.

in which the individual does not have any influence on the course of events.[20] He remarks that, for the market economy, peaceful cooperation of all people is indispensable, as it is more effective than social feuds and disputes. Here we can see Mises' utilitarianism, which takes into account the effect of the labor of particular individuals. It is the ground to assess the usefulness of particular individuals in society, but contrary to appearances Mises does not treat man as an object.

The author of *Human Action* here extends the theory of comparative costs, according to which a participant in exchange gains profits even if he sells goods that call for fewer outlays on production in exchange for goods that call for greater outlays.[21] David Ricardo has proved that the division of labor is profitable for all, even when one party is in every respect more productive than the other.[22] Mises claims that social cooperation is the main source of human successes in the struggle for survival and improvement of material conditions. Putting aside the factors of moral nature, cooperation based on the division of labor and voluntary exchange brings material profits to all and is a foundation of social order broadly understood.[23]

This way of understanding brings us to another natural inclination of rational human nature, which constitutes the ground of rational human action in Mises and which St. Thomas calls concern for the preservation of one's own life and existence. Mises claims that the acting man desires to replace a less satisfactory state of affairs with a better one. The motivation for this action is therefore always a certain state of uneasiness. Mises notes that there is no difference here between satisfaction attained from eating food and that from communing with art, for in man's valuation they are perceived as more or less urgent needs. Man attributes a value to things as means to remove his anxiety and places them all in one scale. This corresponds to the law of decreasing marginal utility. This principle is a praxeological truth that is derived from the nature of the acting man, and shows

[20] Mises, *Human Action*, 195–96.

[21] M. Blaug, *Economic Theory in Retrospect* (Cambridge: Cambridge University Press, 1990), 126–28. In view of an enormous range of application of this law, Mises calls it the law of cooperation.

[22] Mises, *Theory and History*, 27–28.

[23] G. Callahan, *Economics for Real People: An Introduction to the Austrian School* (Auburn, AL: Ludwig von Mises Institute, 2004), 64.

that the first unit of a good will be used in the most valuable manner for us, and each successive unit with respect to its place on our own scale of values.[24] This law refers to the subjectivist value theory, for man will not attain even the most sublime goals if he does not satisfy his most basic needs.[25]

Mises thus discovers and describes human action in the socioeconomic sphere that is manifested in the preservation of one's own life and thereby corresponds with human nature. Man tends to preserve and defend himself; if we denied this law, we would eliminate being itself. It is a manifestation of the natural law in the cosmic dimension and deals with all animate beings that want "to be rather than to have." The preservation of existence-life is according to Krapiec an ontic "base" of other rights.[26] Mises correctly notes that the noblest goals of man cannot be attained by people who have not satisfied the needs of their bodies first.

The last natural inclination, indicated by Aquinas, that we find in *Human Action*, deals with the transmission of life. In Mises, this idea occurs mainly in his work on socialism.[27] In it he objects to Marxism because, by way of social revolution, it tends to eliminate not only private property but also the institution of monogamous marriage, which Friedrich Engels saw as a consequence of concentrating wealth in a male's hands.[28] Mises looks at marriage as an irreplaceable social institution, an element of the individual's adjustment to social order in which woman may, in accordance with nature, fulfill her main task—that is, bear children and care for the family.[29] Mises claims that the institution of marriage is a contract based on a bilateral and free decision whose basis is a free choice in love.[30] This relationship enforces a duty of mutual loyalty in which both parties have the same

---

[24] Mises, *Human Action*, 119–27.

[25] Mises, *Theory and History*, 38.

[26] Krąpiec, [*Man and the Natural Law*], 200–202.

[27] Mises, *Socialism*, 75.

[28] F. Engels, *Origin of the Family, Private Property, and the State*. http://www.marxists.org/archive/marx/works/download/pdf/origin_family.pdf.

[29] J. A. Tucker and L. H. Rockwell, "The Cultural Thought of Ludwig von Mises," in *The Meaning of Ludwig von Mises*, 285.

[30] Mises, *Socialism*, 91.

rights.[31] The Austrian economist is a staunch opponent of free unions because he thinks that they are contrary to nature and result from the pseudo-democratic propaganda of socialists who are in favor of the elimination of natural and socially conditioned inequalities between woman and man.[32]

In considering the latter inclination, St. Thomas does not limit "the right to transmit life" merely to reproductive functions.[33] He adds the upbringing of children, indicating thereby that the life of the human person begins and develops in a family. Mises thinks likewise and says that a child grows to be "a healthy human creature" only when parents teach him or her how to love.[34]

This analysis of the economic system shows that, according to Mises, human action in the socioeconomic sphere is based on the principal inclinations of human nature. The Church teaches that they are universal and recognizable by all people by the natural light of reason. An analysis of human action has allowed Mises to proceed still further and, by way of deduction, come to a formulation of the concept of private property, which belongs to the third kind of the most important principles of the natural law, the so-called operative principles.[35]

---

[31] Mises, *Socialism*, 82.

[32] Tucker and Rockwell, "Cultural Thought of Mises," 296.

[33] St. Thomas Aquinas, *Summa Theologica*, I-II, q. 94, a. 2. Referring to Ulpina's maxim, St. Thomas describes the second inclination of human nature in the following way: "those things are said to belong to the natural law which nature has taught to all animals, such as sexual intercourse, the education of offspring and so forth."

[34] Mises, *Socialism*, 91.

[35] M. Lesniak, ["Natural Law"], in *The Encyclopedia of John Paul II's Social Teaching*, ed. A. Zwolinski (Radom, 2003), 405–6. Mises often criticizes the natural law, but as an economist he does not use precise language in this domain and fails to notice that "natural" refers not to nature in the biological sense but a way in which man recognizes this law. See John Paul II, *Veritatis Splendor*, no. 43.

Freedom of Action in the Frame of Private Property

Private ownership of the means of production is for Mises the fundamental and necessary institution in the market economy.[36] It was conceived by human beings and is an entirely human device. Aquinas thinks likewise: private ownership does not contradict the natural law because it was invented by human reason.[37] In social systems in which economic self-sufficiency of particular family households dominates, ownership of productive or consumer goods means that one owns them for oneself and uses them for one's own satisfaction. In the market system, private ownership fulfills a social function. The owner of productive goods is forced to use them for the satisfaction of consumers' needs.[38]

In the frame of the market economy, each individual is free to act within the orbit of private property, which is the ground of market activity. The coordination of the autonomous actions of many individuals is accomplished through market operations, not through special instructions and prohibitions. Beyond the sphere of private property there is the sphere of compulsion and coercion. According to Mises, the market becomes chaotic if the institution of private ownership, disparaged as selfish by the opponents of the free market, is eliminated. The substitution of state property for private property does not contribute to profitable cooperation or peaceful exchange.[39]

Greater productivity, social order, and autonomy of the human person are also arguments on behalf of private property put forward by the social doctrine of the Church.[40] The Second Vatican Council stresses that private property gives the person an opportunity to perform various tasks in society and in private life.[41] Therefore private ownership does not result from *ius naturae* but from *ius gentium*, a fact that changes nothing in the scope and the categorical character

---

[36] Mises, *Human Action*, 682.

[37] Aquinas, *Summa Theologica*, II-II, q. 66, a. 2.

[38] Mises, *Human Action*, 683.

[39] Mises, *Human Action*, 724–26.

[40] F. Mazurek, ["Property"], in [*A Dictionary of Catholic Social Doctrine*], ed. A. Piwowarski (Warsaw, 1993), 192.

[41] Second Vatican Council, Dogmatic Constitution on the Church *Lumen Gentium* (1964), no. 71.

of the norm expressed by the divine commandment "Thou shalt not steal."[42]

Saint Thomas also uses utilitarian arguments on behalf of private property and elicits it from analysis of human action. First, each man naturally strives more diligently to gain things for himself than he does for a common pool of resources. Second, private property contributes to order and responsible cooperation in society. The third argument emphasizes peace, since conflicts start most often where there is no division of property.[43]

The Subjective Character of Valuation Acts

The analysis so far has shown that the subjectivist value theory, which is for Mises a key term to explain all economic phenomena, is based on the foundation of the natural law. In *Veritatis Splendor*, John Paul II states that the natural law expresses the dignity of the human person and lays the foundation for the law and duties of all people.[44] We may therefore say that up to now Mises' economic system corresponds to the personalist norm as an obligation to affirm the person by an act with respect to the person himself and therefore with respect to his exceptional dignity. Owing to this norm, acting man in the economic sphere is located in a proper place in relation to God and to the sources of the law.[45]

The subjectivist value theory itself as presented by Mises, as we have seen, is rooted in the foundation of three natural inclinations of human reason; in no case does it mean to counter the natural law, because it logically stems from this law. A closer look reveals its further consonance with Church teaching.

The Church teaches that the natural law is objective and immutable, and the role of man consists in reading out this law. The objective character of the natural law does not exclude its dynamic character.[46]

---

[42] S. Skobel, "Real Theft and Apparent Theft," *Communio* 1 (1999): 27.

[43] Aquinas, *Summa Theologica*, II-II, q. 66, art. 2.

[44] John Paul II, *Veritatis Splendor*, no. 51.

[45] T. Makowski, ["The Present Understanding of Natural Law in Light of the Official Teaching of the Church"], *Ateneum Kaplanskie* 81, no. 2 (1973): 196–97.

[46] Makowski, "Present Understanding," 201.

In the contemporary teaching of the Church, attention is focused on the personalist aspect of the natural law. Man is not only active in discovering this law but with his own reason may learn the goals of his life in the economic-social sphere, indicate means, and formulate norms by which they can be attained.[47]

Subjectivist value theory was first formulated by the Franciscan Pierre de Jean Olivi. He claimed that, from the economic point of view, the value of a commodity results from a subjective valuation by particular persons who estimate its usefulness and attractiveness.[48] This theory was accepted by the Late Scholastics. Mises took it over directly from Carl Menger, who based his value theory on the one simple fact that "things are valuable because acting humans consider them to be so."[49] Menger's theory has contributed to the refutation of the value theory held by classical economists, who sought to base it on the amount of work necessary for the production of a given good or on its utility, using some objective measure. Karl Marx thought likewise; he believed that the investment of labor automatically confers value on a product.[50]

For the Austrian economist, the value of market goods is a relationship that is deeply rooted in personal, subjective acts of valuation and depends on an individual assessment and concrete choice made by acting man. Mises' praxeology does not evaluate human action from the point of view of its correctness but explains market behavior on the basis of choices. Value for Mises is a purely formal function and does not say whether the action itself is valuable. Economics does not contain any view on the preferred modes of action, valuation of costs, or profits. Acting man merely asks if the chosen means serve to attain his goals, and he acts according to his own order of values.

According to Mises, economics is not a normative science, and despite the fact that he uses the concepts of gain and profit, he abstains

---

[47] H. Waskiewicz, ["Natural Law in the Encyclical *Pacem in terries*"], [*Learned Fascicles of the Catholic University of Lublin*], nos. 1, 3 (1964).

[48] T. E. Woods, *How the Catholic Church Built Western Civilization* (Washington, DC: Regnery, 2005), 158–60.

[49] Callahan, *Economics for Real People*, 25.

[50] H. Landreth and D. C. Colander, *History of Economic Thought* (Boston: Houghton Mifflin, 2002), 198.

from any judgments of value.[51] Like Menger, he thinks that it is the task of economics to examine and describe nature, principal relations, and economic phenomena, including an analysis of cause-effect relations—that is, the formal implications that may be discerned from the fact that people act purposefully.[52] Economics, therefore, to be precise in its methodology, abstains from the ethical valuation of human behavior, for it describes how people act, not how they should act.[53] From the moral point of view, only concrete human deeds can be judged. The science of economics should therefore be distinguished from political economics, whose task is to indicate what conditions should be fostered for definite goals to be attained and which does not abstain from moral evaluations since it is oriented to values.[54]

It should be stressed that the subjectivist value theory has nothing in common with moral relativism. To understand and explain human choices, economics is indifferent toward values. Mises defines human action as tending to happiness, but in praxeology there is no criterion of a greater or lesser satisfaction except the individual judgment of value.[55] The term *happiness* is used in a purely formal sense. The subjectivist science about human action abstains from passing judgments on the purposes of human action. Neither can it state whether man's act contributes to happiness understood as pleasure or lack of suffering. Therefore it cannot be identified with utilitarianism, whose foundation of morality is the principle of the greatest happiness for the largest number of people.[56] For Aristotle, as for St. Thomas, the purpose of economics was happiness and pleasure, understood as entirely subjective.

Mises claims that the acting man tends to attain his chosen goals and, in consequence, there can be no way to evaluate his act other than by

---

[51] Mises, *Human Action*, 10.

[52] C. Menger, *Problems of Economics and Sociology*, ed. Louis Schneider, trans. Francis J. Nock (Urbana: University of Illinois Press, 1963), 29, 200.

[53] P. A. Samuelson, *Economics: An Introductory Analysis* (New York: McGraw Hill, 1967), 5.

[54] Menger, *Problems of Economics*, 38.

[55] Mises, *Human Action*, 14.

[56] J. S. Mill, *Utilitarianism* (Indianapolis: Bobbs-Merrill, 1957), 10.

the desirable or undesirable effects with respect to the chosen goal.[57] This way of understanding could in a sense indicate teleologism,[58] that is, a direction in ethics which recognizes that the effects of an act testify to its moral value.[59] Mises does not say, however, that in reference to earthly goods there are no absolute or immutable norms and everything is relative. Man may recognize absolute norms, which extend over the sphere of immanent goals of human action, not only through supernatural revelation but also through natural reason.[60]

Subjectivist value theory permits man to discover these norms, to rationally orient his act toward the good in its truth, and to freely tend to this good that has been recognized by reason. Man interprets good subjectively, like any other goal, and thinks it is expedient. Therefore, man in Mises has an opportunity for rational, conscious, and free subordination of his acts to God.[61] This is possible within the paradigm of subjectivist value theory, which treats the acting man's judgments of value as data, does not submit them to further analysis, and thus remains indifferent to conflicts between various dogmatic theories and ethical schools.[62]

The subjectivist theory of human action in the economic sphere cannot be identified with subjectivism, for the latter emphasizes individualism and the individual's total autonomy, claiming that on behalf of personal freedom the individual has a right to make any decision. Only a man who lived in isolation could act this way. All peaceful cooperation in society demands that an individual give up many areas of personal freedom.

Social Harmony

The rules of social cooperation and interpersonal behavior, which the author of *Human Action* elicits from the axiom of non-aggression, are based on human nature. For Mises, the end and principle of the

---

[57] Mises, *Theory and History*, 38.

[58] T. Slipko, [*An Outline of Applied Ethics*], vol. 1 (Krakow, 1982), 19–20.

[59] John Paul II, *Veritatis Splendor*, no. 75.

[60] See John Paul II, *Veritatis Splendor*, no. 72.

[61] See John Paul II, *Veritatis Splendor*, no. 73.

[62] Mises, *Human Action*, 21.

free economy is to maintain and promote social harmony and human life. It is indispensable for social cooperation that rational human creatures endowed with free will should observe individual rights. Mises' utilitarianism is based on the structure of the natural law,[63] which is expressed in the form the natural inclinations of human reason.

A member of society must take into account not only his direct profit but also the necessity to affirm with each action the community as such. The life of the individual in society is possible only due to cooperation, and the greatest loss for each would be the collapse of the social organization of life and production.[64] Utilitarianism understood in this way rejects the philosophy of collectivism and totalitarianism. Mises calls this the utilitarianism philosophy of individualism.[65]

Although Mises' praxeology deals with the choice of means for the realization of intentions and does not evaluate ultimate ends, Mises recognizes that man is not infallible and very often makes mistakes when choosing appropriate means.[66] Subjectivity in praxeology should obviously be distinguished from ethical subjectivism. The concept of subjectivity refers to the person who is a conscious subject in action; it does not imply that moral truth is subjective in the sense that each individual determines what is right or wrong.[67] Subjectivity in Mises indicates the dynamism of human actions that is always a response to new circumstances in which man must constantly make new choices. Such a view stresses the fact that human action is based on a permanent subject, the personal "I" in which each deed is rooted.

The concept of freedom and subjectivity in Mises points to the autonomy of the individual in the economic sphere, in which he is independent of the precepts of foreign individuals or collectivities and in his conduct is governed only by his own will. This autonomy results from human nature itself; therefore, each human person

---

[63] E. W. Younkins, "Mises' Utilitarianism as Social Cooperation," *Le Quebecois Libre*, July 6, 2002, no. 106, http://www.quebecoislibre.org/020706-19.hml.

[64] Mises, *Liberalism*, 37.

[65] Mises, *Theory and History*, 39.

[66] Mises, *Human Action*, 21.

[67] G. Gronbacher, *Economic Personalism: A New Paradigm for a Humane Economy* (Grand Rapids, MI: Acton Institute, 1998), 6–7.

has a space of action in which he is free and independent,[68] and the basis for this freedom in the economic sphere is private property. Additionally, there are immutable laws of praxeology that govern economic and catallactic phenomena. The Second Vatican Council teaches that created things and human communities enjoy their own rights, which man should learn, accept, order, and respect, for such autonomy corresponds with the will of the Creator[69] and in no way undermines the subjectivity of the acting person. Mises' subjectivist value theory therefore does not imply that the autonomy of earthly things excludes dependence on God.[70]

In *Veritatis Splendor*, John Paul II shows that the ethics of personalism based on subjectivity does not weaken human action in accord with objective truth. It would be a distortion to claim that the natural law lays stress on the rationality of the human person and truth, while personalism refers only to freedom and responsibility in the quest for truth.[71] John Paul II teaches that there is no conflict between freedom, understood as subjectivity, and nature. The natural law expresses the dignity of the human person, and its obligations have a universal character, but this universality does not ignore the distinctness of particular human creatures.[72] Moral action is good not only when the subject of action corresponds with the true good of a person, which is the ultimate goal and the highest good of man (i.e., God himself),[73] but also when the person through his deeds in a free manner shapes himself and takes on the form he desires.[74] Man's creativity and freedom are not expressed in finding a law, but in living through the law

---

68 W. Granat, [*Christian Personalism: The Theology of the Human Person*] (Poznan 1985), 526.

69 Second Vatican Council, Pastoral Constitution on the Church in the Modern World *Gaudium et Spes* (1965), no. 36.

70 *Gaudium et Spes*, no. 36.

71 J. Smith, "Natural Law and Personalism in *Veritatis Splendor*," in *Veritatis Splendor: American Responses*, ed. M. E. Allsopp and J. J. O'Keefe (Kansas City: Sheed and Ward, 1995), 194–207.

72 John Paul II, *Veritatis Splendor*, no. 51.

73 John Paul II, *Veritatis Splendor*, no. 72.

74 John Paul II, *Veritatis Splendor*, no. 71.

"written in his heart"—his conscience—where the bond between man's freedom and God's law has its living seat.[75]

Laissez-faireism

Contrary to Mises' views that the idea of the natural law is entirely subjective[76] and is not useful in economics, the foregoing analysis has shown the opposite, namely, that his whole economic system is based on the basic assumptions of the natural law. Such assumptions allow Mises as an economist to speak in favor of laissez-faireism[77] as a result of logical reasoning based on the principles of praxeology. Laissez-faireism is an economic system in which a common man is allowed to choose and act within the system of the social division of labor, in a way that corresponds to his dignity. This choice does not call for a declaration on behalf of any ethical system, and it fulfills Mises' postulate for the economic sciences that they should abstain from judgments of value.

The author of *Human Action* compared laissez-faireism with socialism and state interventionism and concluded that laissez-faireism surpasses other economic systems with respect to the production and distribution of material goods and the attainment of earthly ends.[78] The superiority of laissez-faireism consists not only in that, contrary to socialism and state interventionism, it allows people to accomplish the intended goals, but also in that it contributes to the peaceful cooperation of all people.

As an economist, Mises did not fully work out the term *person*, and we cannot bear a grudge against him for that. Our reasoning up to now has shown that his vision of man is based on the foundation of natural rights expressed in the three principal inclinations of human nature. The Austrian economist by virtue of deduction also comes to the formulation of the right to private property; his subjectivist value theory adds creative dynamism to the human person in the quest for truth and safeguards the dignity of the person.

---

[75] John Paul II, *Veritatis Splendor*, no. 54.

[76] Mises, *Human Action*, 720.

[77] Mises, *Human Action*, 730–31.

[78] J. P. Gunning, "Did Mises Err? Was He a Utilitarian? Reply to Block," *American Journal of Economics and Sociology* 64, no. 3 (July 2005): 939–60.

Mises speaks in favor of the free-market economy. The proper criterion for evaluating a socioeconomic system is therefore based not on the maximization of one's own profit in utilitarian categories, but on the natural law from which the dignity of the person proceeds. In socialism and state interventionism, in which there is no room for subjectivity and free decisions, the good of the individual becomes entirely subordinated to the action of the socioeconomic mechanism. These systems identify man with a certain group of social relations, a fact that leads to the disappearance of the notion of the human person as an independent subject of moral decisions.[79] The free-market economy, however, as described by Mises, gives man the space that is indispensable for free and subjective action.

FREEDOM OF HUMAN CHOICES

Man is endowed by God with free will and he can make decisions concerning his own life. Created in the image and likeness of God, he is called to become an image of the invisible God in the visible world. Man's dignity requires that he act according to a conscious and free choice.[80] God's desire is not only that man, of his own will, seek his Creator, but also that he improve the state of affairs outside himself, building a social order in accord with the true good.[81]

The social doctrine of the Church regards freedom of the person in the area of economics as a basic value and unquestionable right that should be protected and made universal.[82] This freedom pertains not only to individuals, but also to cooperating groups.[83] The Church stresses that a proper use of personal freedom calls for definite conditions in the socioeconomic order. According to Mises, these conditions are fulfilled by the free-market economy.

---

[79] John Paul II, Encyclical Letter *Centesimus Annus* (1991), no 13.

[80] *Gaudium et Spes*, no. 17.

[81] John Paul II, *Centesimus Annus*, no. 13.

[82] *Catechism of the Catholic Church*, no. 2429.

[83] Freedom from external coercion was indicated by the Second Vatican Council also in the declaration *Dignitatis Humanae*, where it speaks about religious freedom (Declaration on Religious Liberty *Dignitatis Humanae* [1965], no. 4).

Mises claims that man has not only an intellect but also a will. This presupposition shows how close he is to St. Thomas. In Mises' works, we do not find the concept of *person*, but the description of acting man contains all the elements that constitute personal action.

Free Will

The Church teaches that man may act or not act, or act in this or that way. He may decide and choose, and also resist pressure from without. The source of this self-determination, one of man's essential attributes, is the will, which is characterized by a natural tendency toward good. It is a mental faculty, tied to reason, that recognizes this good and elicits action under the influence of motives and reasons.[84]

For Mises, the main attribute of the individual is the freedom of choice. It is a just desire, for man should, by his own free initiative, form and rule his personal and social life, taking responsibility for it.[85] Mises defines freedom as a praxeological term and has in mind the sphere of economics and catallaxis, in which the acting man is able to choose between alternative modes of action. Man is free insofar as he has an opportunity to choose the means for the attainment of his chosen ends. Mises does not, however, say anything about the tendency toward good, for he places man's ends—and not only those concerning the ultimate things—beyond the sphere of praxeology.

Mises does not divide people into those who are active and full of energy and those who are passive and submissive. Inaction is also action, because in the socioeconomic sphere it affects the course of events.[86] Mises is right here, for man is continuously required to make decisions, and even abstaining from them is already a decision and fulfillment of human freedom.[87] Mises' reasoning corresponds with Christian anthropology, which says that God has created man as a rational creature, giving him the dignity of the person endowed with the capacity to decide and rule over all his actions, including also

---

[84] T. Zeleznik, ["Freedom"], in *A Dictionary of Catholic Social Doctrine*, 192.

[85] John Paul II, *Veritatis Splendor*, no. 34; *Gaudium et Spes*, no. 17.

[86] Mises, *Human Action*, 13.

[87] M. A. M. Krapiec, [*Man as Person*] (Lublin, 2005), 142.

their abandonment.[88] Freedom is the real possibility to make choices (see Deut. 30:19).

The author of *Human Action* thinks that economic freedom is best made real within the frame of the social system of the division of labor. Primitive man was not completely free, because in the pitiless competition for biological survival the fitter individual had an overwhelming advantage.[89]

Mises is a staunch defender of the individual's freedom in social life. He thinks, however, that man's freedom to choose and act is by nature limited. Man has the power to quell his instinctive desire and choose between incompatible ends. In this sense, he is free, but Mises does not interpret this freedom as independent of the universe and its laws.[90]

Natural Limitations of Human Freedom

First, Mises remarks that there are absolute laws of physics to which man must adjust himself if he wants to survive. Second, there are individual limitations, innate features and dispositions, and the influence of environmental factors. The Austrian economist is aware that they affect the choice of goals and means, although our understanding of the mode of their actions is rather vague and incomplete. Finally, limitations come from the laws that govern the interconnectedness between means and ends. Mises has in mind here praxeological laws, as distinct from physical and psychological laws.[91]

Mises does not address the source of all these limitations, but his conception of freedom can be correctly interpreted within Christian anthropology. The Church also teaches that freedom has never had an absolute and unconditional starting point in itself but lies instead in the conditions of human existence, which constitute at the same time its limitation and opportunity. It is the freedom of a created creature that must be accepted.[92] Man is a contingent being; therefore,

---

88 *Catechism of the Catholic Church*, no. 1730.

89 Mises, *Human Action*, 279.

90 Mises, *Ultimate Foundation*, 52; Mises, *Theory and History*, 119.

91 Mises, *Human Action*, 885.

92 John Paul II, *Veritatis Splendor*, no 86.

his freedom must be in accord with his nature.[93] Aquinas emphasizes that God does not act contrary to nature. The Creator respects human nature and in this manner stimulates man to act in accord with his nature, for only this is a guarantee of his real freedom.[94]

Man must choose between the preservation of some laws, which make his life in society possible, and the poverty and insecurity that result from a life of perpetual warfare among independent individuals. For this reason, it is necessary for government to protect peaceful social cooperation.[95] Mises does not regard this form of coercion as a limitation of human freedom to make choices. Man is up to that moment free, for the laws and the government do not force him to give up his own autonomy to a greater extent than is required by the laws of praxeology.[96]

In no case does Mises make freedom absolute. He is aware of its limitations, the same ones that can be found in Christian anthropology. Adjusting the individual to the requirements of social cooperation is linked with a necessity for sacrifices, but they are only transitory because life in society brings immeasurably greater profits. Mises is not an anarchist; he thinks that society could not function without a government that keeps a tight rein on all asocial elements.[97] The state's task is to protect peaceful interhuman relations. Mises thinks that the social system must be based on two pillars: private property and the moral principles that govern its use.[98]

External Coercion

The limitation of freedom and liberty is most acutely felt in acts of external coercion. According to Stanislaw Olejnik, freedom should also be understood as independence from any physical coercion—that is, liberty permits what behooves man in the external sphere of actions and that to which he is by his natural desires and acquired

[93] C. Bartnik, ["Nature, Person, and Freedom"], *Bobolanum,* no. 4 (1993): 13–29.

[94] Aquinas, *Summa Theologica,* I-II, q. 10, a. 4 corp.

[95] John Paul II, *Centesimus Annus,* no. 16.

[96] Mises, *Human Action,* 280.

[97] Mises, *Human Action,* 171.

[98] Mises, *Human Action,* 724.

habits internally directed.[99] Freedom is a condition of development, in both the individual and social dimensions. In his encyclical *Spe Salvi,* Benedict XVI stresses that, if the world by reason of conditions or structures were deprived of freedom, it would no longer be good, "since a world without freedom can by no means be a good world."[100]

The Church not only teaches that one should respect the basic freedoms of citizens with regard to their private and sociopolitical life, but also shows how to make these freedom aspirations real, so that they can serve the true good of man and society. A concrete expression of these tendencies is the rights of the person to free assembly, to public articulation of his views, to confess religion in private and public, and to own property.[101]

Mises sees the greatest threat to freedom in the institution of the state. The state is supposed to serve an effective functioning of the social system, and this is for the Austrian philosopher the only standard that should be used to trace the boundaries of its competence. It is not the idea of absolute justice, for there is no way of describing justice beyond the social context.[102] The advocates of the so-called "third way" maintain that state intervention in market phenomena is always necessary because a free play of market forces leads to socially detrimental effects. Mises claims that, with the preservation of the right to private ownership such intervention is redundant, for the individual's interests are not and cannot be contradictory to social interests.[103]

This way of thinking shows that Mises perceives the limits of state intervention in the life of its citizens in a way similar to that of Thomistic philosophers. Mieczyslaw Krapiec stresses that man is a sovereign in his acts of decision.[104] Sovereignty deals with the end-good of human actions and personal recognition of the truthfulness of this end. Man is not a sovereign in relation to all means that enable the attainment

---

99 S. Olejnik, [*Moral Theology: Gift, Calling, and Answer*], vol. 2, [*Man and His Action*] (Warsaw 1988), 44.

100 Benedict XVI, Encyclical Letter *Spe Salvi* (2007), no. 30.

101 *Gaudium et Spes,* no. 73.

102 Mises, *Human Action,* 721.

103 Mises, *Human Action,* 725.

104 M. A. M. Krapiec, [*Human Freedom*] (Lublin, 2000), 132–35.

of the goal, because they belong to another sovereign, which is the state. Man will not develop as man in the order of cognition, volition, and creation without the cooperation of others. The aid of the state must always have, however, a complementary character, which consists in the organization and creation of conditions of freedom in the economic, social, and cultural spheres. State sovereignty must therefore always be subordinate to human personal sovereignty.

The author of *Human Action* says that the individual's tendency to attain his own ends integrates his actions with the overall social system of production and serves the common good; therefore, the government's intervention is unjustified. He confirms thereby that the human person is for him the principle and end of political cooperation.[105] It is consumers who decide what is to be produced; in what quantity and quality it is produced; and where and by whom it is produced. The market economy should therefore be the most desired system of social organization from the point of view of justice. According to the classical formula, justice "consists in the constant and firm will to give their due to God and neighbor."[106] Justice understood in this manner means to recognize the other as a person endowed with reason, responsible for his decisions, and capable of realizing his plans that give sense to his life in both the individual and social spheres.[107] Freedom in the frame of social life should be viewed as a gift, not a threat. One should be educated in the nature of this gift so as to use it well and help others in the growth in genuine freedom.[108]

Mises claims that man in the frame of the free market is free to act in the sphere of private ownership and his choices are final.[109] Christian tradition has never maintained the right to private property as an

---

[105] See *Catechism of the Catholic Church,* no 1884; and Congregation for the Doctrine of the Faith, "Doctrinal Note on Some Questions Regarding the Participation of Catholics in Political Life," November 24, 2002, no. 2, http://www.vatican.va/roman_curia/congregations/cfaith/documents/rc_con_cfaith_doc_20021124_politica_en.html.

[106] *Catechism of the Catholic Church,* no. 1807; see also Aquinas, *Summa Theologica,* II-II, q. 58, a. 1.

[107] *Compendium of the Social Doctrine,* no. 384.

[108] S. Olejnik, [*Moral Theology*], vol. 2, 44–45.

[109] Mises, *Human Action,* 724.

absolute and inviolable principle.[110] It understands property rights instead in the context of the universal destination of goods, which does not mean that private ownership is weakened or eliminated, for it is inseparably linked with human freedom.[111] Mises is correct when he writes that beyond the sphere of private property and the market there is the sphere of compulsion and coercion.[112]

Depriving man of the possibility of private ownership is a serious obstacle in free decision making. This leads to captivity and strikes at something essential to the person.[113] John Paul II teaches that a man who is deprived of private property and cannot earn a living through his own entrepreneurship is not able to understand his dignity as a person, nor can he build up an authentic human community.[114]

The Purposefulness of Human Action

Having analyzed freedom as the main attribute of man and at the same time recognized the limits of human choices in the free-market economy, we now move to Mises' main assumption: that man always acts purposefully. Only one who is capable of discovering causal relations may properly *act* in the Misesean sense. Limitations of freedom that flow from without interfere with the process of the choice of end and means to its attainment. This way of reasoning is identical with Thomistic philosophy. The same man who by virtue of natural inclinations freely creates social structures cannot dispense with the purposeful character of his personal actions. Depriving man of his personal goals belittles him and destabilizes the relationship between the means and goals of human action.[115]

Mises defines human action as the will put into operation—that is, transformed into an agency.[116] For Mises, thinking and acting are

---

110 John Paul II, Encyclical Letter *Laborem Exercens* (1981), no. 14.

111 Krapiec, [*Human Freedom*], 188.

112 Mises, *Human Action*, 725.

113 Krapiec, [*Human Freedom*], 188–89.

114 John Paul II, *Centesimus Annus*, no. 13.

115 Krapiec, [*Human Freedom*], 211–12.

116 Mises, *Human Action*, 11.

therefore the specific human features.[117] Similarly, St. Thomas attributes freedom only to a being which is the only cause of its acts.[118] Freedom in Thomistic tradition is linked with the freedom of choice. It is multifarious, multilevel, and primeval.[119] According to Christian anthropology, there can be no talking about freedom in nonpersonal beings. Freedom occurs only in spiritual and reasonable beings.[120]

For Mises, action is a voluntary reaction to stimuli and external conditions.[121] According to Aquinas, a truly free action is preceded by acts of intellectual consideration.[122] The author of *Human Action* does not give a precise definition of human action but stresses that it is a conscious adjustment of man to the state of the universe. One notices here that human action is not limited to the sphere of the intellect but—as in St. Thomas—is a perfect harmony of the intellect and the will.

Mises looks at man mainly as *homo agens*,[123] who can rationalize his behavior and is governed not merely by impulses or instincts. Action is essential for man because it enables him to survive. Mises assumes human action as something given, something that belongs to his nature and existence.[124]

Man acts, for he feels discontented and wants to remove his discontent.[125] This is the main reason why—according to Mises—people want to do something with their life. Acting man constantly subordinates his needs and wishes to his proper scale of values, makes choices, and

117 Mises, *Human Action*, 25.

118 St. Thomas Aquinas, *Commentary on the Letter of Saint Paul to the Romans*, trans. F. R. Larcher, OP (Lander, WY: Aquinas Institute for the Study of Sacred Doctrine, 2012), 7–9, 59–60.

119 C. Bartnik, [*Personalism*] (Lublin, 1995), 267.

120 St. Thomas Aquinas, *Summa contra gentiles*, bk. 3, nos. 47 and 48, http://www.catholicprimer.org/aquinas/aquinas_summa_contra_gentiles.pdf; J. Maritain, [Philosophical Writings], trans. J. Fenrychowej (Krakow, 1988), 85.

121 Mises, *Human Action*, 11.

122 K. Wojtkiewicz, [*St. Thomas Aquinas' Personalism in "Tract on Man"*] (Olsztyn, 1999), 157.

123 Mises, *Human Action*, 14.

124 Mises, *Human Action*, 19.

125 Mises, *Human Action*, 69.

acts. This leads to a belief that in our actions there is a basic order that is expressed in combined acts of our rational knowledge and acts of the will. Having concrete goals, man organizes the means to attain it.

The essential unity of man compels him to harmonize and concentrate his conduct around the superior end. This end may be his awareness that God is a good in himself, and this may be the starting point for the choice of proper goods-means to attain this end. Mises does not say what the goal of man in action is; he only places this end beyond him, so that he can strive after it. In like manner he affirms that man is a fragile and contingent being who cannot be a goal for himself, as the creature who is not the fullness of good.[126]

The author of *Human Action* correctly places the goal beyond the sphere of economics, for the principal end of our life—the good made manifest in the desire to substitute the worse state for something better—is given to man as a contingent and imperfect being, by virtue of nature itself. We may therefore say that each man in the free-market system is free to act on behalf of good.[127]

The Reality of Choice

Praxeology is interested in concrete action that a concrete person has taken in a concrete time and place. Mises rejects philosophical assumptions according to which universal concepts correspond to real beings, for they make it impossible to grasp praxeological problems in a satisfactory manner. The best-known is the paradox of value, which for centuries has hampered the progress of studies of classical economists. The act of decision is always a choice between various opportunities open to the individual. Man never chooses between "gold" and "iron" in general, but only between a definite amount of gold and a definite amount of iron in a concrete moment.[128] In his reasoning, Mises employs the categories of classical philosophy and claims that it is in intellectual knowledge that knowledge in the economic sphere touches reality. The object of intellectual knowledge is always "something that exists." This concrete "something"—which

126 Krapiec, [*Human Freedom*], 44–45.

127 Krapiec, [*Human Freedom*], 49.

128 Mises, *Human Action*, 45.

man perceives and whose reality he states—is called *being* in classical philosophy.

The reality of being has far-reaching consequences that go beyond the interests of economics and affect man's actions in the prospect of the ultimate end. The order of knowledge coalesces with the order of desire and love, for the real being that is known is at the same time a good. Abstractions cannot be objects of desire. Mises' observation is important because the knowledge of the very structure of the real being, which is derivative of the First Being as pure existence, is the way that leads man to be aware of the desire of happiness—that is, God.[129]

According to Thomistic philosophy, freedom made real through a decision presumes that there is an intellectual understanding of the world and oneself and that there is awareness of the choice of the ultimate goal as good.[130] Mises also claims that human action is always rational. A problem appears at the moment of defining a goal. The author of *Human Action* does not say what makes man's concrete goal. He only says that the ultimate goal is always satisfaction of one's desires. Therefore, one cannot use judgments of value to measure actions taken by another man. No one has a right to dictate what causes greater or lesser satisfaction in man or what should make him happier.[131]

Mises says that ultimate goals of action are indifferent to praxeology. People in the free-market economy are not governed only by what makes their living standards better. The ultimate goal of human action may also be eternal life.[132] The most important task of the free-market economy is to create a space for making free decisions, including in the socioeconomic dimension.[133]

For Mises, the subject matter of praxeology is real action. It is man's behavior that is essential, not what he says about his plans or unrealized projects. Real action leads to the attainment of a state that is more desirable than the initial state of affairs. Thomists stress that if a person has acted in a free and conscious manner, then a synthesis

---

[129] Krapiec, [*Human Freedom*], 39–43.

[130] Krapiec, [*Human Freedom*], 124.

[131] Mises, *Human Action,* 14.

[132] Mises, *Human Action,* 15.

[133] John Paul II, *Centesimus Annus,* no. 16.

of knowledge and will—an act of conscious and free choice—has occurred. Moral evil or good came to exist at the moment of decision, which was a conscious choice of the practical judgment about good. Thomists also add that this must obviously be a real decision. Where there are doubts as to how to act, we are in a situation where a decision has not yet been made.[134] In the domain of catallaxis, a human act is a decision that is made, not a series of psychological events that lead to action.

According to the Austrian economist, each decision—until the moment that it is made—is only a speculation. Acting man takes into consideration the current data of the market because these conditions are constantly changing up to the moment when an exchange is made. If a conscious and free decision is made, it no longer refers to hypothetical circumstances but to real conditions in a definite unit of time. Mises is aware that time is passing. Therefore, he claims that the moment of decision converges in praxeology with the moment of making a market exchange. Economics is interested not with a decision made but with actions performed—which were consequences of those decisions because only such a state of affairs affects behavior on the market. What we are dealing with here is *phronetic* knowledge; its task is to govern a person in concrete action and guide him to make a decision to act in this way and not another.[135] It is a unique act and will never be repeated, for its circumstances will never be repeated exactly.

The Choice of Means

The ultimate goals of human action are indifferent to praxeology. Praxeology is a science about means. According to Mises, a means is what serves to attain a goal, and what man in his action regards as a means. Things in themselves are not means, but they become such when human reason plans to use them to attain its goals. The choice of means in relation to the chosen goal is an essential moment of the free choice. It is the choice of the practical judgment of the good-means that takes place in a moment of auto-determination; by way of this good-means we are making our good real. Through a free choice

---

[134] Krapiec, [*Human Freedom*], 55–56.

[135] Krapiec, [*Human Freedom*], 46.

of the practical judgment in relation to the good, man constitutes himself in action as a real cause of his deed.[136]

The ground of human action in the economic sphere is economic goods. The goods that abound in nature are not the object of interest for economics, Mises insists. Economic goods are all material goods produced by man in the process of production in order to satisfy human needs. They are always limited and therefore they are an object of saving. Economic goods, however, do not have to be limited to material things. Nonmaterial economic goods Mises calls *services.* Because these goods and services are always limited, the acting man has created in his mind a scale of needs and values, which helps him to order the decisions he is making.

Man must choose because he cannot use two means at the same time to attain the same goal. The order of concrete action as a choice of means must be manifested in concrete decisions. Each day man is dealing with the sphere of practical life and is making an act of cognition in order generate an act that is always unrepeatable and unique.

A special means for the author of *Human Action* is human labor. Man has at his disposal a limited amount of energy and each unit of labor may produce only a limited effect. On the free market, workers sell their services like other people sell their products. An analysis of Mises' thought shows that we are dealing here with a subject-oriented approach to labor. The worker is a free man because the free market makes him independent of the imperious decisions of the employer. Man is not treated as a nonpersonal element in the organization of production, for he himself makes a decision whether to join the process of the division of labor in society, and for this purpose uses his natural abilities.[137] The employer is a merchant who purchases labor for a market price, but the acts of either employer or employee are entirely human and moral because they are fully conscious and free. Freedom confers on them a subjective character and prevents labor from being a common commodity.[138]

Labor in the objective sense is a contingent aspect of human activity, but it cannot be viewed as something separate from its social dimen-

---

[136] Krapiec, [*Human Freedom*], 47.

[137] *Catechism of the Catholic Church,* no. 2428.

[138] *Compendium of the Social Doctrine,* no. 183.

sion. The labor of one man is naturally interwoven with the labor of other people.[139] Writing on entrepreneurship in *Centesimus Annus*, John Paul II certainly has in mind what Mises calls a social division of labor. Not only material goods but also services fall under catallactic exchange in this social system. They are subject to the process of a market game because they serve as means to attain the chosen ends of both the buyer and seller. In this understanding, labor is always oriented toward man. Each man has a right to use his talents to contribute to social development and earn the just fruits of his efforts.[140]

Self-Possession

While choosing the good-means, which is the man selling and buying his services on the market, the same cognitive forces of reason take part in the act of decision as in the case of exchange of other economic goods. They embrace the subject, which is man in action, and the object of man's action in view of the goal. Knowing himself in action, man possesses himself in knowledge. This conscious and free action presupposes what Wojtyła calls self-possession—possessing oneself in the acts of knowledge and self-government (governing oneself in the acts of will over oneself as the acting being) and self-determination in the context of participation in social life.[141]

For Mises as for St. Thomas, intellect and will are principal elements of a free choice, but they lack yet one element to become a morally good act. Freedom never has an absolute and unconditional point of departure in itself.[142] Mises does not put it in these terms, but this does not mean that he does not think in this way. As we have already seen, he presumes existential limitations determined by nature, but for obvious reasons he limits himself to the laws of nature and makes no mention of sin. In his praxeology, there is no reference to obedience to truth, but a subjectivist theory of value gives man an opportunity to discover and to master this truth and its ethical norms.[143]

---

[139] John Paul II, *Centesimus Annus*, no. 31.

[140] John Paul II, *Centesimus Annus*, nos. 32 and 34.

[141] K. Wojtyła, *The Acting Person*, 106–7.

[142] John Paul II, *Veritatis Splendor*, no. 86.

[143] *Catechism of the Catholic Church*, no. 1956.

One should stress that man is capable of a practical and concrete recognition of truth and evil. This is done through the judgment of conscience, which leads him to take responsibility for the good he has done and the evil he has committed.[144] Using freedom presumes also a reference to natural moral law. This law has a universal character because it is discovered by reason, owing to which we learn what should be done and what should be avoided. We have already shown that the main principles of the natural law exposed in the Decalogue, which make the foundation of man's rights and duties,[145] constitute also the basis of Mises' socioeconomic system. The Church teaches, however, that one may learn moral truths with complete certainty and without any mistake only by virtue of grace and revelation.[146]

The above observations are important because praxeology is a science about the general theory of choice and preferences of human action. We must remember, however, that in Mises it embraces only economics, which he regards as the best-developed branch of praxeology. The Austrian philosopher does not think in the categories of sin, redemption, or salvation, but it is difficult to find fault with him on that account. One must recognize, however, that the Misesian description of the theory of human action and preferences is contained within a broader Christian conception of man and hides in itself a teleological dimension.

Happiness as the End of Human Action

Mises presumes that man possesses intellect and free will and acts purposefully. The motive of human action is constant discontent. Man desires to change this state of affairs, but the end of this action Mises places beyond the domain of economics. Saint Thomas claims that the end to which man strives is good because evil cannot be a conscious goal, unless it is a byproduct.[147] Man comes to attain this main goal

---

[144] John Paul II, *Veritatis Splendor*, no. 61.

[145] *Catechism of the Catholic Church*, no. 1956.

[146] First Vatican Council, Dogmatic Constitution on the Catholic Faith *Dei Filius* (1870), chap. 3; Pius XII, Encyclical Letter *Humani Generis* (1950), introduction.

[147] C. Bartnik, ["Agatic-Telematic Structure of Reality"], *Philosophical Annals*, no. 41 (1994): 9.

through mediate choices. They affect the personal development of one who is making choices, as long as they are free. Man cannot develop or tend to his fullness automatically.[148] Mises is therefore right when he claims that what is needed is the space of freedom limited only by the laws of nature and praxeology.

Saint Thomas observes, however, that man can, but does not have to, choose the good he has recognized as the most proper. He is free and therefore exposed to mistakes. The things desired, which from the subjective point of view seem good, in reality can be improper and may not lead to the ultimate goal. The way to a subjectively understood happiness may overlap with the way of self-realization, but this does not always happen. There is always a danger of non-fulfillment. For this reason, St. Thomas places happiness beyond man, for he identifies it with God. Mises also does this, but for another reason: because the laws of praxeology do not permit him to determine what or who this goal is.[149]

Thomistic theology teaches that numerous choices that man makes throughout his life in order to attain particular goods are always subordinate to one good, which he calls happiness. Man expects a full satisfaction and fulfillment of his own person; therefore, happiness for him must be a personal being, infinitely perfect, which becomes the goal of his striving.[150] The Austrian philosopher does not identify happiness with God, but neither does he deny it. The preservation of a space free from external coercion gives man an opportunity to make a true choice.

Mises is a staunch defender of human freedom from external coercion. This is extremely important, for in each act of decision made in freedom man makes himself more perfect and "sculpts" his personal face.[151] Freedom is therefore something more than a lack of coercion and cannot be limited to social context.[152] It is written in the essence of the human person created in the image and likeness of God.

---

[148] K. Wojtkiewicz, [*St. Thomas Aquinas' Personalism*], 167–68.

[149] Mises, *Ultimate Foundation*, 6.

[150] K. Wojtkiewicz, [*St. Thomas Aquinas' Personalism*], 167–68.

[151] A. Szostek, [*On the Dignity of Truth and Love*] (Lublin, 1995), 75.

[152] Mises, *Human Action*, 279.

TRANSCENDENCE AND PARTICIPATION

The Church teaches that the human person is open to infinity, that is, to God and all created beings.[153] Man is not only a material being linked with this world but also a spiritual being open to transcendence and discovery of the "deeper truth" with respect to his reason, owing to which he participates in "the light of Divine reason."[154]

We shall not learn from Mises' writings whether man is a carnal-spiritual creature. According to Mises, there is the external world of physical, chemical, and physiological phenomena, and the internal world of thoughts, feelings, and purposeful action.[155] The essential statements of monism and materialism are for him only metaphysical postulates devoid of any scientific grounds. Man is not only *homo sapiens* but is above all *homo agens*, for "action is the essence of his nature and existence, his means of preserving his life and raising himself above the level of animals and plants."[156] Although Mises does not pursue it, this way of thinking suggests that man also has spiritual needs.

Maximization of Profits

The majority of Christian critics of liberalism therefore depart from the truth when they say that the leading motive of the free market is materialism.[157] Praxeology, as a branch of a more general domain dealing with human action, deals with all human acts—that is, man's purposeful actions oriented at the attainment of chosen goals, irrespective of what these goals are. Therefore, it is not true that economics postulates or presumes that people aim only at material well-being.[158] Each human action has its cost and profit, but allocation of means to goals depends entirely on the person taking action.

For this reason, thinking about chosen goals in the categories of "rationality" or "irrationality" is for Mises nonsensical. The desire to be rich is not less or more rational than the desire to be as poor as

---

153 *Compendium of the Social Doctrine*, no. 130.

154 *Gaudium et Spes*, no. 15.

155 Mises, *Human Action*, 18.

156 Mises, *Human Action*, 18.

157 T. Slipko, [*An Outline of Ethics*], vol. 2 (Krakow, 1982), 23.

158 Mises, *Human Action*, 884.

a Buddhist monk.[159] Mises notes that more people follow their own ideals rather than the desire to raise their living standard. Subjectivist value theory does not permit us to think about man exclusively in the categories of *homo economicus.*

Getting richer is not the summit of man's economic activity, nor the only reason for his action. Certainly, it is maximization of "profit," but profit does not have to correspond only to material good. Thus Mises rejects the principal assumption of the neoclassical model of economics that speaks about maximization of utility expressed in the specific conception of man as *homo economicus.* It cannot be accepted from the point of view of Christian anthropology,[160] as it is a considerable simplification and reduces man's action to a model used in physics. Morality and values remain outside the area of Mises' interests, but in his economic theory he takes into account the whole man, because every aspect affects economic behaviors.

The Austrian philosopher does not ask about man's origin. He is interested only in man in action and observes that people created by God or nature are unequal and differentiated, a fact that constitutes the general principle of living creatures.[161] People's equality before God or nature consists only in that each person is endowed with an unalienable right to life. Mises decisively opposes the idea of ontological egalitarianism, which undermines the natural order of the universe and is in opposition to harmonious inequality made by God. Moral action—in line with the truth about man created in the image of God—respects natural and lawful differences, appreciates variety, and builds a coherent community in which there is also room for difference.[162] According to Leo XIII, complete equality in human society is impossible. The pope rightly notes that collective life calls for

---

159 Mises, *Human Action,* 884.

160 T. Gruszecki, ["The Enterprise (Firm) and the Market in Contemporary Economics and in the Social Doctrine of the Church"], in [*Centesimus Annus: The Text and Commentaries*], ed. F. Kampka and C. Ritter (Lublin, 1998), 266.

161 Mises, *Human Action,* 175.

162 H. Witczak, ["The Image of God in Man—the Source and Aim of Moral Action"], in [*Theological-Moral Anthropology: Conceptions—Controversies—Inspirations*], ed. I. Mroczkowski and J. A. Sobkowiak (Warsaw, 2008), 36.

various skills and talents, and people are made to perform concrete tasks above all by their respective personal differences.[163]

Man's activity results therefore from his nature and the express will of the Creator: "Be fertile and multiply; fill the earth and subdue it" (Gen. 1:28). The end of man's activity is his good. The Second Vatican Council understood by this an improvement of man's living standards,[164] as well as his development and perfection in all spheres of life.[165] The main axiom of Mises' praxeology is the purposeful action of each person by way of which he wishes to substitute the less satisfactory state of affairs for the more satisfactory. This axiom corresponds fully with the assumption of Thomist philosophy.[166] According to St. Thomas, each being acts with a purpose that is good for it.[167] From the metaphysical point of view, each individual human action consists in changing from the state of potency into the state of action, and reflects the gradual growth of perfection of the acting subject. Rational action presupposes the subject's intelligence and free will. The human person is a rational and conscious creature, capable of self-reflection. The acting man must therefore be aware of the limited means needed to attain the planned ends. This action can be a result only of substantial unity.

There is yet one more property of acting man noted by Mises and St. Thomas. They both think that human knowledge is limited and that man can be wrong in his choice of means for the attainment of intended goals. Ignorance is therefore an important feature of human action, from which—despite its being taken in the conditions of freedom—we cannot exclude evil. This goal could deny man's ultimate goal, which is God,[168] but even then such action has a rational character.

In his *magnum opus* Mises does not entirely develop his anthropology, but his system indicates indirectly the transcendence of the human being. He regards as an unquestionable fact not only the uniformity and immutability, in the course of history, of logical structures in

---

[163] Leo XIII, Encyclical Letter *Rerum Novarum* (1891), no. 14.

[164] *Gaudium et Spes*, no. 34.

[165] *Gaudium et Spes*, no. 35.

[166] Zanotti, "Misesian Praxeology," 60–61.

[167] Aquinas, *Summa contra gentiles*, nos. 1 and 2.

[168] Aquinas, *Summa Theologica*, I-II, q. 2, a. 8c.

thinking, speaking, and acting, but also the fact that logical thinking and acting are not dependent on class membership, historical context, or race.[169] Man is not a puppet of external, social, or economic forces, nor of his inner appetites and senses.[170] Reason is what defines all human action.

In like manner the author of *Human Action* defends human dignity and integrity against deterministic systems that reduce all man's thinking and acting to the sum of internal and external forces that push and attract him in various directions.[171] Intending to explain what is fundamental and common to all human acts, Mises abstains from determining individual and concrete action, because the choice of goal is man's personal, subjective, and individual affair. Mises is aware that the available objectives can be historically, culturally, or environmentally determined; despite that, man can change them at any moment, a fact that shows that he is free in the sphere of action.

Truth-Orientation

We find this way of looking at man—on the one hand limited as a creature, and on the other unlimited in his desires and called to a higher life—in John Paul II's encyclical, *Redemptor Hominis*.[172] This dynamic structure, created by the element of self-determination— that is, conscious freedom and transcendence in action which is shaped in the person through freedom and conscious efficiency—is what makes the person different from nature.[173] "Nature," in scholastic vocabulary, means the world of actors (for instance, animal creatures) whose action does not depend on their own "I."[174] Man is created in the image and likeness of God, but at the same time he is free and capable of rejecting this truth about his existence, living in unawareness, or consciously denying it. Freedom is not merely a momentary whim but something that really belongs to man's structure and constitutes his

169 Mises, *Human Action*, 4–5.

170 Mises, *Human Action*, 16.

171 Gregory R. Beabout et al., *Beyond Self-Interest: A Personalist Approach to Human Action* (Lanham, MD: Lexington Books, 2002), 77.

172 John Paul II, Encyclical Letter *Redemptor Hominis* (1979), no. 14.

173 Wojtyła, *Acting Person*, 229.

174 Wojtyła, *Acting Person*, 163.

becoming good or bad through his acts.[175] While dissociating himself from other varieties of personalism that lay a great emphasis on man's freedom and see in it the main ground of personal dignity,[176] Karol Wojtyła distinctly stresses that transcendence of the person in act is not only a dependence on one's own "I" but also on the truth, and it is this moment that ultimately shapes freedom.[177]

One should stress here that Mises discovers the immutable laws that govern human action in the socioeconomic sphere and claims that their observance safeguards the well-being and peaceful development of man. We are encouraged to this labor by *Gaudium et Spes,* which rightly notes that created things and human community cherish their own laws and values, and man's task consists in discovering and ordering them.[178] John Paul II confirms that "governing over the world" is a great task and responsibility for man, which obliges him to obey the Creator.[179]

Mises is aware that each choice in the area of human action must be based on some system of values, but he posits that it is not the domain of praxeology to define the goal of human action. Mises dissociates himself from valuation and normative judgments not only because the process of production calls for a complicated exchange and supervision would be costly and unreal, but above all because he respects human freedom.

Praxeology is for Mises perfectly neutral to, and free from, any judgments of value, as it refers only to means and never to the choice of ultimate ends.[180] Economics as a branch of praxeology deals with the general theory of purposeful human action irrespective of the goals man intends to accomplish. A person may submit to the disutility of labor in order to serve God, and his behavior will not be different from

---

[175] Wojtyła, *Acting Person,* 147.

[176] A. Szostek, ["Alienation: The Ever-Current Problem"], in [*John Paul II: Text and Commentary*], ed. F. Kampka and C. Ritter (Lublin, 1998), 298.

[177] Wojtyła, *Acting Person,* 198.

[178] *Gaudium et Spes,* no. 36.

[179] John Paul II, *Veritatis Splendor,* no. 38.

[180] Mises, *Human Action,* 885.

other attempts to attain mundane advantages by expending labor.[181] Misesian man may fully realize himself as a carnal and spiritual being through an openness to transcendence. Openness to transcendence and God depends entirely on man possessing in this respect absolute freedom, and he has such capacity because of his reason.

The analysis up to now permits us to state that the reasoning of the author of *Human Action* in the category of negative freedom coalesces with the concept of freedom in Wojtyła. The latter presumes that people are free from external forces and, should they consent to domination in their lives, would lose their personalities. It should be stressed, however, that praxeology is too much reduced to the concept of negative freedom. Contrary to Mises, Wojtyła concentrates on ontological freedom and shows that people are not free merely when they are not subordinate to any external limitations, which interfere in the ends rationally chosen and determined by them, but above all when they enjoy internal freedom to choose what is truly good.

Freedom here is not understood as something given or permitted by someone from without, but as the principal element of the human creature. Man was created in the image and likeness of God, and this implies that, by virtue of the hypostatic union of divine and human nature in the person of the Son of God, man shares the Son's human nature. The lack of coercion therefore is not the only necessary condition to make the human act personal. The human act must be truth-oriented, for only then does it presume action in freedom. Each act that is not oriented toward truth can gradually weaken man's ontological freedom, because all human acts are integrated with their subject.[182] The stress on action in line with truth in no way diminishes the dignity of the human person. Man experiences himself as the agent of his act and, in consequence, is its subject. Wojtyła calls it *integration*, which supplements the concept of transcendence.[183] This means that each decision and each act affect the person who is their author.

---

[181] Mises, *Human Action*, 587.

[182] Beabout et al., *Beyond Self-Interest*, 103.

[183] Wojtyła, *Acting Person*, 189.

Danger of Alienation

It should be stressed that excessive subjectivity in Mises can lead to self-limitation and in consequence to alienation.[184] If we assume that man's ends are subjective and internal to such an extent that he cannot share them with other persons, then he is isolated and alienated from them. Emmanuel Mounier is right when he says that too much concentration on freedom as a possibility for choice may lead to weakening the willingness to make a choice because there are no respective motives in the future.[185] This is important because praxeology is limited to economic or catallactic issues but is supposed to be a general theory of human action.[186] It must therefore take into account not only the negative concept of freedom worked out by Mises on behalf of the economic and social sciences, but also its ontic ground, which is the foundation of true human freedom.

There is yet one more danger inherent in the immanent understanding of the act of decision. We have already shown that Mises does not subordinate the act of freedom to truth. The subjective character of choices cannot be carried out in the void or in an indeterminate horizon, for this standpoint is close to Jean-Paul Sartre's formal principle of authenticity, according to which an act is good only because it is in accord with me, with my freedom.[187] This is important not only in the area of the fundamental option but also at the level of categorical acts, because, without reaching to the truth about the nature of the human person, reason in its self-project writes in only the contents drawn from observation of the world and society; they are products of his individual personality or of historical customs.[188]

John Paul II teaches in *Veritatis Splendor* that total sovereignty of reason leads to a dangerous distinction between "an ethical order, which would be human in origin and of value for this world alone, and an order of salvation, for which only certain intentions and interior

---

[184] Beabout et al., *Beyond Self-Interest,* 89.

[185] E. Mounier, *Personalism* (Notre Dame: University of Notre Dame Press, 1952), 63–64.

[186] Mises, *Human Action,* 4.

[187] See T. Styczen, [*An Outline of Ethics: Metaethics*] (Lublin, 1974), 80.

[188] L. Melina, ["Conscience—Freedom—Magisterium"], *Ethos,* nos. 15/16 (1991): 99.

attitudes regarding God and neighbor would be significant."[189] This dichotomy causes disintegration of the personality of man as a carnal-spiritual and also religious, moral, and cultural creature.[190] Rejection of receptive transcendence based on the objective truth leads, according to Andrzej Szostek, to the destruction of personalism itself.[191]

Transcendent Dimension of Human Action

The Misesian concept of negative freedom, however, does not limit the acting man to creative transcendence, and leaves him an open space to develop receptive transcendence, without enclosing him in the immanence of the acting subject. On the one hand, the danger consists in the fact that the rejection of this freedom to receptive recognition of one's own dignity may lead the acting man to treating himself as a means to realize himself as his own self-project and stretch the truth. On the other hand, the concept of negative freedom guarantees that the other person will never become a victim of someone else's self-project. It is worth emphasizing that negative freedom may be lost without losing ontological freedom or positive freedom.[192]

If praxeology, as Mises claims, "deals with the real actions of real men,"[193] then it must make space for transcendent human action alongside action aiming only at the removal of uneasiness. The Austrian economist's assumption that each human action can be explained in the categories of the pursuit of one's own profit corresponds with many areas of human behavior and refers especially to the principles of the free market but does not deal with all human actions. People are also ready to act in a way that cannot be explained in the categories of their own direct and immediate profit.[194]

Wojtyła shows that an action transcending one's own profit is possible to a certain degree. An obvious instance is giving oneself in love

---

[189] John Paul II, *Veritatis Splendor*, no. 37.

[190] T. Biesaga, ["K. Rahner's Personalism and K. Wojtyła's Personalism in the Debate on Moral Theology"], *Analekta Cracoviensia*, no. 32 (2000): 99.

[191] A. Szostek, [*Nature—Reason—Freedom: A Philosophical Analysis of the Conception of Creative Reason in Contemporary Moral Theology*] (Rome, 1990), 280.

[192] Beabout et al., *Beyond Self-Interest*, 63.

[193] Mises, *Human Action*, 651.

[194] Beabout et al., *Beyond Self-Interest*, 32.

to another person, an example of which is St. Maximilian Kolbe, who offered up his own life for a family's father in a concentration camp. This does not mean, however, that this transcendence denotes neglect of oneself. Wojtyła affirms that human action comes from the acting person; it is his full expression and manifestation. Therefore, it is possible to overcome one's own profits and be attached to them at the same time.[195]

Similarly, Mises emerges from this problem unscathed and claims that giving disinterested gifts without expecting any recompense is not possible, for even here there is an exchange in which the one who gives a gift is satisfied with the improved situation of the one who has received it, up to the point of self-satisfaction, because such was the aim of his action.[196] The question of motives and purposes of action, however, goes beyond the scope of Mises' praxeology, because it transcends what is observable, and the subject matter of praxeology is only human action, not the events that lead to it.[197]

We must finally admit that there is an element of transcendence and one's own profit in each economic relationship because the buyer and seller are persons. When we recognize the buyer as a person capable of self-possession and self-government, then by making a trade agreement the merchant transcends himself—as does the customer. At first glance it may seem that neighborly love is understood mainly in the categories of transcendence and self-giving, while trade exchange is based on exchange and one's own profit. In the light of Wojtyła's understanding of human action, it turns out that, to a certain extent, in both cases there are elements of transcendence and one's own profit.[198] The mirror of consciousness permits us not only to internally watch our acts and their dynamic dependence on our "I," but also to live through these acts as being our own acts.[199]

---

[195] Beabout et al., *Beyond Self-Interest*, 65.

[196] Mises, *Human Action*, 195.

[197] Mises, *Human Action*, 11–12.

[198] Beabout et al., *Beyond Self-Interest*, 65.

[199] Wojtyła, *Acting Person*, 91.

Self-Emptiness of Christ

Mises claims that man's ends are purely subjective, but this approach, without an objective reference to truth, may reduce praxeology to a mere horizontal dimension without human action referring to God as the source of this truth. This complete subjectification denotes that human action has an immanent character and cannot go beyond itself in the vertical dimension. We do not mean here only transcendence, which is an intentional desire oriented at the proper object, which may be a value or goal. Speaking about the person as a transcendent being, we have in mind not only horizontal transcendence, but above all vertical, in the frame of which the subject confirms himself in relation to God, transcending himself, and owes this achievement to the very fact of ontological freedom in action.[200]

Man for Mises is capable of heroic deeds,[201] which from the human point of view are profound and noble. He can give up his life for his homeland because he has some vision of the good and desires to act accordingly. It cannot be compared to the instinctive action of a bee, which gives up its life to save the beehive, but this does not automatically mean that such a man can transcend himself, for he is still limited by his own subjectivity. He can attain the intended goal, but we do not know if he can completely give himself to others, because he does not have an objective reference to his own "I" as an essential element of self-determination.[202]

Mises claims that his praxeology is not fit to describe God's action because God's omnipotence presumes that he cannot feel uneasiness, which is the motive of any action.[203] This theory of action can lead us to dangerous conclusions: that God does not exist or is completely inactive, or that knowledge of him is completely impossible for us. These conclusions can never be reconciled with the Christian point of view. Knowledge about Mises' effective action, however, may be enriched by Wojtyła's praxeology, which permits us to describe each action from the perspective of God and man.[204]

---

200 Wojtyła, *Acting Person*, 485ff.

201 Mises, *Human Action*, 19–20.

202 Beabout et al., *Beyond Self-Interest*, 91.

203 Mises, *Human Action*, 69.

204 Beabout et al., *Beyond Self-Interest*, 94.

According to Wojtyła, God does not follow his own interest and sense of uneasiness, because a disinterested and self-fulfilling act constitutes an integral part of himself and his relation to man and the world. An example of such action is Christ's "self-emptiness."[205] By taking "the form of a slave" and "human likeness," Christ effected *kenosis* (κενόω; Gk. "to empty," "to deprive"). This Greek verb is here used in a reflexive form and indicates that the object of Christ's mysterious and single action (ἐκένωσεν; *aorist*) is himself.[206] Kenosis is therefore a *par excellence* gift of oneself, for, because there is no actualization in God (he is eternally, fully realized being), everything that he does is done out of a pure and disinterested love for man. Love in its radical form is shown in Jesus' death on the cross, the death that is God's turning against himself, through an offer of himself, in order to lift man and save him.[207]

Similarly, like the human creature, the Creator also acts at the same time as an object and subject: God creates people in his image and likeness; he enters into a real, free, and dynamic relationship with them, giving up himself.[208] This relationship is still more apparent in the incarnation, in which God shows us precisely what his omnipotence is. Rocco Buttiglione claims that the almighty God becomes a beggar who in a sense gives up his almightiness in order to respect our freedom—but in reality he gives up only the almightiness of power, the better to show us the power of truth and love.[209] Wojtyła's praxeology therefore offers us a pattern of what people aim at and at the same time a view of what God's eternity and his almighty love are.[210]

---

[205] Philippians 2:6–7: "Who, though he was in the form of God, did not regard equality with God something to be grasped. Rather, he emptied himself, taking the form of a slave, coming in human likeness; and found human in appearance."

[206] A. Jankowski, ["St. Paul's Letters from Prison"], in [*The Holy Scripture of the New Testament: An Introduction—Translation from the Original—Commentary*], vol. 8, ed. E. Dabrowski (Poznan, 2006), 115.

[207] Benedict XVI, Encyclical Letter *Deus Caritas Est* (2005), no. 12.

[208] Beabout et al., *Beyond Self-Interest*, 94.

[209] R. Buttiglione, *Karol Wojtyła: The Thought of the Man Who Became Pope John Paul II*, trans. Paolo Guietti and Francesca Murphy (Grand Rapids, MI: Eerdmans, 1997), 374.

[210] Beabout et al., *Beyond Self-Interest*, 94.

Ontological Freedom

We notice here the limitation of Mises' praxeology and its difference from Wojtyła's view of freedom. Contrary to the author of *Human Action*, Wojtyła concentrates on two kinds of freedom, both of which are indispensable to understand action that is fully human. Aside from negative freedom, Wojtyła describes positive freedom, which presumes that the human ability to act is perceived not only in the categories of a lack of external limitations but also in the categories of goals that man chooses because he regards them as valuable. Aside from negative and positive freedom, Wojtyła stresses especially ontological freedom, which Mises does not take into consideration at all.

No one has to give this freedom to man, because it constitutes the principal part of what it means to be a human creature. Wojtyła rightly notices that freedom is not limited to a free action but is the essence of human existence. For this reason, human action must be oriented at truth. If the goal does not correspond to truth, it will undermine the ontological freedom of the acting man; this freedom, together with his acts, constitutes his integrity as a person.[211]

Wojtyła emphasizes that man's self-fulfillment is carried out not so much by the act itself as by the moral goodness of the act oriented at truth, because by doing an act man also ontologically fulfills himself in it. This understanding leads us to an important perception: that self-fulfillment permits us to think about the human person only as a potential, not actual, being. This, in turn, means that we cannot deny Mises' claim that action results from a wish to substitute a less satisfactory state for a more satisfactory one. Man is never able to avoid thinking and acting in the categories of removing uneasiness. Of such a state of the soul St. Augustine of Hippo writes in the beginning of his *Confessions*: "Restless is our heart until it comes to rest in thee."[212]

The person is also open to another person, because only when he perceives himself in relation to another "you," can he speak of himself as "I."[213] The Bible teaches us that God's love cannot separate us from the love of neighbor because all commandments "are summed up

[211] Beabout et al., *Beyond Self-Interest*, 103.

[212] *Augustine: Confessions and Enchiridion*, trans. and ed. A. C. Outler (Philadelphia: Westminster, 1955), bk. 1, chap. 1.

[213] *Compendium of the Social Doctrine*, no. 130.

in this saying: 'You shall love your neighbor as yourself.' Love does no evil to the neighbor; hence, love is the fulfillment of the law" (Rom. 13:9–10; see also 1 John 4:20). Love of neighbor is therefore the commandment that instructs us to go beyond ourselves, beyond our egoistic behavior, to establish a dialogue and create a community with another person.[214]

The Personalistic Value of Act

Despite the fact that all human actions are always actions committed by individuals, man, for Mises, appears clearly as a social being. An isolated and asocial being is only a fictional construction needed to explain catallactic processes. The Second Vatican Council likewise teaches that the human person out of the depths of his nature is a social being.[215] Communal life is a natural property that makes man different from the rest of earthly creatures. It was God's desire to create man as a social being. From the very beginning the human person is called to live in a community.

Mises claims that man's natural condition is to live in the social system of the division of labor; this system is characterized by an inequality of people with respect to their ability to perform various jobs and unequal distribution of natural resources. Mises does not depart here from Christian anthropology, which teaches that the human person, created in the image of God and after his likeness (see Rom. 1:26), situated in the visible world to live in society (see Rom. 2:20, 23) and subdue the earth (see Rom. 1:26, 28–30), is from the very beginning called to social life.[216] According to the teaching of the Church, the human person may develop his calling only in relationship with other people.[217]

According to Mises, man's social nature is not reduced to being among individuals of the same species or to common action that allows him to attain what for individuals would be impossible. The author of *Human Action* gives each man a free space limited only by the laws

---

[214] *Compendium of the Social Doctrine,* no. 130.

[215] *Gaudium et Spes,* no. 12

[216] *Compendium of the Social Doctrine,* no. 96.

[217] Congregation for the Doctrine of the Faith, *Instruction on Christian Freedom and Liberation* (1981), no. 32; *Compendium of the Social Doctrine,* no. 97.

of nature and praxeology,[218] in which the individual can determine himself. According to Karol Wojtyła, this is not only what the personalistic value of act means,[219] but also the personalistic dimension of participation. By acting together with others, man confirms and realizes himself as one who "cannot fully find himself except through a sincere gift of himself."[220]

Thus understood, the personalistic value of act is the principal criterion by which to evaluate not only socioeconomic systems but also the attitudes of particular citizens of a given community. Wojtyła regards those systems as erroneous and harmful which exaggerate in stressing the development of man as an individual, ignoring or eliminating the dimension of participation or else ignoring the personalistic value of act, and thereby subordinate it to other effects of cooperation. Wojtyła calls these systems, respectively, individualism and totalitarianism, indicating that in both of them a correct relationship between the good of a person and the common good of society have been violated.[221]

Our analysis of Mises' thought permits us to state that this relation has not been violated in a free economy based on the principle of private property, which enables an authentic participation at the individual level. The person in Mises is free and may be in solidarity with the common good in a given community through his own work and enterprise, or he may oppose it through withdrawal from buying or using the services existing on the free market; this is made with the same concern for the common good in which one sees at the same time one's own well-understood good and the way of personal development.[222]

Mises' laissez-faireism therefore appreciates both transcendence as the essence of freedom, unveiling completely the spiritual nature of man, and participation, which is an expression of his profoundly and personalistically conceived social nature. Society for Mises is only a means that allows every individual to attain his own goals. It exists

---

218 Mises, *Human Action*, 278–80.

219 Wojtyła, *Acting Person*, 304.

220 *Gaudium et Spes*, no. 24.

221 Wojtyła, *Acting Person*, 313ff.

222 See Wojtyła, *Acting Person*, 322–29.

only because the wills of two individuals encounter each other in an attempt at a common action, which leads to the division of labor. This division is for Mises the essence of society and removes any contradiction between society and individual.[223] For Mises, as for Wojtyła, the basic condition of the existence, sense, and permanence of any other economic and social ties is a reference to another person.[224] Mises does not speak about the commandment of love as a normative expression of human action, but the space of freedom left to man enables self-fulfillment through the disinterested gift of oneself.

For Mises, socialist central planning means an end to any economic rationality, not only because it refutes private ownership but also because it introduces a false philosophy of man. The latter treats him as being in essence material and determined by external material and social conditions.[225] The collectivist system, subordinating the individual to society, has contributed to man's alienation. The person in that system has no chance to make of himself a gift, nor can he create an authentic community en route to his own destiny, which is God.[226]

John Paul II indicates that alienation also appears in the capitalist system, and shows that it is inherent in its referring to man as *homo economicus.* The preceding analysis of Mises' thought shows, however, that the pope has in mind rather state interventionism in which economic actions are reduced to maximization of utility and, as a result, to reifying man, not Misesian laissez-faireism, for which the most profound act of freedom is an entirely free exchange of goods and services based completely on the system of private ownership. It is worth emphasizing that alienation occurs also among the citizens of well-off societies and may appear in laissez-faireism, but then it comes about without violence and the mass media play an important role.[227]

Mises, as a radical defender of negative freedom, indicates only the external dangers to human freedom. The Church teaches that

---

[223] Mises, *Socialism,* 264–65.

[224] See Wojtyła, *Acting Person,* 292.

[225] K. Marx, *Theses on Feuerbach,* https://www.marxists.org/archive/marx/works/1845/theses/theses.htm; K. Marx and F. Engels, *The Communist Manifesto* (Arlington Heights, IL: Harlan Davidson, 1955), 39–40.

[226] John Paul II, *Centesimus Annus,* no. 36.

[227] A. Szostek, ["Alienation"], 304.

danger comes also from within, from moral weakness; therefore, it is the condition of true freedom to have a reliable relationship to truth. In *Redemptor Hominis*, John Paul II warns us against freedom comprehended superficially, without going deeper into the whole truth of man and the world, and points at the same time at Christ who brings man freedom based on the truth (John 8:32).[228] It is the Christian's task to use this freedom and help others to grow in it. Our analysis has shown that Misesian laissez-faireism creates ideal sociopolitical conditions for the development and use of freedom as a gift. It provides an indispensable space in which Christians can apply the principles of subsidiarity and solidarity not only in the horizontal dimension, but also, and above all, in the vertical dimension.[229] We turn now to an analysis of Mises' socioeconomic system from the point of view of the fundamental principles of Catholic social doctrine.

---

[228] John Paul II, *Redemptor Hominis*, no. 12.

[229] Benedict XVI, *Address of His Holiness Benedict XVI to the Participants in the 14th Session of the Pontifical Academy Social Sciences*, http://www.vatican.va/holy_father/benedic_xvi/speeches/2008/may/documents/hf_ben-xvi_spe_20080503_social-sciences_en.html.

3

The Communal Character of Human Calling in the Free-Market Society*

Mises claims that action is always taken by an individual person. His point of departure in the analysis of social life is therefore the individual dimension of man. This does not mean, however, that individuals isolated from social context constitute for him the only reality. Mises recognizes the indispensable character of social life and its ontological foundation. Cooperation among people is a result of human action and of the conscious pursuit of an end. The economy, therefore, is not understood as an abstract being composed of mechanic elements that correspond only to the category of *homo economicus.* The previous chapter's analysis of the personalist foundation of the economy shows that Mises' individual in action may draw interpersonal relations in the economic space through participation and desires in like manner to fulfill his various tasks, including his calling to entrepreneurship.

*Parts of chapter 3 previously appeared as J. Gniadek SVD, ["The Social Dimension of Private Ownership in the Free-Market Economy According to Ludwig von Mises"], *Forum Teologiczne* 11 (2010): 51–66; and J. Gniadek, SVD, ["Christianity Hospitality for the Stranger as a Challenge for the Restrictive Policy of Immigration of the States of European Commonwealth"], *Nurt SVD* (no. 3/4, 2007): 119–35.

In this chapter, we shall further describe the subject-oriented dimension of human labor in the free-market economy. Then we shall analyze the liberal conception of the right to private property. We shall show its social dimension in the free-market economy and see to what extent it corresponds to the principle of the common destination of material goods. In the final part, we shall present the market not only as a space in which the external conditions necessary for people to safeguard their material welfare have been created but also as a space of freedom for the development of man in his full personhood, taking into account its intellectual, spiritual, and social aspects.

THE CALLING TO ENTREPRENEURSHIP

The most frequent objection raised to the free-market economy is the claim that human labor ought not be treated as a common commodity. Mises describes labor as a tool but does so only to explain market behavior in the field of catallactics. He treats human labor, along with other material means, as a specific factor of production. The purpose of the analysis below is to prove that subordinating human labor—as a factor of production in the free-market economy—to the economic process does not lead to man's reification. In an unhampered labor market, man as an entrepreneur decides himself how to join the social division of labor.

The Character of Human Labor

From the theological point of view, work is a human act performed in a free and conscious manner.[1] According to Mises, labor has all the marks of a free exchange. Not every human act is labor for him. Man's labor is the work he undertakes to make a living for himself and his family. One might arrive at the same definition by observing the lives of Jesus, Mary, and Joseph, and using one's own experience (see also Gen. 3:17).[2] Human labor is therefore a group of activities that are

---

[1] J. Wolkowski, ["Man and Work: The Anthropological Context of the Christian Conception of Work"], in [*Man and Work*], ed. J. Wolkowski (Warsaw, 1979), 41.

[2] J. W. Galkowski, ["The Encyclical on Human Labor"], in [*John Paul II, Laborem Exercens: Text and Commentaries*], ed. J. W. Galkowski (Lublin, 1986), 65.

performed in a conscious manner and that trigger effects that are intended and anticipated.[3] Mises has in mind here an exchange in which man seeks to substitute a less satisfactory state of affairs for a more satisfactory. Labor is therefore an intended action linked with a need to earn a living and does not embrace leisure or religious activities, such as prayer.[4] Mises describes these kinds of action as *introversive labor* and includes them in the sphere of consumption.

This does not mean, however, that Mises reduces the rich contents of human labor and its goals exclusively to the economic dimension. The Church teaches as well that labor is basically an economic activity, consisting in creating and exchanging new goods or providing economic services.[5] The purpose of human activity is above all gaining means for the maintenance of life.[6] This necessity results from the scarcity of means for survival—hence the goal of human activity is to subdue matter.[7] The Austrian economist uses precisely the same arguments as the Church does in this respect.

The Church does not view work only from the technical and social point of view, and the same can be said of Mises. Work from the Christian point of view is a conscious use of physical faculties to create value, which enables man's development and helps him to carry out God's plan in the world.[8] Mises makes no mention of such goals, for praxeology does not concern itself with the goals of man's action. He stresses, however, that work is purposeful, and this suffices to make it a personal decision. Labor in Mises therefore has an obviously personal character. The force of labor, as the Church teaches,[9] is inherent in the person and is revealed in a conscious and free action.[10] Praxeology therefore enables a view of work from two aspects, just as it has been

---

[3] J. Troska, ["The Christian View of Work"], *Poznan Theological Studies* 4 (1983): 133.

[4] S. Olejnik, [*Moral Theology*], vol. 2, 261.

[5] *Gaudium et Spes*, no. 67.

[6] Leo XIII, *Rerum Novarum*, no. 34.

[7] J. Galkowski, ["Labor and the World"], *W drodze*, no. 5 (1977): 10.

[8] Troska, ["Christian View of Work"], 133.

[9] Leo XIII, *Rerum Novarum*, no. 34.

[10] J. Galkowski, ["The Problem of Labor in Papal Encyclicals"], *Annals of the Social Sciences* 1 (1991/1992): 67.

presented by Wojtyła. It is at the crossroads of two levels: human participation in man's social nature and human participation in the royal power of Christ.[11]

The Church teaches that toil is attendant on work. Mises claims the same. Daily experience shows that labor is associated with disutility. The Bible says that toil results from man's revolt against God—it is an effect of original sin—and from that time man must get his bread to eat "by the sweat of [his] brow" (Gen. 3:19).[12] According to the author of *Human Action,* man must work because he wants to improve his unsatisfactory situation. The burden of labor is therefore exchanged for its products, which constitute for him a direct gratification. This conception of exchange is written into the Christian understanding of labor: on one hand, gratification for the toil of matter that has been transformed into things that are tactile and useful for man; on the other hand, labor as a means of personal perfection. Through its difficulty work saves, liberates, and ennobles.[13] We may say that in this way there appears in human labor a close relationship between creation and redemption. Work directs man toward the new heaven and new earth, making a magnificent image of history in the prospect of the kingdom of God.[14]

Our analysis of the Christian point of view on work compared with Mises' position has shown that human labor assumes transcendence. It is a common point that makes the two views diametrically different from the Marxist concept of work.[15] One of the socialist myths was the claim that work in socialism would become a pure pleasure. Mises rightly remarks that socialists failed to notice that what man enjoys about work is that it provides the basis of his existence and the sense of being useful for society—the creation of things that people pay for on the free market. In a socialist society, there is no room for

---

[11] J. Galkowski, ["Labor according to Cardinal K. Wojtyła"], *Philosophical Annals* 2 (1979): 87.

[12] John Paul II, *Laborem Exercens,* no. 9.

[13] S. Wyszynski, [*The Spirit of Human Labor: A Thought on the Value of Labor*] (Warsaw, 2001), 59.

[14] M. Riber, [*Labor in the Bible*], trans. from the Italian into Polish by Z. Zwolska (Warsaw, 1979), 91.

[15] Riber, [*Labor in the Bible*], 91.

such joy because the interdependence between the profit of labor and the laborer's income is blurred. All values and human work in such a system are only factors of history, and they act by themselves as automatic forces.[16]

The Christian view is precisely the opposite of the socialist understanding: The former presumes that human labor draws its character from God's plans and has significance with respect to the kingdom of God which is already present on earth—although it is still to come in its fullness, overcoming the limits of time and space. The Second Vatican Council confirms that the progress and organization of human society contribute to the fulfillment of the kingdom of God.[17] Mises does not indicate the goal at which man aims, but his understanding of work as an exchange in which man seeks to substitute a less satisfactory state of affairs for a more satisfactory one points to the transcendence of human acts in relation to work. Similarly, like Christian hope, labor is rooted both in the matter of this world and in transcendence as the goal at which it aims.[18]

Leisure as an Economic Good

The climax of biblical teaching on work is the commandment of Sabbath rest.[19] The Church teaches that holiday rest is a right.[20] Man, created in the image and likeness of God who "rested on the seventh day from all the work he had undertaken" (Gen. 2:2), should respectively make use of his free time. An analysis of the sense of human labor in Mises shows that, for Mises too, rest is written in human nature and is desired by man.

The Austrian economist introduces a new perception of the character of human labor, which permits us to better understand the sense of the third commandment. The state in which man does not have to work is thought to be more satisfactory than the one in which he must work. Mises notices that man treats rest as an economic good of the first order. Similarly, Mises introduces the concept of labor into

---

16 Riber, [*Labor in the Bible*], 91.

17 *Gaudium et Spes*, nos. 38 and 45.

18 Riber, [*Labor in the Bible*], 8.

19 *Compendium of the Social Doctrine*, no. 258.

20 *Gaudium et Spes*, no. 67.

catallactics equally with other factors of labor and considers it in its aspect of marginal usefulness.[21] According to the laws of praxeology, man works until the moment in which he realizes that usefulness linked with further work will not be a sufficient recompense for the uneasiness that results from performing this work. Mises explains from the economic point of view the relationship between work and rest, which has a profound grounding in the Bible.[22]

The book of Genesis shows us God who, having finished his work, rests and blesses the seventh day as predestined for rest. Rest here does not mean only abstinence from daily matters and dedication to God. The story about creation and rest indicates the purposeful character of man's existence—the man who has been *created* in the image and likeness of God and through work is oriented to God's rest, a pattern and fulfillment of his existence.[23] Rest is therefore written into human nature, and this commandment reminds us that a necessary harmony should be introduced in our life.

The Complementary Character of Capital and Labor

The Church teaches that work, because of its personal character, surpasses every other factor of production and assumes priority over capital.[24] In his encyclical *Laborem Exercens*, John Paul II understands capital to be an instrument used to improve the process of production, and he treats work as the efficient cause of this process. An analysis of the relationship between work and capital calls for explanation of how the terms are used by the social teaching of the Church and by Mises, because they do not have an identical meaning.[25] According to the Austrian economist, work is the use of man's forces and abilities as the means to remove uneasiness, and capital is the primary and intellectual tool of actions taken in the market economy,[26] which exists beyond the minds of those who plan such actions. Despite this

---

[21] Mises, *Human Action*, 131.

[22] Riber, [*Labor in the Bible*], 12.

[23] Riber, [*Labor in the Bible*], 12.

[24] John Paul II, *Laborem Exercens*, no. 2.

[25] *Compendium of the Social Doctrine*, no. 186.

[26] Mises, *Human Action*, 260.

conceptual difference, both the social teaching of the Church and Mises agree that the efficient cause in the process of production is always man.

Leo XIII taught that capital cannot exist without work, nor work without capital,[27] indicating thereby their complementarity. In accord with his predecessor, Pius XI states that it would be unjust to separate capital from labor in the process of production, or to attribute the fruits of production only to one of the two factors.[28] John Paul II stresses that all means of production, starting from the most primitive and ending at the most modern, were gradually worked out by man and are the fruit of his experience and intelligence.[29] Later the same pope states that the basic capital and "decisive factor" that man has at his disposal is man himself, and his value is expressed in knowledge, creativity, and entrepreneurship.[30] All this contributes to a new perspective for understanding the relations between labor and capital, where the subject-oriented character of the acting man's labor is clearly emphasized.[31] The documents of the Church do not talk explicitly about capital as an element of economic calculation, but such a concept of capital is implicitly entailed in the subject-oriented dimension of labor, which is the foundation of all action in the market economy.

Michael Novak observes that, although the papal definition of capital may at first seem too narrow, excluding the person, a more profound analysis reveals that John Paul II's principal intention was to show that both capital and labor concentrate on the same object: the primary position of man.[32] Mises and the pope therefore hold a view that is exceptionally anti-Marxist, proving that there is no antinomy between labor and capital in the structure of the very process of production.

John Paul II claimed that the relation between labor and capital often bears the signs of the ancient conflict that, together with changes

---

[27] Leo XIII, *Rerum Novarum*, no. 15.

[28] Pius XI, *Quadragesimo Anno*, no. 54.

[29] John Paul II, *Laborem Exercens*, no. 12.

[30] John Paul II, *Centesimus Annus*, no. 32.

[31] John Paul II, *Centesimus Annus*, no. 43.

[32] M. Novak, *Freedom with Justice: Catholic Social Thought and Liberal Institutions* (New York: Harper & Row, 1984), 154.

in the social and economic situation, take on new attributes.[33] Historical experience shows that that this conflict was rather a consequence of the socialization of the means of production in communist countries and was due to the fact that people were deprived of capital—that is, in the papal understanding, the factors of production. This made it impossible for them to carry out an economic calculation and depersonalized the process of production. At the same time, the lack of a formal system of property that could grasp the economic potential of resources and confer on it a form easy to transfer and control, prevented the creation of capital understood as an abstract idea.[34] This situation naturally led to conflict between labor and capital, because the principle of their complementarity had been destabilized.

The Subjective Dimension of Labor

John Paul II also warns of new dangers in separating labor as an efficient cause from capital as a superior cause, the separation that takes place in the era of globalization and scientific and technical progress.[35] The pope does not say it directly, but our analysis so far has shown that the danger of exploiting laborers by the machine of economics and the uninhibited search for productivity are not linked with technical progress or the globalization process themselves but with state interventionism, which for Mises is the main threat to the subject-oriented and personal character of human labor.

For Mises, labor is the employment of the physiological functions and manifestations of human life as a means of production designed to eliminate uneasiness and attain the intended goal.[36] Thinking about labor in the categories of means does not mean that Mises' concept of labor automatically takes on an object-oriented dimension. Labor for him has primarily a subject-oriented dimension, because in the free-market economy man may independently take on various activities that belong to the process of labor and at the same time correspond to

---

[33] *Compendium of the Social Doctrine*, no. 279.

[34] H. de Soto, *The Mystery of Capital: Why Capitalism Triumphs in the West and Fails Everywhere Else* (New York: Basic Books, 2000), 48–49.

[35] John Paul II, *Address to the Participants in the Fifth General Assembly of the Pontifical Academy of Social Sciences* (March 6, 1999).

[36] Mises, *Human Action*, 131.

his personal calling. Mises takes into account this double dimension of human labor, for he knows well that man is not only a provider of the factor of production, which is labor, but also a human creature from whom his activity cannot be separated. From this follows his exceptional and specific character in the world, a recognition that prevents the reduction of man to the object-oriented dimension as a tool of labor.[37]

In the market economy there is no economic dictatorship that can reduce an employee to the level of a pure tool of production. Mises affirms that the employee sells his services as others sell their commodities, but the employer is not the employee's master; he is someone who buys these services and must pay a definite price for them.[38] In no case can we say here that the axiological qualification of such an exchange has been reduced only to the criteria of effectiveness and economics. We are dealing with a true criterion of personalism. Labor is understood and treated as an act of the person (*actus personae*) and at the same time an act toward a person (*actus erga personam*).[39] This is so because the laborer is a free man. The market defends him against self-centered actions of the employer who—like the employees—depends entirely on the discretion of consumers. One can see here that human labor not only results from the person but is also oriented to the person and tends to him.[40] In the system of the division of labor it also has an essential social dimension, because to work "is a matter of doing something for someone else."[41]

Labor for Mises is only a means, not an end in itself.[42] This ability of purposeful action to use one's own resources to eliminate uneasiness indicates a causal relationship between labor and the human "I"—that

---

[37] S. Olejnik, [*Moral Theology*], vol. 5, [*Service to God and Openness to the World*] (Warsaw, 1991), 264.

[38] Mises, *Human Action*, 633–34.

[39] T. Styczen, ["The Personal Dignity of the Subject of Labor as a Source of its Sense and Value"], in [*John Paul II, Laborem Exercens: Text and Commentary*], ed. J. Chmiel and S. Ryłko (Lublin 1986), 109.

[40] *Compendium of the Social Doctrine*, no. 272.

[41] John Paul II, *Centesimus Annus*, no. 31.

[42] Mises, *Human Action*, 131.

is, the priority of the subject of labor vis-à-vis the act of labor.[43] Aside from the metaphysical priority, there is also praxeological priority. Labor, as defined by Mises, has transitive and intransitive dimensions. The transitive dimension is manifested when labor is objectified in an external artifact. The intransitive dimension is what remains in the subject and constitutes its immanent quality or value—the subject's auto-teleogical dynamism that Woytyla calls "*fieri*."[44] This is possible because praxeology assumes as a fact that people wish to rest, and for this reason they perceive their ability to cause effects in a way different from that which pertains to material factors of production. Praxeology treats rest in the same way as all other economic goods. According to Mises, working is always associated with discomfort; therefore, each man, considering his own work, thinks not only about whether to expend the same amount of effort with greater benefit but also about whether it would be more beneficial to abstain from it. For this reason, work in Mises takes on a subjective dimension, and we may say that it is *actus personae*, which has a character that is permanent and independent of whatever kind of activity it is.[45]

Catallactic and Institutional Unemployment

God enjoined man to work, but he did not put his will in a legal category. The Bible is silent on this, for it regards work as the right proper to human nature and the very fact of being persons imposes on each of us the duty to work.[46] The Church teaches that work is

---

[43] Styczen, ["Personal Dignity of the Subject"], 98.

[44] K. Wojtyła, ["The Problem of Constituting Culture Through Human Praxis"], *Roczniki Filozoficzne* 1 (1979): 12. Through *fieri*, Wojtyła explains, one can understand this aspect of human dynamism that "is directed towards man himself—as the subject of this dynamism.... This necessary directing of dynamism to the subject is therefore the auto-teleological dimension of the human dynamism. Dynamism not only 'comes out' of a man, but also 'returns' to him. In this the subject is both the cause of his dynamism and his effect." Amadeusz Pala, "Structure of Man-Person Dynamism in the Adequate Anthropology of Karol Wojtyła," *Logos i ethos* 47, no. 1 (2018): 144.

[45] John Paul II, *Laborem Exercens*, no. 6.

[46] Riber, [*Labor in the Bible*], 28

necessary to establish and maintain the family,[47] to have the right of property,[48] and to participate in the building of the common good of the human family.[49] Labor should therefore be available, and only systems that provide a possibility of reaching "satisfactory levels of employment" are economically justified.[50] The Church regards unemployment as "a real social disaster,"[51] not only because of the moral consequences it has for social life, but first of all because it injures man's personal dignity.[52]

Generally, Church documents make distinctions among several kinds of unemployment: economic, structural, seasonal, functional, and regional.[53] This is most often the statement of an existing fact, not a more profound economic analysis of the phenomenon and its cause. Mises distinguishes between catallactic and institutional unemployment. The former occurs only in the free-market economy, where man for various reasons remains unemployed of his own choice, and the latter is an effect of the government's intervention in market phenomena. The Austrian economist demonstrates that on the unhampered market unemployment is always voluntary.[54] The reason for this is that job-seekers can and do sometimes wait, because they prefer inactivity or choose self-employment.[55] Unemployment appears therefore when the individual appreciates the marginal usefulness of self-employment or the pleasure of inactivity more than wages, which reflect the marginal productivity of his or her job.[56] This line of reasoning shows that voluntary unemployment never undermines human dignity, because it has all the signs of a decision free from

---

[47] John Paul II, *Laborem Exercens*, no. 10.

[48] Leo XIII, *Rerum Novarum*, no. 11; John Paul II, *Laborem Exercens*, no. 14; John Paul II, *Centesimus Annus*, no. 31.

[49] John Paul II, *Laborem Exercens*, no. 18.

[50] John Paul II, *Centesimus Annus*, no. 43.

[51] John Paul II, *Laborem Exercens*, no. 18.

[52] *Catechism of the Catholic Church*, no. 2436.

[53] W. Piwowarski, ["Unemployment"], in [*Dictionary of Catholic Social Doctrine*], 20.

[54] Mises, *Human Action*, 598.

[55] Mises, *Human Action*, 598.

[56] Hoppe, "Misesian Case against Keynes."

external coercion, which is a consequence of psychic processes and choices made by the employee.

Speaking about unemployment, therefore, the Church has in mind enforced unemployment. The first example of such unemployment is that which occurs in the recession stage of the economic cycle,[57] when there is a sudden decrease in the demand for jobs on the part of employers. Fooled by the decrease of interest rates due to an artificial credit expansion, they make wrong investments and set wages higher than those that would be current on a genuinely free market. The second case is when the demands of labor unions impose wage rates higher than the marginal productivity of labor in a given job.[58] A potential employee becomes forcibly unemployed, and a potential employer must transfer complementary factors of production from the applications that serve the production of a higher value to the production of a lower value.[59]

A Just Wage

It should be stressed once again that a minimum wage rate has nothing in common with a just wage of which Catholic social doctrine speaks.[60] The latter should suffice for a workman to support himself and his family.[61] A free-market wage fulfills this condition because an employer took a job at the moment when he ceased to value the marginal usefulness of self-employment or pleasure flowing from inactivity more than remuneration. This decision reflects the marginal productivity of his job, discounted by time preference. Two conditions of work are satisfied here. First, it has a personal character, for each is endowed with the right to freely use his own abilities and energy. Second, it is determined by the grave duty of every individual to preserve his life.[62] The underlying fact for such a claim is that the law of decreasing marginal usefulness—as we have shown in the pre-

---

[57] Hoppe, "Misesian Case against Keynes."

[58] Mises, *Human Action*, 769–77.

[59] Hoppe, "Misesian Case against Keynes."

[60] *Compendium of the Social Doctrine*, no. 302.

[61] John Paul II, *Centesimus Annus*, no. 8.

[62] John Paul II, *Centesimus Annus*, no. 8.

vious chapter—is based on natural inclinations of human reason to preserve one's own life and existence. Time preference is a reflection of the acting person's subjectivity, and the lack of external coercion safeguards free decision. The free-market wage on an unhampered market also fulfills the condition of natural justice, which is more important and prior to the will of the contracting parties.[63]

It is obvious for the author of *Human Action* that the wage rate depends on the demand for labor, which may be determined only by the market. Mises does not differ in this respect from the Late Scholastics, for whom just wages are determined in the same way as just prices, namely by free consent of individuals.[64] Leo XIII, however, does not share this view. Thomas E. Woods thinks that this pope introduced into the Catholic discourse a fatal conception according to which wage rates determined in the market process become targets of moral criticism on the part of external observers on the grounds of whether they are sufficient for the workers to satisfy their material needs.[65] This view has become part and parcel of later Church documents. This means that even if wages are a function of unhampered market processes, they are not necessarily bound to fundamental economic realities but may be "improved" by state intervention.[66]

This view presumes that the government not only supervises the effective functioning of the market economy but also interferes in the wage rate, so that as many people as possible can find work and thereby achieve a proper living standard.[67] According to Mises, such intervention forces entrepreneurs to use the means of production in a different way than they would without these orders. Market laws become disturbed, and entrepreneurs are no longer able to abide by the current consumers' needs. Mises reminds us that those who ask for state intervention at the same time ask for more coercion and less freedom.[68] In *Quadragesimo Anno*, Pius XI notes that attempts to raise

[63] *Compendium of the Social Doctrine*, no. 302.

[64] Chafuen, *Faith and Liberty*, 107.

[65] Woods, *The Church and the Market*, 54; *Catechism of the Catholic Church*, no. 2434; Leo XIII, *Rerum Novarum*, no. 34.

[66] Woods, *The Church and the Market*, 55–56.

[67] Pius XI, *Quadragesimo Anno*, no. 71.

[68] Mises, *Socialism*, 491.

living standards without regard to cost can cause more harm than benefit by creating an unbearable burden for employers,[69] but except for an arbitrary method, which leads to unending complications, he does not provide any alternative solution for the determination of wage rates.

Woods bemoans that, in the documents that are supposed to be the core of Catholic social teaching, economic laws are as a rule rejected as a rationalization of greed.[70] The Jesuit Heinrich Pesch, founder of solidarism, had an enormous influence on this conception of economic laws. Solidarism is a variation of the corporatist doctrine on which Pius XI modeled his work in *Quadragesimo Anno.* Pesch held that advocates of the existence of economic laws presume that man acts always from purely economic motives.[71] Mises proved that this is a false conception, for there are laws of economics that determine the limits of the economy without positing that purely economic concerns (*homo economicus*) constitute the whole of human motivation. The general theory of choice and preference shows clearly that in his choices man is not governed only by economic interests. There is also one more aspect of human nature, of which Mises does not speak because he is not a theologian. We are dealing here not with man in the abstract but with man in his concrete reality as both sinful and righteous.[72] Praxeology is therefore a science about each kind of real human action, its internal logic and respective consequences for the economic sphere, which cannot be separated from other spheres of man's life and activity. The formal relations between ends and means are universal and binding in praxeology irrespective of the nature of ends, which need not have a material character.[73]

Mises gives yet one more important argument against the arbitrary determination of wage and price rates. Labor is a scarcer factor than most of the naturally available material factors of production, for other-

---

[69] Pius XI, *Quadragesimo Anno,* no. 71.

[70] Woods, *The Church and the Market,* 57–58.

[71] Woods, *The Church and the Market,* 68.

[72] John Paul II, *Centesimus Annus,* no. 35.

[73] M. N. Rothbard, *Man, Economy and State: A Treatise on Economic Principles* (Auburn, AL: Mises Institute, 1993), 63.

wise there would not be any unutilized and marginally unused soil.[74] Employers must therefore compete with one another for scarce labor, and employees have in consequence a choice among many employers who are vying to gain their services. The price of a given kind of work is therefore determined by an interaction of the forces of demand and supply, while the liberty of all parties in question is preserved. The Church teaches that the dignity of persons is the criterion of labor evaluation,[75] but this dignity can never be isolated from freedom. Labor, from the Church's point of view, should be characterized by two principles. The first—the principle of causality—overlaps with Mises' point of view; according to it, there should be a relationship between wages and an employee's efficiency.[76] Following Mises' argumentation, it is more difficult to agree with the second principle—the principle of finality—which says that labor should provide a man and his family with a dignified material, social, cultural, and spiritual status.[77] Mises is well aware that each person has his own opinion on what he deserves on account of status, position, or tradition, but he is right when he claims that this subjective opinion can have no relation to the determination of wage rates by the employer. Nor can economic theory be determined on the grounds of "historical categories." A similar mistake is inherent in Marx's doctrine, which approaches the question of wages as a fact historically conditioned and something that does not exist as a market phenomenon.

The reason that advocates of just prices and wage rates do not allow for a market determination of prices is that they fear that each change could deteriorate the current state of affairs, which, in their opinion, is the best possible. Mises noticed that this kind of thinking was absurd; he demonstrates that the motor of progress is the flexible character of prices. Rigidity and stagnation always lead to the deterioration

---

74 Mises, *Human Action*, 596.

75 Congregation for the Doctrine of the Faith, *Instruction on Christian Freedom*, no. 86.

76 W. Terpilowski, [*The Problem of Labor in the Church's Post-Conciliar Teaching: The Moral-Social Aspect*] (Swidnica, 2006), 185.

77 See *Gaudium et Spes*, no. 67; John XXIII, *Mater et Magistra*, no. 70; John Paul II, *Laborem Exercens*, no. 19.

of economic conditions.[78] In the real world, the number of people, tastes, and needs, as well as the supply of the means of production and technological methods, constantly undergo change.[79] The only method to adjust production to the changing condition of the market is price, and it is not only utilitarian or materialistic arguments that come into play here. The fear of allowing changes on the market leads above all to the limitation of human freedom, and this constitutes an obstacle to the development of entrepreneurship.

Criticism of Labor Unionism

Labor unions are often strident defenders of legal minimum wage rates. Mises carries out a devastating criticism of the syndicalist movement, calling it "the economic philosophy of short-sighted people."[80] He demonstrates that if a labor union insists on determining a minimum wage above the level that it would reach for a given kind of job should the union not exist, it contributes to limiting the number of people whom the employer could employ. As a result of labor unions' pressure and coercion, institutional unemployment appears. The action of labor unions does not differ in any important way from the government's intervention in the job market. Mises demonstrates that the phrase "collective bargaining" does not mean substitution of individual negotiations for a contract negotiated by a labor union, for genuine group negotiations should not differ in any catallactic respect from individual negotiations. This catallactic aspect of labor unionism is a serious challenge for Catholic social doctrine, because it shows clearly that by means of enforcement and coercion one cannot make the wages of all willing to work increase above the level determined by the unhampered market.

The social teaching of the Church in the sphere of solidarity among employees lacks a more profound analysis on the basis of understanding market mechanisms. The Church teaches that relations in the world of labor should be characterized by cooperation and concern for the proper common good.[81] She is decisively against using labor

---

[78] Mises, *Human Action*, 728.

[79] Mises, *Bureaucracy*, 31.

[80] Mises, *Human Action*, 814.

[81] John Paul II, *Laborem Exercens*, no. 20.

unions as a political party and instrument of struggle.[82] In the face of increasingly rapid processes of economic-financial globalization, the pope calls labor unions to work out new forms of activity and enlarge the scope of their solidary action over those employees who work on the basis of atypical or part-time contracts.[83] The Church's concern for an employee is obvious—he should have an opportunity to defend and pursue his rights—but the concern itself does not suffice, if one does not know the cause of the disease and there is no effective medicine to cure it. The reduction of the role of labor unions to "the struggle for social justice" may be wrongly interpreted in political categories and make people think that entrepreneurs and capitalists are irresponsible autocrats. Woods rightly remarks that this way of thinking in Catholic social teaching may lead to a belief that it is only the lack of wise legislation that separates us from a perfect society of the future, whereas it is in fact only capital investments that are capable of multiplying the resources of wealth.[84]

Human Entrepreneurship

The Church teaches that everyone has a right to economic initiative and should take advantage of his talents to contribute to universal development and thus gain the just fruits of his efforts.[85] Using his own creative talents, man is obedient to the will of the Creator, "that work should enable man to achieve that 'dominion' in the visible world that is proper to him."[86] Human creativity manifests itself above all in the capacities of planning and innovation.[87] Such capacities presume that man thinks in the categories of gains and losses. A consequence of this kind of thinking must be rejection of economic systems in which there is no element of uncertainty, for under such circumstances the

---

[82] John Paul II, *Laborem Exercens*, no. 20.

[83] See John Paul II, *Address to an International Conference for Representatives of Trade Unions* (December 2, 1996), www.vatican.va/holy_father/john_paul_ii/speeches/1996/December/documents/hf_jp_ii_spe_19961202_giustizia-pace_enhtml.

[84] Woods, *The Church and the Market*, 79–80.

[85] *Catechism of the Catholic Church*, no. 2429.

[86] John Paul II, *Laborem Exercens*, no. 9.

[87] John Paul II, *Centesimus Annus*, no. 32.

function of the entrepreneur is redundant. For Mises, this function is not a specific trait that characterizes a definite class of people but is instead inherently linked with each human action. Each behavior on the market—even the action of a consumer who aims at satisfying his future predictable needs—has a speculative character, for it is embedded in the flux of time and uncertainty.[88] Each human action aims at a profit; therefore, it is difficult to imagine a situation in which people could function on other principles. John Paul II speaks in a similar vein: in *Centesimus Annus* he approves of profit as the first indicator of the development of an enterprise, for it is the sign that factors of production have been properly applied and human needs are being satisfied.[89]

Contrary to socialism, which makes man dependent on the central planner, the individual in the free-market economy is free and makes his own decisions about his own life; therefore, he may act in a planned, intelligent, and creative mode. This understanding of human action is fully personal and provides a foundation for the theology of creation. Michael Novak rightly notes that man is a creator and he is never one to such a great extent as when he is undertaking daily economic tasks.[90] One should stress, however, that according to Mises work itself is not creation. Man's ability to work is given in the world in the same way as the original and natural capacities inherent in natural resources.[91] Only the human mind has creative capacities. Material changes result exclusively from spiritual and intellectual changes.

Here we can observe some convergence of the Austrian economist's thought with John Paul II's theology of creation. The pope claims that man is obedient to the will of the Creator; therefore, he uses his creative talents to achieve through work "dominion" in the visible world.[92] The pope stresses in particular the close relationship between man as the subject of work and his right to the fruits of this work, including the right to ownership, which allows man to mani-

---

[88] Mises, *Human Action*, 253.

[89] John Paul II, *Centesimus Annus*, no. 35.

[90] Novak, *Freedom with Justice*, 162–63.

[91] Mises, *Human Action*, 141.

[92] John Paul II, *Laborem Exercens*, no. 9.

fest his inherent creative capacities. In human work understood in this way, which corresponds with the personalistic norm, there is an element of cooperation with God through which man contributes to the revelation of the Creator's perennial and wise intentions, and at the same time he expresses his recognition and admiration for the Creator's perfection.[93]

Totalitarian systems deprive man of the right to economic initiative. Mises shows that human entrepreneurship is also limited in the system of the unhampered market, where governments have at their disposal various tools to exert pressure on people; as a result of this pressure, entrepreneurs are forced to use means of production in a way different from the one they would choose under free-market conditions. John Paul II noticed the same problem. In *Solicitudo Rei Socialis*, he states that in today's world the right to economic activity is more and more often suppressed in the name of an alleged "equality." The policy of interventionism followed by contemporary governments destroys entrepreneurship (that is, the creative subjectivity of the citizen).[94] Later, the pope touches on the same problem and rightly notes that, where individual profit is suppressed by coercion or limited by government intervention, it is always replaced by a system of bureaucratic control that deprives man of economic initiative.[95] In the socialist and interventionist system man is identified with a certain collection of social relations. Accordingly, the concept of his own person as an independent subject of moral decisions—the subject that takes a job, changes it, or voluntarily abstains from it—disappears.[96] Mises' and the pope's points of view are therefore convergent.

There is another reason that human entrepreneurship should not be limited by governments' bureaucratic actions: work from the Christian point of view has a redemptive dimension. John Paul teaches that work is related to the mystery of the Incarnation: it imitates Christ and joins in the work that Christ performed during his life on

---

[93] S. Nowak, ["The Bond with God through Work"], in [*Laborem Exercens: Text and Commentary*], 146.

[94] John Paul II, *Solicitudo Rei Socialis*, no. 15.

[95] John Paul II, *Centesimus Annus*, no. 25.

[96] John Paul II, *Centesimus Annus*, no. 13.

earth.[97] The Son of God, in order to redeem the world, descended to earth and voluntarily assumed sweat and toil, which are linked with human labor. The work of redemption was made through suffering and death on the cross. The man who each day consciously takes on himself the cross of activity to which he has been called becomes a true disciple of Jesus.[98] Overcoming the arduousness of work gives him an awareness of victory over his own weakness, contributes to the increase of his spiritual maturity,[99] and enables him to collaborate in the work of the redemption of the world. The redemptive prospect permits us to notice a more profound dimension of man's calling to entrepreneurship, which is not limited only to earthly economics but is also written in all God's works, through which he reveals himself to man and allows man to share in the divine life.

The foregoing analysis allows us to better understand man's calling to entrepreneurship in the socioeconomic sphere. On one hand, Mises points to many areas of human labor that can be deepened from the theological point of view. This analysis, however, calls for a proper understanding of market mechanisms that are part of the divine plan of creation.[100] On the other hand, the social teaching of the Church traces out a proper anthropological ground for understanding man in the perspective of his ultimate destiny. Man transcends the material world and expresses and makes himself real through his creative use of this world, conferring a personal dimension on his work. The ground for man's economic activity, according to Mises, is private ownership of the means of production.

---

[97] Nowak, ["Bond with God"], 145–46.

[98] John Paul II, *Laborem Exercens*, no. 27.

[99] J. Majka, [*Considerations on the Ethics of Labor*] (Wroclaw, 1986), 75.

[100] J. Sadovsky, *The Christian Response to Poverty* (London: Social Affairs Unit, 1985), 5.

The Social Dimension of Private Ownership

The Church teaches that the principle of the universal destination of material goods lies at the foundation of the universal right of their usage.[101] This teaching is in its whole scope apparent in Mises, who claims that in capitalism the ownership of the means of production is linked with social duty.[102] The effectiveness of productive effort is only one of the arguments on behalf of capitalism and private property. The purpose of the analysis below is to show that besides a personal aspect there is also a social dimension of private property in capitalism, which is wrongly identified by some Catholic writers as elevating the right of private property to the rank of a "sacred" right, inviolable and contradictory to the "good of all."

The Right of Private Ownership

For Mises, private ownership of the means of production is a basic institution of the market economy. The catallactic concept of ownership means full control of the applications of a given good.[103] According to Mises, private property is a human invention that appeared at the beginning of history when people appropriated what was no one's before. This mode of reasoning is close to that of St. Thomas Aquinas, who thought that private property came from the establishment of human positive law.[104] The Second Vatican Council adds that property gives a person an opportunity to perform various tasks in society and in social life.[105]

From the economic point of view, an owner for Mises is someone who physically disposes of a certain economic good.[106] This way of thinking is part of the Catholic tradition. Leo XIII, for example,

---

[101] *Compendium of the Social Doctrine*, no. 172.

[102] L. von Mises, "Liberty and Property," Mises Institute, http://mises.org/libprop.asp. Originally published in *Two Essays by Ludwig von Mises: Liberty and Property* (Auburn, AL: Mises Institute, 1991).

[103] Mises, *Human Action*, 682.

[104] Woods, *The Church and the Market*, 194; St. Thomas Aquinas, *Summa Theologica*, II-II, q. 66, a. 7.

[105] *Gaudium et Spes*, no. 71.

[106] Mises, *Socialism*, 27.

reminds us that the right to use material things to satisfies man's real needs is a fundamental human right.[107]

The Church teaches that the beginning of individual property resides in human work. Mises holds the same view. For him any property is derived in the first place from appropriation and lasts until the owner voluntarily gives it up or loses it against his will.[108] This distinction is implied in the Christian tradition in the ban on theft. The seventh commandment, "Thou shalt not steal," has a negative form, but this ban should be understood as a norm deriving from the positive order (Ex. 20:15). It constitutes strong evidence that it is the will of God, expressed in the inspired biblical word, that people should own earthly goods.[109] Questioning private ownership and attempting to limit it are therefore contradictory to God's commandments. On the basis of the Misesian definition of private ownership we may say that the seventh commandment defends the natural bond between man, the material things he needs, and the products of his work, for no man can do without earthly goods.[110]

Catholic social teaching stresses that there is a close relationship between man as the subject of work and the right to the fruits of his work in the form of private property.[111] According to Mises, this relationship has been seriously violated by the introduction of the system of fractional reserves and fiduciary money, which are imposed on citizens by their government without any support in material goods (precious metals, for instance), encourage artificial creation of money, and cause hazardous and recurring economic recessions.[112] The best monetary system, both for the free-market economy and from the perspective of the Church, would be commodity money with a 100 percent cover.[113]

---

[107] Leo XIII, *Rerum Novarum*, no. 7.

[108] Mises, *Socialism*, 36.

[109] M. Wojciechowski, ["Private Ownership in the Bible"], in [*Theft and Economic Development*], ed. A. A. Chafuen et al. (Warsaw, 2006), 109.

[110] A. A. Chafuen and L. P. Liggio, "Cultural and Religious Foundations of Private Property," in *The Elgar Companion to the Economics of Property Rights*, ed. E. Colombatto (Cheltenham, UK: Elgar, 2004).

[111] John Paul II, *Laborem Exercens*, no. 14.

[112] Mises, *Human Action*, 793ff.

[113] Woods, *The Church and the Market*, 122.

Making such a requirement for the contracts of banking deposits on demand would contribute to establishing a system completely in accord with the principles of private property by preventing the double accessibility of the same amount of money on the market,[114] which thereby gives rise to a typical *tragedy of the commons*—the phenomenon that appears when the property rights of third parties are insufficiently defined or protected.[115]

Illegal appropriation of someone else's property therefore does not occur only in totalitarian systems. Mises rightly notes that all who hold political power have an inborn inclination to extend the sphere of their domination to control the lives of their citizens. The only obstacle in their way is the institution of private ownership. It sets limits on the authoritarian actions of governments, creating for the individual an indispensable space for his autonomous intellectual and material development.[116] Beyond the sphere of private ownership and the market there lies the sphere of coercion and violence. The same way of perceiving the role of private property is present in the teaching of the Second Vatican Council. According to the Council Fathers, private possession of goods ensures the indispensable space for each person's personal and family autonomy, encourages the fulfillment of tasks and obligations, constitutes a condition of civil liberties, and is an extension of the space of human freedom.[117] For this reason, the Church demands that the property of goods be justly accessible to all and rejects resorting to arrangements that mandate a "community of goods."[118]

---

[114] H. J. de Soto, *Money, Bank Credit and Economic Cycles* (Auburn, AL: Ludwig von Mises Institute, 2006), 748–49ff. It should be stressed that understanding the proper role of money, which involves an evaluation of contemporary banking and is related to other economic phenomena, is continuously a real challenge for Catholic social teaching. For more about the moral implications of banking with partial reserve, see another contemporary economist from the Austrian School: J. G. Hülsmann, *The Ethics of Money Production* (Auburn, AL: Mises Institute), 2008.

[115] Soto, *Money*, 394.

[116] Mises, *Liberalism*, 69.

[117] *Gaudium et Spes*, no. 71.

[118] John Paul II, *Centesimus Annus*, no. 6; Leo XIII, *Rerum Novarum*, no. 15.

The Church teaches that the right to property is not absolute or untouchable. Christian tradition has always understood it within the broader context of the right common to all to use the goods of the whole of creation.[119] Private property is only a tool by which to respect the principle of the universal destination of material wealth—that is, it is the means, not the ultimate goal.[120] The Church thinks that this norm does not oppose the right to property but instead indicates the necessity of its regulation. Mises' reasoning will be helpful in this respect: when discussing the nature of property from the economic point of view, he introduces a division into the property of consumer goods and the property of the means of production.

Individual Property

The goods of the first degree (i.e., consumer goods), serve to accomplish the immediate gratification of their owner's needs. Of their nature, they may be used only once and with their consumption or usage they cease to exist, thereby losing their quality as goods. Their owner can also exchange them for other goods or voluntarily give them up. The possession of consumer goods excludes the possession of these goods by others and is understood as private ownership *par excellence,* for it deprives others of the benefits associated with the right of their possession. Therefore, for Mises, it is impossible even to consider removing or reforming the principle of the ownership of consumer goods. The consumer's ownership must be exclusive. In the Bible, we find examples of collective ownership, but they are always realized through individual property. The best illustration is the moment when the Israelites received Canaan as their property (Gen. 12:1–7); then it was divided into the tribes and families (Num. 26:52–56; Josh. 18:1–10). Even in such an idealized interpretation, the division of a common estate leads to the individual ownership of land.[121]

Things look different in the case of durable goods, which may be used many times and serve many persons.[122] Ownership of the means of production, unlike that of consumer goods, can be divided in a

---

[119] John Paul II, *Laborem Exercens,* no. 14.

[120] Paul VI, Encyclical Letter *Populorum Progressio* (1967), nos. 22–23.

[121] M. Wojciechowski, ["Private Ownership"], 112.

[122] Mises, *Socialism,* 28–32.

natural manner depending on the divisibility of the services they can provide. Mises stresses that the essence of private ownership of means of production in a society based on the division of labor is decisively different not only from those systems in which the division of labor does not occur but also from any other economic systems.

The Church teaches that the right of private ownership is subordinated to the right of common use.[123] This norm is not opposed to the right of property, however, which should not be regarded as absolute and untouchable.[124] Analyzing Mises' way of reasoning, we can see that such conditions are fulfilled in the free-market economy and determined by consumers' behavior. Consumers constantly control the factors of production and convey it to the hands of those entrepreneurs and capitalists who best fulfill their wishes.[125] The Second Vatican Council teaches that man should regard the things that he legally owns as his own but also as common in the sense that they can bring benefit to others.[126]

A total confiscation of private property, which is coequal to the introduction of socialism, was unambiguously rejected by Leo XIII in *Rerum Novarum*.[127] John Paul II supplements the arguments of his predecessors from the personalistic point of view, adding that the principal error of socialism is anthropological in character, for the abolition of private ownership deprives man of the space in which he can earn for his own living with his entrepreneurship and hinders progress toward the building up of an authentic human community.[128] Mises poses a completely different moral problem that deals with a partial confiscation of private property made by taxation. State interventionism, which burdens its citizens with excessive tax, is an indirect kind of breaking the right to property.

---

[123] John Paul II, *Laborem Exercens*, no. 14.

[124] Leo XIII, *Rerum Novarum*, no. 12.

[125] Mises, *Interventionism*, 2–3.

[126] *Gaudium et Spes*, no. 69.

[127] Leo XIII, *Rerum Novarum*, no. 6.

[128] John Paul II, *Centesimus Annus*, no. 13.

The Limits of Tax Burdens

The social teaching of the Church refers us in this question to Jesus' disputes with the Pharisees about the tax paid to Caesar and reminds us that Jesus does not condemn it (Mark 12:13–17; Matt. 22:15–22; Luke 20:20–26). Saint Paul lays stress on the duty to pay taxes to the civil authority (Rom 12:17) because it serves God for the good of the human person and is "the servant of God to inflict wrath on the evildoer" (Rom. 13:4). We find a similar teaching in St. Peter's first letter (1 Peter 2:13–14). In the biblical teaching, therefore, the point is free and responsible obedience toward the authorities, which respects justice and ensures the realization of the common good.[129] John XXIII addresses the question of tax policy and states that tax burdens should be adjusted to citizens' ability to pay, but at the same time he adds that the authority should be ruled by wisdom and justice in determining taxes.[130] Separately, the pope indicates that by means of the proper amount of taxes the economic balance of the country should be restored. For Mises, this position is unacceptable, for the purpose of levying taxes cannot be an attempt at a just shaping of social conditions.[131] John XXIII's view seems to diverge from John Paul II's later teaching, where the latter proposes that the supervision of the observance of human rights in the economic sphere does not belong to the state but to particular people and various groups and associations of which society is composed.[132] Leo XIII also teaches that the state is unjust if it makes it difficult for its citizens to make use of private property through burdensome taxation.[133]

Mises totally rejects the idea of just taxation. For him, taxes are linked with the market economy and should be invested in maintaining a modest government, absorb a small part of the general incomes of each citizen, and not exceed a moderate level, for otherwise they may turn into weapons that destroy the market economy.[134] He reminds

---

[129] *Compendium of the Social Doctrine*, nos. 379–80.

[130] John XXIII, *Mater et Magistra*, no. 132.

[131] Mises, *Human Action*, 738.

[132] John Paul II, *Centesimus Annus*, no. 48.

[133] Leo XIII, *Rerum Novarum*, no. 35.

[134] Mises, *Human Action*, 741.

us that the character of a free-market economy is precisely that the government does not interfere in economic phenomena. High taxes are not only a threat to the free market but also fail to reach the end for which they have been established. The progressive tax, whose purpose is to introduce financial equality among citizens, paradoxically strikes the less wealthy and is self-destructive, for it hampers the process of capital formation.[135] This happens because only the unconsumed part of incomes may be accumulated as capital, and people with higher incomes, unlike the poor, save and consume only a part of their income, investing the rest. Collecting high taxes from people who earn more and using them to finance public expenditures is a direct consumption of capital, which causes a decline in the marginal efficiency of labor and, in turn, a decline in wages.

Some commentators on Catholic social teaching think that income tax should be progressive to serve as an instrument by which the social good can be realized. But if tax progression is too high, citizens have a sense of injustice and tend to evade it by hiding their incomes, a move that hinders economic development.[136] We should especially be careful when taxing *income* progressively, for people who earn their living from labor should not be deprived of the right to save. Mises' earlier analysis has already shown that a regime of progressive taxation that would satisfy such conditions does not and cannot exist.

The Protection of Private Property

The free-market economy tends to create an area in which the individual is free to think, choose, and act. Mises does not dispute that people can use their freedom in an egoistic manner, but tax policy cannot be reduced to moral intuition referring to social justice.[137]

---

[135] Mises, *Interventionism*, 51.

[136] Mises, *Interventionism*, 247.

[137] Hayek rightly notes that this term becomes a real equivalent of distributive justice. The apparent goal of social justice is to eliminate economic inequalities without taking into consideration the simple fact that disproportions mainly result from the individuals' own choices. F. A. von Hayek, *The Fatal Conceit: The Errors of Socialism* (Chicago: University of Chicago Press, 1989), 117–19. The Second Vatican Council teaches that economic activity must be conducted within the frame of moral order and in accord with

Therefore one should take into account the serious reasons against state intervention into private property. One of Mises' arguments on behalf of capitalism and private property is the incomparable effectiveness of productive effort. This efficiency has made possible a rapid population increase alongside a rising standard of living. Aquinas claimed that private ownership is necessary for three reasons: Man is more concerned about private things than common ones; he treats material affairs in a more ordered manner when he owns property; and private property promotes peaceful interhuman relations.[138] In like manner, the Late Scholastics argued on behalf of private property; they thought that an ordered society and a peaceful division of labor are impossible without the institution of private property.

The *use* of external goods is related to their possession, but it is nevertheless a distinct matter. The right to personal ownership is subordinate to the right of universal usage, as has already been discussed, but it is worth emphasizing yet another aspect here. The possession of external goods enables man to fulfill the commandment to clothe the naked, feed the hungry, and give shelter (Matt. 25:35–36). Distributing someone else's property is not charity. Benedict XVI reminds us that a just ordering of society and the state is a central task of politics, but the view that just structures make charitable works redundant is based on a materialistic and humiliating conception of man.[139]

Mises asserts that the coordination of independent actions by all individuals in the free-market economy is made through the market and there is no need to enforce cooperation by means of special orders and prohibitions.[140] Eliminating private property or enforcing certain limitations on it through government policy is illicit, according to Mises, because it imposes on the market economy a direction of development different from that taken when profit is the only stimulus. Private property is for the Austrian economist an inviolable value, for beyond its sphere there is only coercion and violence. Leo

---

social justice, so that each man can respond to God's plan (*Gaudium et Spes*, no. 64). It is difficult, however, to agree with the assumption that this can be achieved without an indispensable space in the economic and social sphere for making free choices.

[138] St. Thomas Aquinas, *Summa Theologica*, I-II, q. 66, a. 2.

[139] Benedict XVI, *Deus Caritas Est*, no. 28.

[140] Mises, *Human Action*, 244–45.

XIII takes a similar view of private property as a sacred right and basic principle.[141] Pius XI adds that even abusing or abstaining from using private property cannot be justification for its confiscation.[142]

These are affirmations of the principle of respect for the goods of another man, which forbids theft, but contemporary teaching, referring to the principle of solidarity, imposes certain limitations on private property. The Second Vatican Council teaches that it is not theft when someone's goods are taken and used to satisfy the urgent and basic needs of another.[143] The Council Fathers refer here to the teaching of St. Thomas, but they emphasize that all required moral conditions must be satisfied. Martin de Azpilcueta, who remained—like all scholastics—under Aquinas's influence, adds that one who takes a thing in utmost need is obliged to compensate, if and when he has such an opportunity.[144]

The traditional teaching of the Church says that the right of property is not absolute, but justice, which imposes certain norms on the use of property, cannot undermine the commandment "Thou shalt not steal." Michal Wojciechowski rightly notes that life in the Bible has a greater value than property; therefore, the hungry man does not sin what he is forced to steal (Prov. 6:30).[145] Property has only a material character and cannot be given priority over other values.

The Bible warns us against the worship of property, which is a form of idolatry. This danger affects not only the wealthy, for excessive concern about material things threatens all who possess wealth. The biblical criticism of wealth is directed against unrighteous profits

---

141 Leo XIII, *Rerum Novarum*, no. 46.

142 Pius XI, *Quadragesimo Anno*, no. 47.

143 "The seventh commandment forbids theft, that is, usurping another's property against the reasonable will of the owner. There is no theft if consent can be presumed or if refusal is contrary to reason and the universal destination of goods. This is the case in obvious and urgent necessity when the only way to provide for immediate, essential needs (food, shelter, clothing, etc.) is to put at one's disposal and use the property of others." *Catechism of the Catholic Church*, no. 2408.

144 Martin de Azpilcueta, *Manual de confesores y penitents* (Salamanca 1556), 206, as cited in Chafuen and Liggio, "Cultural and Religious Foundations of Private Property," 40.

145 M. Wojciechowski, [*Private Ownership*], 114.

and those who have gained great wealth and turned away from God and neighbors. Saint Paul says that a man concentrated on God rises above material questions and is able to live in poverty (Phil. 4:12). In the light of biblical teaching, private property is normal and right, although the love of God and neighbor stands higher. Property therefore is protected by God's law, and the person to which this property belongs is responsible for its use. Our analysis so far has shown that the subjectivist theory of value, according to which the acting man on the basis of his own scale of values chooses out of various available possibilities, completely overlaps with biblical teaching.

Limitations of Private Ownership

The problem of which Mises is speaking is not the abuse of the right to property but its limitation in the name of state property. By means of its laws and regulations, the state may indeed interfere in various ways in the shaping of property relations. It should be stressed that the state's ordering tasks in the sphere of material goods must be carried out with a complete respect for private ownership.[146]

Generally speaking, the Church does not approve of practices that, directly or indirectly, would make the right to property illusory.[147] The only serious exception from the point of view of the free-market economy is expropriation through the state, allowed in the teaching of the popes after respective conditions have been fulfilled, one of which is just compensation to the original owners for the property they have lost.[148] Pope Paul VI has in mind here mainly the expropriation of land that "impedes the general prosperity."[149] The popes stress that this is to be done only when required by the common good, but it is difficult to defend this line of reasoning because the decision is based on an arbitrary reference to "the good of all." According to

---

146 *Gaudium et Spes*, no. 71; John Paul II, *Sollicitudo Rei Socialis*, no. 42; John Paul II, *Centesimus Annus*, nos. 40, 48.

147 A. Rauscher, SJ, ["Private Ownership in the Service of Man"], in M. Novak, A Rauscher, SJ, and M. Zięba, OP, [*Christianity, Democracy, and Capitalism*] (Poznań, 1993), 103.

148 Pius XII, "On the Economic Order," March 11, 1945, *Utz-Groner*, no. 2919, as cited by A. Rauscher, ["Private Ownership"], 107.

149 Paul VI, *Populorum Progressio*, no. 24.

Mises, such intervention may be contradictory to the social interest, because the state seeks to authoritatively determine new borders for the use of the rights to property, undermining the borders naturally established by the private ownership of the means of production.[150] Mises reminds us that the state has the power to put such expropriation into practice, but it will never be able to accomplish the intended goals by such coercive means.[151] In the free-market economy, force is used only to protect private property and the market against violence.[152]

This is not the only limitation that Catholic social teaching imposes on private property. Pius XI claimed that some kinds of goods should be reserved for the state because their possession confers power that could endanger the state. From the point of view of the free-market economy, what John XXIII wrote in *Mater et Magistra* can no longer be held; namely that the state should conduct economic activity to a certain degree and should entrust its economic enterprises to citizens who are professional and honest. The experience with workers' self-governments has shown that an attempt to degrade private property to the sphere of possession and consumption, ignoring the whole function of ordering, has brought pathetic results. Private ownership has its own inherent power to dispose of and effectively use material goods, which nothing can replace.[153] Hernando de Soto writes: "Property, then, is not mere paper but a mediating device that captures and stores most of the stuff required to make a market economy run."[154] According to Mises, private property occurs only where the individual can use his property as a factor of production in a way that he deems to be the most profitable.[155]

In Catholic social teaching there has been a slow evolution of the view of the relationship between private property and the common destination of material wealth. In *Centesimus Annus*, John Paul II stated that private property guarantees jobs and human development. Earlier, in *Laborem Exercens*, he showed that the taking over of the means of

[150] Mises, *Interventionism*, 13–14.

[151] Mises, *Interventionism*, 27.

[152] Mises, *Interventionism*, 31.

[153] A. Rauscher, ["Private Ownership"], 109.

[154] de Soto, *Mystery of Capital*, 63.

[155] Mises, *Socialism*, 245.

production by the state is not equivalent to "socialization," for one can speak about socializing only when the subjective character of society is ensured. According to the pope, this goal can be achieved only when, on the basis of his work, each person can consider himself a part-owner of the "great workbench at which he is working."[156] According to Mises, this takes place only in the free-market economy, in which the subjective character of society is ensured by the sovereignty of consumers. It is not the entrepreneurs, the farmers, or the capitalists who determine what has to be produced but the consumers.[157] They determine not only the prices of consumer goods but also those of all factors of production. Ownership of the means of production therefore is not a privilege but a social liability.[158] Capitalists and landowners are compelled to take care about consumers' needs as best they can and thereby to fulfill the common destination of material wealth. John Paul II has noticed as much, writing that the capability of recognizing in time the needs of others and the most appropriate factors of production to their satisfaction is an important source of wealth.[159]

John Paul II teaches that the ownership of the means of production is just only if it serves useful work.[160] This function of private ownership can be fulfilled only in the free-market economy. Mises indicates that one who does not use his property to serve consumers as best he can is penalized by losses, and if he does not learn the lesson and does not reform his conduct of affairs, he loses all his wealth.[161]

Contemporary Catholic social teaching often states that public authorities have the right to supervise so that no one abuses their private property to the detriment of the public good.[162] John Paul II explains that the supplementary interventions of the state must be as brief as possible, so as to avoid creating, in a sense, a new type of state—the so-called "Welfare State."[163] The Council Fathers suggest

---

[156] John Paul II, *Laborem Exercens*, 14.

[157] Mises, *Human Action*, 270.

[158] Mises, *Human Action*, 311.

[159] John Paul II, *Centesimus Annus*, no. 32.

[160] John Paul II, *Centesimus Annus*, no. 43.

[161] Mises, *Human Action*, 311–12.

[162] *Gaudium et Spes*, no. 71.

[163] John Paul II, *Centesimus Annus*, no. 48.

that ownership often becomes an opportunity to greed, which is a pretext to question the law itself. Mises regards this kind of thinking as improper, for its authors fail to perceive the significance of the forces they condemn as immoral.[164] The market is not dealing with ideal individuals; it must take into account man as he is. Should we replace the motive of profit, which is the key factor of the private ownership of the means of production, with "moral" motives, we would destroy the purposefulness and efficiency of the market. Egoism, greed, and the individual's inclination to accomplish his own goals are not contradictory to the overall social process of production so long as man in action on behalf of his own interests remains in the space determined by private ownership.[165]

Private Ownership as a Guarantee to Maintain and Protect the Family

In the social teaching of the Church, one of the main arguments on behalf of private property declares that it is essential for the maintenance and protection of the family. Leo XIII taught that family property is a factor of the family's unity and strengthens the permanence of family community.[166] Family property ensures autonomy for the family and protects it against the state's interference, which may take place only when the family needs such support.[167] Private property gives the family a life-space necessary for the accomplishment of the ultimate end, which is eternal bliss.[168] Mises does not speak about the ultimate end of man's action, for this question goes beyond the sphere of catallaxis. His way of reasoning, however, is similar: because private property is the basis of free action in the free-market economy, it safeguards the attainment of intended goals by the person acting within its framework.

---

164 Mises, *Interventionism*, 14–15.

165 Mises, *Interventionism*, 33.

166 Leo XIII, *Rerum Novarum*, no. 6.

167 Leo XIII, *Rerum Novarum*, no. 28.

168 Pius XI, *Quadragesimo Anno*, no. 118.

The Austrian philosopher lays stress on the individual, but he treats marriage as a free contract between woman and man with equal rights.[169] It constitutes a natural adjustment of the individual to the social order and a natural way to fulfill all the tasks and duties toward the family that results.[170] Every attempt to abolish or limit private property is therefore directed not only against the individual's freedom but also against the model of a traditional family. Private ownership helps to consolidate and protect the family; therefore, as Mises rightly notes, Marxism has always struggled against the idea of a traditional family together with the right to private property.[171]

Mises thought that the idea of private property was in accord with Christianity. Much room in his work on socialism is devoted to a criticism of those who sought to combine their uncompromising condemnation of egoism and the desire of possession, as well as the dictates of social justice and neighbor's love, with the socialist system of norms and values.[172] Mises, like some historians, doubts whether Jesus put forward any program of social reform.[173] Instead he called people to prepare themselves for the advent of the kingdom of God. The gospel is full of condemnation for the rich (Matt. 19:24) and calls to sacrifice, but in his private life Jesus was not an ascetic, did not despise property, visited the homes of wealthy people, and allowed them to have him as their guest.[174]

Mises criticizes the interpretation of the book of Acts according to which in the primitive Church everything belonged to all (Acts 2:44; 4:34–35). This was not a form of "communism," he insists, for communism is not aimed at participation in consumption and usage of goods but instead at collective work and production, which is associated with

---

[169] Mises, *Socialism*, 82.

[170] Tucker and Rockwell, "Cultural Thought," 292–93.

[171] Mises, *Socialism*, 75.

[172] Mises, *Socialism*, 369–87.

[173] Mises, *Socialism*, 376; R. Pipes, [*Property and Freedom*], trans. L. Niedzielski (Warsaw, 2000), 33.

[174] See M. Hengel, *Property and Riches in the Early Church: Aspects of a Social History of Early Christianity*, trans. J. Bowden (Philadelphia: Fortress Press, 1974), 26–28.

the common ownership of the means of production.[175] The Church in the first centuries regarded private property as a component of eternal life and called the faithful to charity. The monastic life, too, is not a form of socialism, in Mises' view, because the monks lived off various forms of property.[176]

This analysis shows that Mises supports private ownership because it may be used in a more efficient and practical manner, owing to the fact that the essence of private ownership consists in creating an indispensable space of freedom for economic and social initiatives. Consideration of the Austrian economist's thought has brought us to the conclusion that in a society in which there is the division of labor no one is *de facto* an exclusive owner of the means of production and their possession always has a social character. A society based on private ownership is more peaceful, more productive, and more ethical in conduct. Private ownership allows people to create an indispensable space for the fullness of personal development.

The Common Good in the Free-Market Economy

According to Mises, society emerges as a result of peaceful cooperation among people who recognize that they have goals that they cannot attain alone. The end of laissez-faireism is to promote the welfare of all rather than of particular groups or social classes.[177] Welfare in liberalism, however, cannot be reduced solely to the state of material-cultural goods and economic services. The free market, as Mises claims, "seeks to produce only outer well-being because it knows that inner, spiritual riches cannot come to man from without, but only from within his own heart."[178]

Nowhere in Mises' writings do we find the concept of the common good itself. The purpose of our analysis therefore will be to prove whether and to what extent the liberalism presented by Mises creates

---

[175] Mises, *Socialism*, 374; see also E. Troeltsch, *The Social Teaching of the Christian Churches*, vol. 1 (Chicago-London, 1976), 115–16; A. Rauscher, ["Private Ownership"], 64.

[176] Mises, *Socialism*, 384.

[177] Mises, *Liberalism*, 7.

[178] Mises, *Liberalism*, 4.

an indispensable space that permits particular people to attain full personal perfection.[179] The *Catechism of the Catholic Church* stresses that the common good must be based on three essential elements: respect for the person as such, welfare and social development, and peace (the permanence and safety of the just order).[180] These three elements therefore will determine the framework of the analysis of Mises' thought.

The Good as a Motive of Human Action

According to Mises, basic human rights include the right to an independent determination of one's own actions and a free choice of the means for its attainment. The whole sociopolitical system should be oriented at the protection of political, economic, and religious liberties that emerge from this basic right.[181] He says nothing about what constitutes the motive of human action. We can surmise, however, that it is the good of the individual, for action in Mises is the desire to replace a less satisfactory state of affairs with a more satisfactory. What attracts man to action, says Mieczyslaw A. M. Krapiec, is good. Krapiec stresses that each action calls for a motive, and this motive can only be a good that can "move" the forces that trigger action.[182]

Obviously, there arises a question whether what is my good can also be the good for others. Krapiec refers to St. Thomas Aquinas, who claims that the common good can be called a *common end*.[183] Mises does

---

[179] By the common good we should understand "the sum of those conditions of social life which allow social groups and their individual members relatively thorough and ready access to their fulfillment." (*Gaudium et Spes*, no. 26).

[180] *Catechism of the Catholic Church*, nos. 1906–1909.

[181] Mises, *Liberalism*, 37–39.

[182] M. A. M. Krapiec, ["The Common Good and the Threat of Alienation"], in [*At the Source of the Identity of European Culture*], ed. T. Rakowski (Lublin, 1994), 68–72.

[183] In his *Summa Theologica*, St. Thomas writes: "Actions are indeed concerned with particular matters, but those particular matters are referable to the common good, not as to a common genus or species, but as to a common final cause, according as the common good is said to be the common end" (I-II, q. 90, a. 2, ad. 2).

not say anything about a man who tends to his own perfection, for the goals of human action remain beyond the domain of praxeology's interest, but he leaves the space of freedom limited only by praxeological laws. Mises stresses that praxeology is interested in the whole man, not only in man thinking in economic categories. In laissez-faireism, through his rational action and free decisions, man can actualize and perfect himself because he does not live in a vacuum, and the sphere of economics cannot be separated from other spheres of human life. For Krapiec, the development of personal human potentialities within knowledge, love, and free decision-making is the "common good," which is the real reason for the personal being of action. The good understood in this way is not only a personal good of each man but becomes the property of all people, for the whole community is made rich with the personal wealth of its members.[184]

Mises stresses that God has endowed man with reason, the desire to aim at happiness, and this permits him to discover that society and the state are the most important means by which to attain the goals in accordance with his needs. The common good for Mises therefore consists in the conditions in which people find the most complete capacities to develop their own personalities. The free-market system of the division of labor and social cooperation performs social tasks, and through a positive reference to human needs it gains sense and usefulness in relation to the common good.[185] One can say that the principle of the common good consists in assuming the attitude of giving, which is the contribution of particular people in social life.

Pluralism of Goals

This attitude is possible only when we are dealing with free persons. Freedom implies, however, pluralism of goals. The society of free persons certainly is, as Mises claims, based on practical cooperation. But can one claim that it is also founded on common goals, if one does not claim at the same time that particular free persons have common goals? Michael Novak notes that in the traditional understanding, the common good was thought of as the terminus of human action.

[184] M. A. M. Krapiec, ["The Common Good"], 69–70.

[185] J. Krucina, ["The Common Good"], in [*The Catholic Encyclopedia*], vol. 3, ed. R. Lukaszyk, L. Bienkowski, and F. Gryglewicz (Lublin, 1979), 1379–82.

To discern that endpoint was to ensure good life both to oneself and to the whole community.[186] The modern social order, however, is too complicated to grasp by means of one act of insight—not only because of the lack of a commonly understood terminology but also because of the lack of the requisite knowledge.

A modern concept of the common good must therefore be open to change, and—above all—to the invention, enterprise, creativity, and free choices of multitudes of free persons.[187] Novak notes that in traditional societies each member knew all others owing to their closeness. The relations in modern societies are entirely different, because citizens do not know about the life and labor of other citizens. Many people, according to Hayek, discerning no supreme ruler who is dictating affairs, regard such a spontaneous form of undirected order as illusion or magic.[188] The complicated action of demand, supply, and prices is today the product of intelligence but, as Novak claims, it is not one intelligence but many acts of intelligence.[189] For Mises, the participants of the free market, governed by their own good, seek to satisfy the claims of other participants and adjust their behavior accordingly. The ultimate result of market actions is the attainment of a high level of free cooperation.

An analysis of the conception of the individual in the context of the common good in Mises can be interpreted within the personalistic perspective initiated by Pius XII. In a well-known definition of the common good, the pope states that "every other sphere of cultural activity represents a universal and most exalted center of activity, very rich in its variety and coherent in its harmony, in which men's intellectual equality and diversity of occupation come into their own and secure adequate expression."[190] Pius XII diverges here from Leo XIII's concept of the common good of a moral and religious character based entirely

---

[186] M. Novak, *Free Persons and the Common Good* (Lanham, MD: Madison Books, 1989), 22.

[187] Novak, *Free Persons*, 81.

[188] F. A. von Hayek, *Law, Legislation and Liberty*, vol. 1: *Rules of Order* (Chicago, 1978), 38ff.

[189] Novak, *Free Persons*, 98.

[190] Pius XII, *The Internal Order of States and People: Christmas Message of 1942*, www.papalencyclicals.net/Pius12/ P12CH42.HTM 2.HTM.

on the thought of St. Thomas Aquinas, according to which material goods have a functional character in relation to spiritual values and the common good is better than the good of the individual—and, of its nature, more loved than a private good.[191] In a new political, social, and religious situation, when political communities are no longer Christian, this hierarchic relation loses its *raison d'être.* The public authorities must respect the pluralism of values and opinions, and therefore they can no longer be responsible for the support of common material goods, including spiritual and religious goods.

The Personalist Conception of the Common Good

In the social teaching of the Church there has been a decisive evolution in the understanding of the common good, confirmed by the teaching of the Second Vatican Council. It is not the political authority but citizens as persons endowed by nature with reason and freedom, created in the image of God—subjects conscious of their rights and duties—who are primarily responsible for their own material and spiritual development.[192] The task of the state therefore consists in creating respective social conditions so that this integral development of the person is possible. In a similar personalist spirit, the common good is also defined by John XXIII, who goes beyond the conception of the common good limited only to one political community and expands it practically over the whole world.[193]

The personalist conception of the common good has been made more profound by John Paul II, who placed it in a new context: the mystery of the Trinitarian life of God—the Creator, the Redeemer, and the Sanctifier of man. The pope speaks about the Holy Trinity in interpersonal categories, which for him are always a point of reference for the understanding of communication and interhuman relations.[194]

According to John Paul II, the good is itself only when it is created and shared with others, for "by its nature it is 'diffusive of itself'" (*bonum*

---

[191] R. Rybka, OP, ["The Common Good: A Relict of the Past or a Concrete Task for Today and for Tomorrow?"], *Teofil* 2 (1998): 43–44.

[192] *Dignitatis Humanae,* no. 6; *Gaudium et Spes,* nos. 26, 74.

[193] John XXIII, *Pacem in Terris,* no. 56.

[194] M. Waldstein, "The Common Good in St. Thomas and John Paul II," *Nova et Vetera* (English edition) 3 (2005): 569.

est diffusivum sui).[195] In the creative act the Triune God has called man in his image and after his likeness—that is, he has endowed the human person not only with capacities that we identify as the ability to know and make a free decision but also the ability of such decisions to reflect the relationship of the Three Persons of the Holy Trinity. John Paul speaks of the diffusion of good as instanced in the family, but there is no obstacle to extending the same mode of reasoning to the socioeconomic sphere.

Economic actions on the free market are not zero-sum games in which every gain must bring someone's loss.[196] Mises has clearly shown that transactions in the system of an unhampered market economy are always profitable to both the buyer and the seller; otherwise they would never happen.[197] The condition of exchange is always the space of freedom. Through freedom the market becomes a social instrument to realize the common good, for man—as a rational and free person—may decide about himself and become a gift for others.

The pope's reasoning permits us to grasp the proper and more profound sense of the common good, which differs from the individual good by its universality and ease of diffusion.[198] The pope states that a good becomes more common when it is also more one's own.[199] He invokes directly a passage from *Gaudium et Spes* that was the leading idea of his pontificate: "Man … cannot fully find himself except through a sincere gift of himself."[200] This way of reasoning permits us to discover the Holy Trinity not only as a paradigm of unity, whose reflection is the unity of the sons of God in truth and love, but also as the model of a perfect gift of self.

John Paul speaks about the trinitarian character of human love in the context of the gift of life that spouses give to their child. The

---

[195] John Paul II, Letter to Families *Gratissimam Sane* (1994), no. 10.

[196] Novak, *Free Persons*, 100.

[197] Mises, *Human Action*, 664–66.

[198] C. de Koninck, "On the Primacy of the Common Good against the Personalists," *Aquinas Review* 4 (1997), 16.

[199] John Paul II, *Gratissimam Sane*, no. 10.

[200] P. Ide, *Une theologie du don: Les occurences de Gaudium et spes, n. 24, § 3 chez Jean-Paul II*, A, 17 (2001): 149–78, 313–44.

giving of life is for him part of "the logic of the disinterested gift."[201] The pope posits that the common good of parents is their child. Michael Waldstein remarks that St. Thomas Aquinas, who came to the same conclusion earlier, makes an interesting distinction between the *proper* and *external* common good, which ensures an easier grasp of the pope's way of reasoning.[202]

Saint Thomas cites an example from Aristotle's *Metaphysics*, which helps illustrate the universal principle of the common good. For an army, the proper common good is its internal order and unity, which lead to its external good, which is victory. Waldstein notes that the same principle may be used in relation to marriage: the proper common good, which is unity in love between husband and wife flowing from their marital oath, is directed at their child as the external good of marriage. We can transplant the same idea into the economics of enterprise. The proper common good of the free market, which is peace and free enterprise, determined by the praxeological law, becomes directed at the creation of material goods, which are its external good. The common good of spouses, according to the pope's letter, is love, loyalty, and marital honesty, and the stability of their relationship unto death. Analogically speaking, in the socioeconomic dimension the common good of society is peace, which ensures the preservation of the institution of the division of labor and free enterprise, which in turn liberates the creative potential in man.

Mises stresses that economics' *raison d'être* lies in the fact that the well-being of man is limited by the scarcity of external factors.[203] We must constantly bear in mind this scarcity, analyzing man's actions in the economic sphere so as to better grasp the trinitarian dimension of participation of each person in social life, a dimension that is written in the logic of gift of oneself, which is labor. Man struggles against limitations in this world, for his life is conditioned by natural factors. The rare character of these factors is not an artificial product established by human action. This, and not another world, is the place created and given by God to man, where he is supposed to aim at his perfection and salvation. The acting man wants to know how to

---

[201] John Paul II, *Gratissimam Sane*, no. 11.

[202] M. Waldstein, "Common Good," 575.

[203] Mises, *Human Action*, 234.

use the available means, so as to remove felt uneasiness in the most economical way,[204] and he knows well that he can accomplish this end owing to a peaceful and intelligent division of labor. If each human act shapes and builds man created in the image of God as person, then this refers also to economic life.[205]

The Significance of the Free Market for the Realization of the Common Good

Man for Mises is a special being, although, as an economist, he ignores in his writings the whole sphere of transcendence as unavailable to scientific knowledge. The individual in action, as has been shown in the previous chapter, nevertheless possesses in full the traits of the transcendent being. All the rights in laissez-faireism—political, economic, and religious liberties—emerge from the basic right to an independent determination of the goal at which man aims, and to a free choice of the means to attain it. The point of reference for Mises, the objective reality of praxeology, is founded on the natural law and perfectibility and thereby on the dignity reserved for man by reason of creation in the image of God. Therefore we may speak about the immanent common good in Mises' work, analogously to how it is understood in the teaching of the Church: as the state in which all people can accomplish their own goals, including transcendent ones that can be a point of reference for human action in the economic sphere.

In Mises' writings one can also easily find the concept of the instrumental common good (i.e., the means to attain the immanent good). First, it is the minimal state, whose only task consists in the protection of citizens and their possessions against external aggression. The state has no right to interfere in the world of goals and means created by particular individuals. These views, up to the moment when the encyclical *Centesimus Annus* appeared in 1991, remained in tension with much of what had been said in the social teaching of the Church before John Paul II. The magisterium of the Church strongly emphasized the role of the state as a designer of the common good, one that is responsible for its attainment. *Centesimus Annus* rejects the omnipo-

---

[204] Mises, *Human Action*, 207–8.

[205] A. Szostek, [*On the Dignity of Truth and Love*] (Lublin, 1995), 75.

tence of the state in designing the common good and attributes a very limited right of the state to interfere in the sphere of economics,[206] which does not mean, however, that John Paul II reduced the role of the state to purely negative functions.[207]

The second element of the instrumental common good is, according to Mises, the free market, as the only natural system independent of external circumstances. The laws that govern it have an objective dimension, and each intervention of the government disturbs its function and limits human freedom. In the social teaching before *Centesimus*, the Church was cautious about accepting capitalism as an economic system. There were also elements in this teaching that affirmed the far-reaching policy of interventionism. John Paul II clearly speaks on behalf of the free market as "the most efficient instrument for utilizing resources and effectively responding to needs."[208] We can observe here a further convergence between Mises' thought and the teaching of the magisterium.

The concept of the common good calls for welfare and social development, but it is often used only in reference to economic actions and, in practice, denotes redistribution. Mises levels a stringent criticism against this type of thinking, characteristic of a centrally controlled economy. Karl Marx, who was absorbed by the idea that profits gained by people are determined only by their biological nature, thought that man is interested only in multiplying his possessions.[209] The (classical) liberal conception of the common good liberates us from the image of a concrete good expressed in the categories of a particular state of affairs.[210] This image is characteristic of collectivist society, in which the governing wish by force to bind each individual will with collective goals; that is, in reality, with the goals of those who govern. This manner of attaining the common good is foreign to the society of free persons.

Unfortunately, some contemporary schools of Catholic social thought tend in this direction of the common good understood as

---

[206] John Paul II, *Centesimus Annus*, no. 48.

[207] John Paul II, *Centesimus Annus*, no. 46.

[208] John Paul II, *Centesimus Annus*, no. 34.

[209] Mises, *Theory and History*, 93.

[210] Novak, *Free Persons*, 82.

redistribution.[211] The Second Vatican Council taught that the state authority should ensure that all persons have access to what is needed to live a truly human life.[212] Mises stresses that on the free market, consumers themselves choose and define both the amount and quality of produced goods. In the real world of human action there is no such thing as profit independent of an idea and preceding it in time and logic. What man regards as his own profit is a reflection and effect of his way of understanding and valuing, and this way shapes his goals. It is difficult to speak about redistribution of definite goods through the state, if one of the basic problems of production in the free-market economy is not only the question how much to produce but, above all, what to produce. The civilized man must face the problem of choice between the ways of satisfying various needs and various methods of satisfying the same needs. The profits of the contemporary person are varied and defined by the ideas that shape his choices. In socialism, it is the government that is concerned about these matters and does not give its citizens what they want but instead what the authorities think they should receive.[213] It should be stressed that the accumulated consumer goods are results of concrete people's actions, and in the free-market economy their current supply cannot be determined or regulated in advance.[214]

Mises indicates that consumers' behavior on the free market affects the income and wealth of the individuals who deal with production, and the government should not change their decisions. The entrepreneurs' profits are always derivatives of a better satisfaction of consumers' needs. If governments regulate incomes, this results from a metaphysically false doctrine; namely that the introduction of income tax will equate citizens' incomes, which in consequence will improve their lives. Mises shows that the effect of such action in the long run

---

[211] C. E. Curran, "The Common Good and Official Catholic Social Teaching," in *The Common Good and U.S. Capitalism*, ed. O. F. Williams and J. Houck (Lanham, MD: University Press of America, 1987), 122–24.

[212] *Gaudium et Spes*, no. 26.

[213] Mises, *Theory and History*, 94.

[214] H.-H. Hoppe, *Democracy—the God That Failed: The Economics and Politics of Monarchy, Democracy, and Natural Order* (New Brunswick: Transaction, 2001), 9–10.

is always the reverse, for a considerable part of what is subtracted as taxes on incomes could be used for the accumulation of additional capital.[215] Slower accumulation of capital reduces the invested capital on one employed laborer, and this impedes the increase of labor productivity and its related increase of wages. Once the individual is deprived of the right to a free disposal of his property, which always forces the individual to serve consumers, the development of the economy is impeded. Mises' utilitarian ethics goes decisively in the direction of rejection of the distribution of income tax, and the only way to eliminate poverty and scarcity is to increase production.[216]

Social welfare, like history, cannot be planned.[217] According to Mises, history is one great record of changes. Humankind can never attain perfection. Benedict XVI teaches that anyone who promises a better world that comes into existence once and for all makes a false promise, for he neglects human freedom.[218] The pope reminds us that the construction of a socioeconomic system is not a finished and closed task.[219] It is a tiresome effort made by each generation that contributes to the determination of a persuasive order of freedom and good. In Mises' view, a completely permanent adjustment of production to all consumers' expectations constitutes a utopian vision and does not correspond with human nature; man is constantly seeking to replace less satisfactory conditions with more satisfactory.[220] Mises rightly observes that people create history but cannot influence the direction of the development of the world. It is the complex result of conscious action by all free subjects in society. All that an individual can plan and introduce into his life is his action; only action in combination with the actions of other free persons has the power to create historical processes.

---

215 Mises, *Human Action*, 807.

216 D. Gordon, "Justice and Redistributive Taxation: James Buchanan versus Ludwig von Mises," *Review of Austrian Economics* 1 (1994): 130.

217 Mises, *Theory and History*, 131.

218 Benedict XVI, *Spe Salvi*, no. 24.

219 Benedict XVI, *Spe Salvi*, no. 25.

220 Mises, *Theory and History*, 240–41.

Private Property as a Condition to Preserve Peace

The third element on which the concept of the common good is founded is peace. *The Catechism of the Catholic Church* understands by peace the permanence and safety of the social order. This task rests on rightful authority, which for this purpose may use fair means to make this safety real.[221] Mises also thinks that the state is the institution called to defend peaceful interhuman relations.[222] Only under such protection can the division of labor develop.[223] Without the protection of the state the division of labor would not go beyond the limits of a local community or even a single household. The *Catechism* similarly states that peace on earth cannot be achieved without the protection of the goods of the human person, a free exchange of thought between people, respect for the dignity of persons and nations, and the enduring struggle to foster brotherhood.[224] According to Mises, labor creates wealth and thereby creates the "outward preconditions for the development of the inner life."[225]

It should be stressed here that peace means more than lack of war.[226] The Second Vatican Council teaches that peace is not the state of balance between hostile forces. Peace calls for authentic respect for the dignity and rights of all, so as to ensure the full development of personality.[227] What safeguards peace is the construction of a social order on the foundations of justice and love. Justice is understood here as respect for all dimensions of the human person. The principal aspect of human freedom in the economic sphere is the right to free enterprise, which is guaranteed in full in the system of the free-market economy. Mises claims that the substitution of liberalism with socialism, nationalism, protectionism, imperialism, statism, or militarism always leads to war, because of their faulty conception of the person.

---

[221] *Catechism of the Catholic Church*, no. 1900.

[222] Mises, *Human Action*, 149.

[223] Mises, *Liberalism*, 28.

[224] *Catechism of the Catholic Church*, no. 2304.

[225] Mises, *Liberalism*, 5.

[226] *Gaudium et Spes*, no. 78.

[227] John Paul II, *Message for the XXVII World Day of Peace: The Family Creates the Peace of the Human Family*, January 1, 1994.

Collectivist systems do not respect human dignity, and interhuman relations are not directed at the common good, which is man himself.[228] The limitation of state authority to a necessary minimum, determined by the laws of praxeology, would alleviate antagonisms between nations.[229]

For Mises, war is always something bad, although he does not exclude, under exceptional circumstances, the use of force, permissible only for the defense of the highest value (freedom). The fact that the government of a free country imposes the duty to defend the country against aggressors does not go beyond the tasks that the laws of praxeology dictate. The taxes levied for this goal therefore are completely in accord with the freedom which the individual uses in the free-market economy.[230] The social teaching of the Church, drawing on the tradition of teaching on just war, also states that there are situations in which one should resort to weapons to defend man and his dignity, standing in defense of the common good, which is man himself and his freedom.[231]

The Church teaches that peace is built day by day, preserving the order established by God.[232] The first condition of such an order, according to Mises, is respect for private property. The social teaching of the Church, although it does not put it in the first place because the necessary condition to preserve peace is to live it in one's heart,[233] demands that private property be justly accessible to all as a safeguard of the proper social order.[234] Mises brilliantly stresses that what is meant here is not only respect for someone else's property but also the ownership of the means of production, for then the motive for war is removed. In such a world the whole area of land constitutes one economic territory. Liberal political institutions are designed in such a way that the passing of sovereign authority over a given territory

---

228 *Compendium of the Social Doctrine*, no. 494.

229 Mises, *Nation, State and Economy*, 79.

230 Mises, *Human Action*, 282.

231 S. Olejnik, [*Moral Theology: Gift, Calling, Response*], vol. 7, [*Morality of Social Life*] (Warsaw, 1993), 343.

232 Paul VI, *Populorum Progressio*, no. 76.

233 *Compendium of the Social Doctrine*, no. 495.

234 *Compendium of the Social Doctrine*, no. 176.

by one government to another is indeed a matter of secondary importance.[235] It is possible only because the liberal governmental apparatus has no other function than protection of the life, freedom, property, and health of its citizens. This refutes another argument on behalf of waging war: the expansion of the state's activity always leads to the policy of protectionism, which, according to Mises, is the main cause of all military conflicts.

The second condition, which is a logical consequence of building social structures on the private ownership of the means of production, is the liberal state whose limits do not depend on military, historical, or legal elements. The liberal policy of peace is based on the assumption that humankind in each territory has the right to determine what kind of state it wants to live under. According to Mises, it is liberalism that created the legal structure of a plebiscite, owing to which the people's wishes concerning their state membership could be articulated.[236] Ethnic, racial, or religious minorities often experience membership in a state is as second-class citizenship. Mises admits that this is a source of uneasiness in a liberal state. But it is even more troublesome in a state where the administrative authorities have the right to intervene in everything as they wish. The life of the people who belong to national minorities in such a state becomes unbearable, for they are subjected to arbitrary judgments and oppression on the part of public functionaries who belong to the ruling majority.[237] Mises notes that the construction of society on the basis of liberal principles, not the attempt to discover the natural causes of violent antagonisms between nations, leads to peaceful cooperation. Liberalism understood in this manner ensures that a nation does not become a shapeless crowd and passive mass that may be manipulated and treated instrumentally. This kind of reasoning finds its reflection in the teaching of the Church, which constantly reminds us that the human person is always the principle and aim of political coexistence.[238] The nation is a collectivity

[235] Mises, *Liberalism*, 144.

[236] Mises, *Liberalism*, 110.

[237] Mises, *Liberalism*, 164.

[238] *Compendium of the Social Doctrine*, no. 1881; *Gaudium et Spes*, no. 25.

comprising persons who preserve inviolable autonomy on the level of personal life and intentions.[239]

Freedom of Migration

Another presupposition is the opening of borders for the transfer of capital and labor to new and more profitable locations. The migration of capital and labor presumes not only a complete freedom of trade but also migration from one country to another. David Ricardo's classical doctrine of free trade provided powerful evidence that the international division of labor and specialization is worthwhile. The branches of production are divided into particular countries in such a way that each sacrifices its resources to the domains of industry in which it has the greatest advantage over the others. Mises is aware that the countries with relatively better conditions of production will be richer than others, but this fact cannot in any case be changed by political means. According to the Austrian economist, the essence of society based on the private ownership of the means of production is that each person can work and spend money where he thinks is best for him.[240] *Gaudium et Spes* practically states the same when it maintains that various reasons make people change their place of living and their way of life.[241]

Mises thinks that, once the right to private property is preserved, the individual's interests are not and cannot be contradictory with social interests.[242] The individual's tendency to attain his own goals, including the maintenance of the family, from which the right to migration results, integrates his actions with the overall shape of the social system of production and serves the common good; the government's intervention is here not only unjustified but even harmful. This kind of reasoning shows that for laissez-faireism the human person is the principle and goal of political coexistence, which corresponds to Christian anthropology.[243] The market economy, which presumes

---

[239] *Compendium of the Social Doctrine*, no. 385.

[240] Mises, *Liberalism*, 137.

[241] *Gaudium et Spes*, no. 6.

[242] Mises, *Human Action*, 726.

[243] *Catechism of the Catholic Church*, no. 1884.

a free migration of workforce, should therefore be the most desired system of social organization from the point of view of justice.

According to the classic formula, justice consists in recognizing the other as a person endowed with reason, responsible for his decisions, and capable of realizing plans that give his life sense both on the individual and social levels.[244] Freedom within the frame of social life consists of the right to change one's place of living and way of life, and should be viewed as a gift, not a threat, stipulating that one should be educated in order to make good use of it and help others to grow in true freedom.[245] An action is morally good not only when its object corresponds with the true good of the person, which is God himself,[246] but also when through his own acts of the person can freely shape himself.[247]

Raising living standards does not of itself mean that migration is good, because material welfare is not the only value. For Mises, physical and mental welfare are subjective concepts. The value of market goods is a relation profoundly rooted in personal and subjective acts of valuation and depends on individual assessment and a concrete choice; such is also the case in immigration and emigration. Subjectivity understood in this way indicates the dynamism of human action, which is always a response to new situations and circumstances in which man must constantly make choices. The dynamic relationship between person and act, which in this case refers to the right to emigration, is realized on the level of human subjectivity. The experience of the efficient relationship between person and act, which is the change of the place of residence or work, expresses the moral value that is shaped and matures in this dynamic set.[248]

The immigrant as person is a whole in himself, not a part of the greater whole.[249] In other words, he cannot be in the same measure a part and a means to reach a goal by the hosting country. A person can join the community as its member, but life in community can in

---

[244] *Compendium of the Social Doctrine*, no. 384.

[245] S. Olejnik, [*Moral Theology*], vol. 2, 44–45.

[246] John Paul II, *Veritatis Splendor*, no. 72.

[247] John Paul II, *Veritatis Splendor*, no. 71.

[248] Wojtyła, *The Acting Person*, 105–7.

[249] Wojtyła, *The Acting Person*, 27.

no way threaten the personal being himself. Man should never be the servant of the state, for the state is for him.[250] The space of freedom and independence from state coercion is created by private property. In this space, the individual is autonomous to make choices, one of which is the liberty to migrate. Being oneself means self-possession of the subject as such in a conscious and free relation to the whole reality. The sphere of private property together with the person constitute the whole in itself, conferring a new quality on the personal relation in society. Property certainly refers to the objects, but the rights of property refer to the reciprocal relationship between person and thing.[251] John F. Crosby rightly notes that the state frequently treats an innocent person as if his life belonged to it, whereas in reality it belongs to the person. The violation of the rights of a person is an attempt to dispose of what is that person's own and commits a kind of theft against the very being of the person.[252]

The combination of freedom with subjectivity guarantees that man's action corresponds with his dignity, which belongs to him as person. A restrictive immigration policy and protectionist actions subordinate the good of the individual to the economic and social mechanism. In such a system, man is reduced to a series of social relationships and, consequently, the concept of the person as the autonomous subject of moral decisions disappears.[253] The free-market economy described by Mises safeguards in social life the benefits of a free collaboration, giving an indispensable space for free action regardless of state borders and national identity.

Our analysis of the social character of the right to free entrepreneurship, which for Mises is based on private property and division of labor, show us very clearly that the classical liberal tradition does not lay stress only on liberal rights but also on the importance of a community for the preservation of the freedom and dignity of the human person. Mises frequently stresses that the interests of human persons and the common good are profoundly convergent. For him,

---

[250] J. Maritain, [*Man and the State*], trans. A. Grobler (Krakow, 1988), 19.

[251] W. Kwasnicki, [*History of Liberal Thought*] (Warsaw, 2000), 246.

[252] J. F. Crosby, *The Selfhood of the Human Person* (Washington, DC: Catholic University of America Press, 1996), 22.

[253] John Paul II, *Centesimus Annus*, no. 13.

"everything that serves to preserve the social order is moral; everything that is detrimental to it is immoral."[254] The observance of the moral law therefore brings profit to each individual because everyone profits from a peaceful social cooperation.

Mises is aware that this attitude must be accompanied by a sacrifice of one's own particular personal good at a given moment, for in the long run such behavior brings an incomparably greater profit. John Paul II, speaking in Uruguay in May 1988, stated that contemporary economic actions arouse a new and profound spirituality in people, spirituality based on sacrifice, cooperation, and solidarity.[255] The common good cannot be attained in a simple manner by means of perfect instruments that do not exist. This is confirmed from various points of view by the liberal and Catholic traditions. An analysis of the elements of the common instrumental good, composed of a conception of the state and economic life, and the attractiveness of Austrian economics for Catholics from the moral point of view, will be the topic of consideration in the chapter that follows.

---

[254] Mises, *Liberalism,* 34.

[255] John Paul II, *Address to Workers in Melo* (Uruguay, May 8, 1988), "Origins," May 26, 1988, 26.

4

Economic Life in the Market Economy

Mises was an uncompromising and staunch advocate of market rationality and logic. He was brave enough to follow logic and reason wherever they led, which permitted him to discover and describe real human action in the socioeconomic space. On the one hand, he believed in the power of human reason, and on the other he was aware that to persuade the opponents of private ownership by way of reasonable and logical arguments would not be easy. We shall try to give a moral justification of the free-market economy and show the significance of the culture of freedom for the proper development of the person in society.

In the first part, we shall describe market mechanisms, in particular Austrian price and money theory, and their importance for a proper moral evaluation of free-market mechanisms. Further, we shall analyze the conception of the state, its limited role in relation to market processes, and Mises' argument on behalf of the democratic system. Finally, we shall present the relationship of economics—as an autonomous science—to morality, and the reasons behind Mises' positive view of laissez-faireism.

THE ROLE OF THE FREE MARKET

According to Mises, the market economy is the social system of the division of labor under private ownership of the means of production.[1] Its establishment resulted from a long evolutionary process in which man tended to adjust his action, as far as possible, to the given conditions of the environment that he was not always able to change. The main purpose of economics, says the Austrian economist, is therefore a conscious endeavor to effectively remove as far as possible felt uneasiness.[2] Catholic social teaching views the main goals of economic similarly: After the appearance of John Paul II's encyclical *Centesimus Annus*, the most important question of economics is how to take advantage of the world's resources in accordance with the logic of the principle of economic specificity.[3] Maciej Zieba stresses that this is an essential novelty in the teaching of the Church, for up to that time the popes had mostly criticized the negative symptoms of capitalism, and only passing efforts were made to address the positive elements in the "economics of enterprise."[4]

Methodological Anthropocentrism

According to Mises, the social system is maintained by the market itself, which gives it sense and meaning. This does not mean, however, that the market is an independent collective being. All changes on the market are a result of individual human actions. The principle of methodological individualism is for the Austrian economist a way to learn the market processes, which consist in adjusting the individual actions of the members of market society to the demands of cooperation.[5] A similar analysis of reality, based on methodological anthropocentrism, led John Paul II to take a positive stance toward

---

[1] Mises, *Human Action*, 257.

[2] Mises, *Human Action*, 235.

[3] John Paul II, *Centesimus Annus*, no. 34.

[4] M. Zieba, [*The Popes and Capitalism*] (Krakow, 1998), 123.

[5] Mises, *Human Action*, 41–44.

free-market economics.[6] For the pope, the basic measure of economic systems is human labor, which in the free economy becomes more fruitful and productive, because man can better learn the productive potentialities of the earth and is more profoundly cognizant of the needs of the person for whom his work is done.[7] John Paul II rightly notes that the wealth of nations does not depend on natural resources but on technique and skills. The pope's anthropocentrism, like Mises' methodological individualism, avoids the ideologization of socioeconomic problems and leads to the discovery of the true principles of the free market.[8]

The anthropological attitude of methodological anthropocentrism can be found in *Gaudium et Spes,* where all social and economic institutions are oriented at the final realization of man as person.[9] Man is a social creature. This follows from his dynamic nature and the tasks entrusted to him by God in realizing a new community of those saved by Christ. Man fulfills this task by entering interhuman relations, overcoming barriers of his individual existence, and developing the values hidden in him as the image of God and of the Son.[10] We can also find in the document attitudes similar to Mises' methodological individualism. The Council teaches that man is the creator and goal of the whole of socioeconomic life.[11] It follows that the initiative of individuals and social groups, not the state, contributes to the realization of the economic process.

The principle of methodological individualism is often misunderstood as positing atomized individuals. But the acting individual, as Hayek rightly notes, is never a being isolated from others. Methodological individualism is only a tool to understand social phenomena.[12] No one can deny the obvious fact that man, from the

---

[6] M. Jaworski, ["The Endangered Man and the Merciful God: An Anthropological Method in the Encyclical *Dives in misericordia*"], *W drodze* 4 (1981): 64.

[7] John Paul II, *Centesimus Annus,* no. 31.

[8] Zieba, [*The Popes*], 125

[9] *Gaudium et Spes,* no. 25.

[10] *Gaudium et Spes,* no. 22.

[11] *Gaudium et Spes,* no. 63.

[12] F. A. von Hayek, *Individualism and Economic Order* (Chicago: University of Chicago Press, 1948), 6.

moment of coming into this world, is not entirely self-sufficient. This lack of self-sufficiency leads to cooperation with other members of society. Cooperation on the economic level begins when man notices that the means to satisfy his needs are not simply and perpetually given to him by others. He learns that in order to satisfy these needs he must give others something in exchange.[13]

The free market arises when acting persons are freely committed to the exchange of some goods or services for others. This process starts spontaneously on the basis of the logic of choice, the logic inscribed in human nature.[14] People know from experience that action based on cooperation is more efficient and productive than the isolated action of a self-sufficient individual.[15] In accord with David Ricardo's law of association, the division of labor brings profits to all who participate in it.

The Autonomy of Earthly Affairs

For Mises, the discovery of the natural harmony of the market order through the social philosophy of eighteenth-century rationalism and liberalism and contemporary economics means that we do not have to resort to miraculous intervention by supernatural powers to explain social relations. The pioneers of political economics had noticed some regularities in the functioning of the market and recognized that human action may be analyzed from a perspective other than a purely ethical one.[16] Seeking the laws governing human action, Mises rejected the conception according to which economics would have to imitate physics and the exact sciences in this respect. The existence of the free will and the ability to choose makes it impossible to study social interactions in the same way as we study inanimate objects. In

---

[13] A. J. Santelli et al., *The Free Person and the Free Economy. A Personalist View of Market Economics* (Lanham, MD: Lexington, 2002), 68.

[14] Santelli et al., *Free Person,* 69.

[15] Mises, *Human Action,* 157.

[16] Ludwig von Mises, "Social Science and Natural Science," in *Money, Method,* 3–4.

human action there are no constants, and it does not correspond with mathematical principles.[17]

Mises is correct: in the spirit of a proper autonomy of earthly affairs, created things and societies enjoy their own rights and values approved by man.[18] Autonomy understood in this way—called "normative autonomy" by the Council—is in accord with the will of the Creator, and man should respect it, recognizing the methods proper to the social and economic sciences.[19] Contrary to mathematical economists, Mises does not present man as a creature acting only from economic motives. He takes into account man's uniqueness in the world and perceives in him what the Council called the person's dignity. This ontological autonomy means that man, who has been given the dignity of the person in the image of and likeness of God, is called to continue the work of creating the world and subduing it to himself with respect to the moral law made by the Creator.[20]

This autonomy is apparent above all in the conception of consumers' sovereignty,[21] which, as we have seen, is essential for the understanding

---

[17] J. G. Hülsmann, "Facts and Counterfactuals in Economic Law," *Journal of Libertarian Studies* 17 (Winter 2003): 86.

[18] *Gaudium et Spes*, no. 36.

[19] See S. Kaminski, ["Autonomy"], in [*The Catholic Encyclopedia*], vol. 1, ed. F. Gryglewicz, R. Lukaszyk, and Z. Sulowski (Lublin, 1973), 1160.

[20] J. Gocko, ["The Moral Problem of the Principle of the Autonomy of Earthly Realities"], *Roczniki Teologiczne* 3 (2004): 109.

[21] One should agree with Robert Murphy that "the term is inaccurate because it implies a condition of violent submission where none exists, and because it seriously underrates the treatment of 'minorities' in a market economy. More seriously, the application of consumer sovereignty to real-world producers cannot rely on their objective actions, but must instead probe into their subjective intentions. For these reasons, many modern Austrian economists reject the doctrine of consumer sovereignty." R. P. Murphy, "The Rothbardian Critique of Consumer Sovereignty," Mises Institute, April 13, 2018, http://direct.mises.org/library/rothbardian-critique-consumer-sovereignty.

The most obvious drawback of this theory is, according to Murray N. Rothbard, its name itself. As he explains, "The term 'consumers' sovereignty' is a typical example of the abuse, in economics, of a term ('sovereignty') appropriate only to the political realm and is thus an illustration of the dangers of the application of metaphors taken from other disciplines. 'Sovereignty' of Mises' free-market economics.[22] Mises did not think that producers always and everywhere must behave in such a way as to ensure the highest financial profits. In some cases, the producer himself can play the role of a consumer; then the principle of the sovereignty of the consumer is not violated.[23] The profits from the mechanisms of the free market have been appreciated by the social teaching of the Church. John Paul II taught that in many situations the free market is the most efficient instrument for utilizing resources and responding to needs.[24]

There is no doubt that the conception of the sovereignty of the consumer affects the harmony of interests existing on the free market between the owners of resources and consumers. What in reality, however, preserves the order of free-market interests and stimulates them is the institution of private ownership, which in the free-market economy is always subordinate to the common destination of material wealth. The owners of the means of production are in fact only their transitory stewards. In any given moment they may be dismissed, if they fail to satisfy the expectations of their true masters, the consumers.

According to Mises, the only theoretical exception to the principle of consumer power is the monopoly price.[25] Mises noticed the effects

---

is the quality of ultimate political power; it is the power resting on the use of violence. In a purely free society, each individual is sovereign over his own person and property, and it is therefore this self-sovereignty which obtains on the free market. No one is 'sovereign' over anyone else's actions or exchanges. Since the consumers do not have the power to coerce producers into various occupations and work, the former are not 'sovereign' over the latter." M. N. Rothbard, *Man, Economy, and State: A Treatise on Economic Principles; with Power and Market: Government and the Economy*, Scholar's Edition (Auburn, AL: Mises Institute, 2004), 630.

[22] I. M. Kirzner, "Mises and His Understanding of the Capitalist System," *Cato Journal* 19, no. 2 (Spring 1999): 220.

[23] R. Murphy, "Consumer Sovereignty: What Mises Meant," Mises Institute, April 4, 2018, https://mises.org/library/consumer-sovereignty-what-mises-meant.

[24] John Paul II, *Centesimus Annus*, no. 34.

[25] Mises, *Human Action*, 358. Rothbard, the most outstanding disciple of Mises, criticized the conception of "monopolist price," indicating that there is no satisfactory definition of this term, correcting Mises, who only partly

of monopoly price, but he did not support governmental intervention to remove this defect of the free-market economy. He was aware that monopoly pricing occurs very rarely and that the unfavorable effects are nothing in comparison with coercive government monopolies.

Except for one case, of which Mises writes in *Human Action*, the appearance of monopoly price is, as he says, always brought about by government policies, for instance by imposing customs barriers.[26] John Paul II is of the same opinion; he stresses that barriers and monopolies are obstacles in the realization of the principle of the universal destination of material wealth. They should be removed to allow all people to join the general process of development and furnish them with the basic conditions of participation.[27] Catholic social teaching adds that monopolies take part in undermining the principle of subsidiarity[28] and decisively resists especially the educational monopoly of the state, which violates parents' right to educate their children and establish educational institutions.[29] The Congregation for the Doctrine of the Faith claims explicitly that the state that reserves for itself the exclusive authority to run schools "oversteps its rights."[30] Mises and the

---

accepted this theory. Rothbard notes that a singular seller of goods or services, a recipient of a governmental privilege, or an enterprise that can establish a monopoly price is called a monopolist. The first part of the definition makes no sense because in these terms everybody is a monopolist. The second part is justified because it concentrates on a governmental intervention that interrupts the shaping of market prices. The third part is empty because we understand that there is no such thing as "monopoly price." On the market, each price is competitive, and we would not be able to conceptually differentiate it from a monopoly price. Monopoly price exists only when it is an effect of governmental interventionism. Rothbard, *Man, Economy, and State*, 661–704.

[26] Mises, *Human Action*, 361.

[27] John Paul II, *Centesimus Annus*, no. 35.

[28] It should be added here that, according to John Paul II, the state has the right to intervene when concrete circumstances, caused by existing monopolies, create delays or obstacles to development. *Centesimus Annus*, no. 48; *Catechism of the Catholic Church*, no. 2431.

[29] Second Vatican Council, Declaration on Christian Education *Gravissimum Educationis* (1965), no. 6.

[30] *Instruction on Christian Freedom and Liberation*, no. 94.

Church thus both regard monopoly profit as the result not of a weakness in the market but of the power of the state.

The Price as a Market Phenomenon

It was already the Late Scholastics who warned against the state's interfering in market phenomena. They claimed that, if the authorities regulate prices, the result is always disturbance of prices and distortion of the market.[31] According to Mises, the shaping of prices is inseparably linked with the market process.[32] Market prices are determined only by subjective valuations made by people acting in the free market. John Paul II expressed the same opinion; he taught that people produce something so that others may use it, having paid a price mutually agreed upon through free bargaining.[33] After the publication of *Centesimus Annus* it no longer makes sense to speak about regulated prices, for a just price is simply a market price.

John Paul II distanced himself from a capitalism that leaves the solution of all problems to a free game of market forces.[34] This evaluation of capitalism, different than in Mises, results from the fact that the pope does not speak about capitalism as a mental construction corresponding to an unhampered market, but about the contemporary form of capitalism, whose operation departs widely from true free-market rules. John Paul II stresses that many economic difficulties can be traced not only to the desire for profit but also to the thirst for power and the intention of imposing one's will on others.[35] He warns that man's sinful nature may be manifested in capitalism; this threat has not disappeared despite many positive transformations in the contemporary world.[36] Following the teaching of Leo XIII, the

---

[31] L. Baeck, "Spanish Economic Thought: The Social School of Salamanca and the Arbitristas," *History of Political Economy* 20, no. 3 (Spring 1988): 385; M. Rothbard, *An Austrian Perspective on the History of Economic Thought*, vol. 1, *Economic Thought before Adam Smith* (Auburn, AL: Mises Institute, 2006), 120.

[32] Mises, *Human Action*, 332.

[33] John Paul II, *Centesimus Annus*, no. 32.

[34] D. R. Finn, "The Economic Personalism of John Paul II: Neither Right Nor Left," *Journal of Markets & Morality* 2, no. 1 (Spring 1999): 83.

[35] John Paul II, *Sollicitudo Rei Socialis*, no. 37.

[36] John Paul II, *Centesimus Annus*, nos. 41, 33.

pope repeats that the "just wage" cannot be decided only by "free contract" because the employee may not have any other choice. The pope refers to this teaching, for he is aware that in the contemporary world man is subjected to structures of sin wherein politics still has too much power over economics, without leaving any due space for making free decisions. Therefore he reminds us that the state's task is to create legal frameworks for the development of free economics in which there will be equality between parties.[37]

This space of freedom is indispensable to the formation of prices, which constitute the core of the market economy. As we saw in chapter 1, prices arise as a result of a constant interaction of two forces: demand and supply. Mises thinks that there is no concept of real costs independent of subjective value judgments. There is no impartial judge who could measure and give an objective price, for prices cannot be conceived other than through a reference to value judgments. Therefore, it is difficult to see how some commentators on the social teaching of the Church can think that the basis for the formation of a just price from the moral point of view is the cost of production broadly understood.[38] Such a conception of price is not only an unconscious approval of the Marxist theory of value but also a complete depersonalization of the process of the exchange of goods and services.

According to Mises, government interference with the structure of prices and their formation at a level different from the one that would be determined by the unhampered market is not only wrong from the moral point of view but above all evokes effects contrary to its purpose, worsening the living standards of the person who must always struggle with the scarcity of external factors in his quest to eliminate want.[39] The introduction of minimal and maximal prices lowers supply and introduces a new principle of the allocation of goods and services, which ultimately ends up rationing those goods in order to avoid violence and chaos.

John Paul II claims that the state under exceptional circumstances can fulfill substitute functions, and adds that this may take place only in a strictly determined time, so that economic and civil liberties are

---

[37] John Paul II, *Centesimus Annus*, no. 15.

[38] J. Majka, [*The Ethics of the Economic Life*] (Warsaw, 1982), 205.

[39] Mises, *Human Action*, 764.

not infringed.[40] From the point of view of the Austrian school, however, one cannot agree with this assessment, for such intervention does not encourage the most economical possible management of resources for which there is highest demand at the moment of crisis. The raised prices determined on the free market force people to ration things for which there is highest demand at the given moment. In like manner we go back to the concept of scarcity, which reminds us that external factors are limited and resources must be rationed. The best way for this is the market economy with a free fluctuation of prices, a method that gives us a chance for uncoerced sharing and cooperation at all times, above all in times of crisis.[41]

For many critics of the market, *profit* has become a pejorative term, a synonym of exploitation and abuse,[42] and *speculation* is an unjust profit that arises as a difference between the price of purchase and the price of the sale of commodities or services.[43] They condemn the prices determined by the unhampered market and advocate limiting the free decisions of individuals. But Mises is right when he says that if we try to substitute the egoistic drive for profit within the frame of the free-market economy with social justice, then government, by means of an apparatus of violent compulsion, would have to give the individual unambiguous instructions as to what he should do, what prices to demand, and how much to pay in each concrete case; and this deprives man—as John Paul II rightly understands—of initiative and creativity.[44] The condemnation of speculation is also a negation of the conditions of the real world in which no participant of the market can have perfect knowledge of market data.[45] For Mises, each entrepreneur is a speculator, rewarded with profit only when he can better adjust his production to the needs of the future structures of

---

[40] John Paul II, *Centesimus Annus*, no. 48.

[41] Woods, *The Church and the Market*, 46–50.

[42] A. Lindenberg, *The Free Market in a Christian Society*, trans. D. H. Sandin (Washington, DC: St. Antoninus Institute for Catholic Education in Business, 1999), 142–43.

[43] A. Zwoliński, [*Ethics of Growing Rich*] (Krakow, 2002), 144–45.

[44] Mises, *Human Action*, 728–29; John Paul II, *Centesimus Annus*, no. 25.

[45] Mises, *Human Action*, 327.

the market.[46] These conditions cannot be reduced to a set of rules that can be easily learned and applied.

The attempt to regulate prices results from incomprehension of the market economy, in which speculation intent upon profiting is the driving force of the market and production.[47] Profits and losses are essential phenomena of the market economy, indicating success or failure of the entrepreneur in adjusting production to the needs of the consumers.[48] John Paul appreciated the positive role of profit as an indicator of a well-functioning enterprise.[49] In the pope's teaching, profit embraces also moral and human factors that cannot be ignored in economic calculation, for they are also essential for the enterprise's action.

Moral Implications from the Lack of the Conception of Time Preference

Eliminating the phenomenon of prices in the catallactic sense is carried out not only by way of interference in the structure of market prices in the form of imposing minimal and maximal prices, but first of all through the governmental introduction of fiduciary money. An analysis of the free market as one of the elements of the common instrumental good cannot do without a discussion of indirect exchange. Mises has in mind here money, which is a universal means of exchange and tool of economic calculation. It occurs in every economy that has advanced beyond the stage of barter exchange. Mises regards money within the frame of the theory of indirect exchange and medium of exchange, for all theorems concerning money are valid also in reference to any other media of exchange.[50] Such an approach to the theory of money in the Austrian school of economics permits us to grasp more easily the main moral problems that follow from the acceptance of false contemporary monetary theories, which provide an opportunity for the arbitrary creation of currency.

---

[46] Mises, *Human Action*, 585.

[47] Mises, *Human Action*, 328.

[48] Mises, *Human Action*, 297.

[49] John Paul II, *Centesimus Annus*, no. 35.

[50] Mises, *Human Action*, 398.

According to Mises, the lack of understanding of the proper role of money and the contemporary usage of fiduciary money lead to serious moral implications that pose a challenge for Catholic social teaching. On the one hand the Church stresses that finance economics must serve real economics—that is, the development of persons and human communities— but on the other hand it indicates the necessity of the intervention of international economic institutions in the sphere of financial systems, so as to prevent any serious disturbances in economic life and ensure safety for the weakest and defenseless.[51] Lack of proper economic knowledge makes a proper moral evaluation difficult. This can be seen in the historical case of usury, wherein the Church has been accused of curbing the development of capitalism through forbidding loans at interest.

This prohibition was introduced by the Church in the Middle Ages under the impact of the Old Testament and Geek thinkers, especially Aristotle, who regarded charging interest as contrary to nature.[52] Benedict XV was the first who sought to make precise the doctrine referring to interest-bearing loans in his encyclical *Vix Pervenit* in 1745, and under its impact in France in the beginning of the nineteenth century, a rate of 5 percent was legally introduced.[53] Taking into account changes in economic conditions, especially the fact that the decisive majority of loans in the Middle Ages were for the purpose of consumption rather than investment, the Holy Office issued in the years 1820–1836 a series of decrees that permitted taking moderate commissions on borrowed money.[54] Thomas E. Woods rightly notes that in the Church's discussion one essential issue was missing: the notion of *time preference*, which is the basic principle of human action.[55] Failure to recognize time preference prevented accurate understanding of basic economic phenomena.

---

[51] *Compendium of the Social Doctrine*, nos. 369, 371.

[52] Y. M. Hilaire, ["Catholics Did Not Always Abhor Money"], *Communio* 6 (1997): 80; I. Jaruzelska, [*Property in Biblical Law*] (Warsaw, 1992), 70–72, 112–20.

[53] Hilaire, ["Catholics Did Not"], 82.

[54] A. Karkowski, ["Usury"], in [*Dictionary of Catholic Social Doctrine*], 97.

[55] Woods, *The Church and the Market*, 115.

Mises stresses that time preference is a category inherent in human action, expressed in the phenomenon of "originary interest," the discount of future goods against present goods.[56] People in reality do not treat a given amount of good today and an equal amount of good in several years as the same good. This means that they do not save unless there is interest to be gained. Mises shows that interest occurs in every pricing of the objects of the external world and cannot be wished away.[57] The interest is the ratio of the value assigned to particular present goods as against future value.[58] The prohibition of computing and paying interest forces people to treat the present and future good as the same, which is a manifest violation of time preference and of the dignity of the human person who calculates his own ratio of the value of goods over time. Determining the rate of interest therefore should not take place through the loan market but through the adjustment of the rate of interest on loans to the rate of originary interest as manifested in the discount of future goods.[59]

We should admit that a serious obstacle to describing the positive aspects of the free market, as well as threats to it, is the lack of sound knowledge of money and inflation on the part of Catholic theologians.[60] For Mises, money is simply a means of exchange,[61] not a measure of economic value, as Majka tries to define it.[62] Majka is unwittingly in favor of the labor theory of value, claiming that things have value in themselves. The medium of exchange is a good

---

[56] Mises, *Human Action*, 524.

[57] Mises writes that "there cannot be any question of abolishing interest by any institutions, laws, or devices of bank manipulation. He who wants to 'abolish' interest will have to induce people to value an apple available in a hundred years no less than a present apple. What can be abolished by laws and decrees is merely the right of the capitalists to receive interest. But such decrees would bring about capital consumption and would very soon throw mankind back into the original state of natural poverty." Mises, *Human Action*, 532.

[58] Mises, *Human Action*, 526.

[59] Mises, *Human Action*, 527.

[60] Woods, *The Church and the Market*, 87.

[61] Mises, *Human Action*, 401.

[62] Majka, [*Ethics of Economic Life*], 219.

acquired in order to exchange it in the future for goods needed for consumption or production. Mises has in mind here commodity money, which in itself is a commodity or represents the title to such a commodity in the form of paper currency. This currency must be exchangeable on demand for a commodity that is the ground of currency (e.g., gold). Money in the economy appeared on its own, without the state's intervention or any central management, because man can use reason and perceives profits he can attain when some discovered good becomes a medium of exchange. Money therefore is not, as Majka seeks to present it, paper banknotes, whose essence is based on trust in the state and its banking institutions.[63] Majka has in mind here fiat money, which is a substitute of money, but in this case does not refer to the medium of exchange, is not a commodity, and does not represent title to a commodity.[64]

Contrary to Catholic theologians who mainly stress the danger of the cult of money as the highest social value, Mises indicates the effects of the introduction into circulation of cheap money, and the serious and profound moral implications that result from the acceptance of false monetary theories. The fatal mistake that has led monetary policy astray in almost all governments is the concept of the so-called neutrality of money. Its consequences are the establishment of the notion of the "level" of prices and a belief that this level changes in proportion to the quantity of money in circulation.[65] It is obvious to every economist that the proportions of exchange between money and commodities change, but these changes in purchasing power—and here is the essence of the myth of its neutrality—do not affect simultaneously all the prices of various commodities and services.[66] Mises brilliantly notices that the point of consideration is wrongly assumed to be government action (*Volskwirtschaft*),[67] not the action of individuals (catallaxis), which should be the starting point.

---

[63] Majka, [*Ethics of Economic Life*], 221.

[64] H.-H. Hoppe, "How Is Fiat Money Possible?—or, The Devaluation of Money and Credit," *Review of Austrian Economics*" 7, no. 2 (1994): 49.

[65] Mises, *Human Action*, 398–99.

[66] L. von Mises, "The Non-Neutrality of Money," in *Money, Method*, 70.

[67] By this term Mises defines "a sovereign nation's total complex of economic activities directed and controlled by the government" (*Human Action*, 323).

This faulty presupposition of the neutrality of money is the reason why mathematical economists introduced the equation of exchange, which on the one hand is a fruitless attempt to deal with changes in purchasing power, and on the other represents its dangerous depersonalization. The changes in the structure of prices and in the supply and demand of money do not arise in *Volskwirtschaft* as such but are triggered by the interaction of individuals who are the only and proper subject of the market game. As our previous analysis showed, the deregulation of the financial markets in some parts of the world, of which John Paul II spoke to the members of the Papal Academy of Social Sciences in 1997, is not ethically troubling.[68] A serious moral problem does arise from the opposite of such deregulation: the attempt to find institutional solutions for the instability of financial systems.

Free Banking

It is obvious for Mises that the free market cannot exist without free banking, which would defend it against crises and depressions related to credit expansion.[69] Andrzej Zwoliński surprisingly states that "the creation of money is a social good through the creation of economic wealth." The belief in the fact that the increase of money supply is socially beneficial is, Sennholz points out, "one of the greatest economic illusions of our times."[70]

Mises proves that giving fiduciary loans increases the amount of substitute money on the market and thus the purchasing power of debtors, irrespective of the real state of the market. This additional demand inflates the prices of commodities and the level of wages. The introduction of an additional amount of money offered for loans contributes to the lowering of interest rates below what would occur on the unhampered market. This type of irregularity would not happen with a commodity loan, for a bank could increase the number of loans only to the degree that savers would entrust their deposits. Mises rightly claims that no government now is willing to give up the existing system because it ensures a handy source of revenue, and in

---

[68] Address of Pope John Paul II to the Academy Social Sciences, April 25, 1997, no. 3.

[69] Mises, *Human Action*, 433.

[70] H. F. Sennholz, *Age of Inflation* (Belmont, MA: Western Islands, 1979), 19.

a time of state interventionism nobody questions that the banks' task is to lend money to the state.[71]

The author of *Human Action* avers that it was a deadly blow to the free-market economy when liberalism abandoned the principles governing free enterprise in the field of banking.[72] The interest rate is a market phenomenon that cannot be manipulated by free market actors. In an unhampered market economy, the interest rate falls when people economize. The credit that banks are ready to offer is therefore a natural derivative of human savings. The lowered interest rate is a signal to investors that consumers are ready to put off consumption and thus investments should be made in more time-consuming stages of production. A similar process may be triggered by an artificial lowering of the interest rate and increasing credit availability. This misleads entrepreneurs, who direct their resources to time-consuming stages of production while consumers are not changing their preferences to delay consumption. The economy is thus pulled in two extreme directions and exceeds its productive capacities, a fact that causes collapse as a result of malinvestments from the period of the artificially induced boom.[73]

The Austrian theory of economic cycles explains why there is a sudden accumulation of mistakes by entrepreneurs, concentrated in the sector of capital goods. Mises thinks that boom leads not only to impoverishment—for there must be a reduction of consumption up to the time when the capital wasted in the period of the boom is restored—but also to moral ravages.[74] The process of readjustment to new conditions generates frustration, for while people do not want to lower their living standard, neither are they willing to shun their belief in unreal development. The worst thing is that they are not aware of the proper cause of the economic crisis and do not blame the authorities for creating the boom, only for the collapse. Therefore, they believe the only way out of recession is increasing inflation and further credit expansion.[75]

---

[71] Mises, *Human Action*, 442.

[72] Mises, *Human Action*, 443.

[73] Mises, *Human Action*, 575.

[74] Mises, *Human Action*, 576.

[75] Mises, *Human Action*, 578.

Regular booms, busts, and recessions are not, as previously thought, inevitable phenomena in an unhampered market economy. The economic cycle is generated by the arbitrary production of money, which would not occur in a commodity money regime. The question of the economic cycle has utmost importance for a moral evaluation of the principles of the free market, because it shows that economic knowledge helps to avoid purported solutions that in reality only make the problem worse.[76]

Mistakes in economics and their improper moral evaluation result from a neglect of the basic postulates of economic reasoning, which surveys human action as it affects the whole economy. The free market is a natural order that developed spontaneously on the basis of free human action based on private property and a free exchange of goods and services. Experience shows that this is the best tool to improve the conditions of human life, but it is not the only institution that makes up society.

The Tasks of the State

Society is a necessary condition for the existence and development of man. Mises, in line with the social teaching of the Church, claims that the state must safeguard man in everything he needs for life and development in the earthly dimension. For both Mises and the Church, the existence of the state is a necessity. In this section we discuss the tasks of the state and the threats resulting from its overactivity in citizens' lives, observing similarities and differences between Mises and Catholic social teaching.

Political Community

According to Mises, society is an excellent means for the attainment of man's ends.[77] The Second Vatican Council teaches likewise, stating that political community exists with a view to the end that man could not otherwise attain.[78] This goal is the most complete growth of all members of the political community, who are called to

[76] Woods, *The Church and the Market*, 105–6.

[77] Mises, *Human Action*, 165.

[78] *Gaudium et Spes*, no. 74.

permanent cooperation in the realization of the common good. The state safeguards the external conditions necessary so that all citizens can develop their abilities, their material, intellectual, and religious life.[79] The state is in all its basic dimensions directed to service on behalf of the human person, who in the Christian vision is always superior to the state, although in the sphere of actions on behalf of the common good is subordinated to the state in accord with the principle of solidarity.[80]

Mises claims that man is of his essence a social being and, conceived as an isolated and asocial being, is only a mental construction. Praxeology indeed speaks of the solitary individual, acting exclusively on his own behalf and independently of others, but it does so only for the sake of a better explanation of the problems of social cooperation.[81] This corresponds to the teaching of the Church that social life is not something imported from without but an essential and inseparable dimension of human existence.[82]

Mises claims that social cooperation has nothing in common with love, mercy, or other positive sentiments toward one's neighbor. *Prima facie*, this statement is surprising, but the Austrian philosopher wishes only to stress that society is the result of man's purposeful action and is not based on a passing sentiment or a social contract. People cooperate with one another in the system of the division of labor because it serves their own interests. Like St. Thomas, Mises proves the need for social life and the state on the basis of the individual's insufficiency.[83] Mises refers here to man whom the Creator has endowed with reason and the urges toward the pursuit of happiness, and for this reason there is no need to appeal to miraculous interventions of supernatural forces.[84] Political community therefore was not established in response to sin,

---

[79] Pius XII, "The Internal Order of States and People," Christmas Message, 1942, https://www.papalencyclicals.net/pius12/p12ch42.htm.

[80] T. Slipko, [*Outline of Ethics*], vol. 2, 282.

[81] Mises, *Human Action*, 165.

[82] *Gaudium et Spes*, no. 25.

[83] St. Thomas Aquinas, *On Society and Reign* (*De regimine princium*), in *Aquinas' Political Writings*, ed. R. W. Dyson (Cambridge: Cambridge University Press, 2004), 5ff.

[84] Mises, *Human Action*, 147.

as Augustine thought, but has its special dignity resulting from the plan of God itself. According to St. Thomas, man is a social creature by nature.[85] The state's regulation of multifaceted dimensions of social life is therefore based on principles rooted in Christian anthropology.

The main and only task of the state is, according to Mises, the protection of private property, citizens' freedom, and civil peace.[86] Mises' liberalism therefore has nothing in common with anarchism. He is well aware that the existence of society would be in danger if there were no threat of the use of power behind the rules of conduct necessary for the protection of the individual's freedom. He calls the state "the social apparatus of compulsion and coercion"[87] that serves to make people observe the rules of living in society. Mises holds that society cannot rely solely on voluntary compliance with the law and contracts. Like St. Thomas, he thought that the law should forbid sins that destroy social order, such as murder and theft. The state should be intent on justice and social peace.[88] According to the social teaching of the Church, it is the state's obligation to prevent conduct that strikes at the basic principles of social cooperation, and it has the right prevent disorder caused by delinquent actions through a system of punishments.[89]

Mises decisively criticizes universalist and collectivist doctrines as theocratic systems that postulate the existence of a superhuman entity to which the individual is bound to submit. The terms *social* and *state* represent in those doctrines imperishable entities possessing their own ends that are different from those of the individuals who comprise them.[90] Mises refuses to acknowledge the independent personal existence of society, a view that corresponds with the Christian conception. According to the latter, lower societies are subordinate to higher ones, but only to the extent of aiming at the common good, which is a common end. In other aims the individuals preserve full autonomy. In the moral order, the good of the individual is prior to

---

85 W. Giertych, ["Unused Capital"], *W drodze* 2 (2008), 34.

86 Mises, *Liberalism*, 38.

87 Mises, *Liberalism*, 62.

88 Giertych, ["Unused Capital"], 38; Aquinas, *On Society and Reign*, I, 1.

89 *Compendium of the Social Doctrine*, no. 402.

90 Mises, *Human Action*, 151.

the social good. The social good can never be attained to the detriment or neglect of the good of the individual or lower societies, for they are genetically prior to the state.[91]

The Principle of Subsidiarity

The social teaching of the Church has worked out the principle of subsidiarity, which defends the members of a given community and smaller associations against the ambitions of the totalitarian social order.[92] Pius XI formulated this principle in *Quadragesimo Anno* (1931) as the most important law of social philosophy, defining the essence of social life, which consists in a respect for the initiative and freedom of action of individuals in relation to society, and lesser associations in relation to larger associations.[93] We find this aspect of the principle of subsidiarity in Mises' thought: He says that freedom is a situation in which government coercion does not restrict individual decisions more than the commonly obliging praxeological principles of any human action.[94] The ability to attain the chosen ends is restricted and depends on the fulfillment of definite conditions determined by the laws of praxeology. Mises bemoans the fact that the governing class very often ignore those conditions, without noticing that their troubles and failures are related to the violation of the laws of economics. They make a mistake that derives from devoting attention only to "what is seen,"[95] forgetting that economic reasoning calls for taking into account long-term effects across the entire economy.

---

[91] *Gaudium et Spes,* nos. 25–26; J. Zabielski, ["Building a City Worthy of Man: The Inspiring Role of the Social Teaching of the Church in the Creation of Stable Foundations of Social Life"], *Lomzynskie Wiadomosci Koscielne* 1 (2005): 172–87.

[92] M. Pokrywka, ["The Primacy of the Human Person in Social Life"], *Roczniki Teologiczne* 47, no. 3 (2000): 221.

[93] Pius XI, *Quadragessimo Anno,* no. 79.

[94] Mises, *Human Action,* 761–62.

[95] F. Bastiat, "What Is Seen and What Is Not Seen," in Bastiat, *Selected Essays on Political Economy,* trans. S. Cain (Irvington-on-Hudson, NY: Foundation for Economic Education, 1995), 9.

We have already said that praxeology as a science cannot encroach upon the individual's right to choose and to act.[96] For this reason, private property is for Mises an inviolable value, for beyond it there is only coercion and violence. Within the confines of private property, the individual is independent of the state.[97] The Misesian principle of abiding by the laws of praxeology is linked with making the human person more valuable as a subject of action—an aim similar to that of the principle of subsidiarity.

Subsidiarity also contains a positive aspect, which consists in helping where it is necessary, but this means help that is temporary rather than permanent, so that the individual or social group will be able to attain its ends and complete its tasks independently.[98] It means help in a supplementary form to persons and associations, help that does not kill initiative but fosters it.[99] Richard J. Neuhaus rightly notes that the essence of subsidiarity does not entail the passing of state functions to lower levels of society, for this action would be based on an assumption that these functions belong to the state in the first place.[100] John Paul II speaks about intermediary structures, which have their origin in the family.[101] These structures provide the individual with a free space and protect him against the anonymous forces of the state apparatus, which always tends to transform people from subjects into objects.

The principle of subsidiarity allows us to understand the essence of a subsidiary state as distinct from a welfare state. Mises counters the criticism of classical liberalism that believes it would deprive the needy of assistance.[102] He stresses that capitalism brought about an increase in the standard of living and that the poverty of the masses is

---

[96] Mises, *Human Action*, 174.

[97] Mises, *Liberalism*, 69.

[98] Pius XI, *Quadragesimo Anno*, no. 79; W. Piwowarski, ["The Principle of Subsidiarity"], in [*Dictionary of Catholic Social Doctrine*], 198.

[99] Pokrywka, ["Primacy of the Person"], 222.

[100] R. J. Neuhaus, *Doing Well and Doing Good: The Challenge to the Christian Capitalist* (New York: Doubleday, 1992), 244.

[101] John Paul II, *Centesimus Annus*, no. 13.

[102] W. Piwowarski, ["The Subsidiary State in Catholic Social Doctrine"], *Chrzescijanin w swiecie* 2 (1993): 164.

not caused by capitalism but by the absence of capitalism.[103] Laissez-faireism converted the employable poor of feudal times into wage earners. In a subsidiary state, there is particular concern for people who for various reasons are not able on their own to provide for their elementary needs.[104] Mises notices this problem and stresses that provision for such people has always been a duty of charitable organizations and should remain in private hands.[105]

Mises effectively wards off attacks on charity that claim that its means are too modest, by pointing out that these means would be greater if state interventionism through credit expansion and inflation growth did not make it difficult for people to economize and accumulate reserves for the future. And he criticizes all those who think that the poor deserve help by virtue of the law and at the same time accuse capitalism of indifference and impersonal transactions; they condemn the system of charity just because it is based on love of neighbor. Mises notices precisely what John Paul II wrote about in *Centesimus Annus*: people need the spirit of love and interhuman solidarity; therefore, when offering man material assistance, those assisting should not reduce him to an object of social security.[106] As an economist, Mises provides no solutions in this area, for these problems have no praxeological character. He thinks, however, that substituting charitable assistance with a state guarantee not only contradicts man's true nature but is also undesirable for practical reasons, as it reduces incentives to pursue or return to productive work.[107]

Mises' criticism of socialism and interventionism demonstrates that he was an opponent of the excessive presence of the state in social life. His assessment supports the Church's view that, if private initiative is refused, the principle of subsidiarity dies, while an attitude of passivity is cultivated and involvement in social life is discouraged.[108] He also proves that actions taken by interventionists cause worse effects

---

[103] Mises, *Human Action,* 836.

[104] Pokrywka, ["Primacy of the Person"], 224.

[105] Mises, *Human Action,* 837.

[106] John Paul II, *Centesimus Annus,* no. 49.

[107] Mises, *Human Action,* 839.

[108] *Compendium of the Social Doctrine,* no. 187; J. Szymczek, ["What State: Welfare or Subsidiary?"], *Chrzescijanin w swiecie* 2 (1993): 218–20.

than the conditions they are trying to prevent. John Paul II similarly writes that the enlargement of state intervention brought about the establishment of "the Welfare State," which not only fails to respond to poverty and deprivation unworthy of the human person but also causes many abuses.[109]

Direct Government Interference with Consumption

Touching upon the question of economic interventionism, we must stop a while on the problem of direct government interference with consumption, even though this issue has no catallactic character. Economics examines only the influence of production on consumers' behavior, not the motives that govern them when choosing a concrete commodity on the market.[110] Mises, however, takes up this problem with reference to drugs, for this is an important issue both for the individual and for society. The *Catechism of the Catholic Church* teaches that it is the duty of a political community to protect the security and health of the family, especially in view of such threats as drug addiction.[111] Drug addiction is for Mises a mortal threat, but this does not mean that the state authorities must interfere to put down this evil by a ban on trade.[112]

Mises is afraid that the state, when it interferes with citizens' privacy, in reality will deprive individuals of freedom. He asks rhetorically whether the protection of the government should in this case be limited exclusively to the protection of the body, or whether it should be extended over minds and souls by preventing them from reading inappropriate books. The mischief done by such ideologies may in the long run be more pernicious than the damage done by narcotic drugs. The Austrian philosopher forces us to consider not only whether

---

[109] John Paul II, *Centesimus Annus*, no. 48. Woods remarks that the documents of the Church are very ambiguous on this question; this refers also to John Paul II's earlier encyclicals, which recommended a broad and expensive package of government social programs. A strong and unambiguous criticism of the welfare state appeared only in *Centesimus Annus*. Woods, *The Church and the Market*, 147.

[110] Mises, *Human Action*, 733.

[111] *Catechism of the Catholic Church*, no. 2211.

[112] Mises, *Liberalism*, 35.

this interference is good or bad but also whether it actually leads to the state's desired ends.[113] This argumentation is in accord with the thought of St. Thomas Aquinas, who claimed that the ethical level the state can enforce is lower than that offered by the Church through the sacraments and the living word of God. The state's task is not to lead people to holiness but only to virtue through securing a just functioning of social life. If the state authority enforces too-stringent ethical demands on a morally immature society, it may cause revolt and negation of the state's authority.[114]

Social Justice

Mises stresses that the problem of contemporary governments consists in seeking a just tax that would allow a reform of social conditions according to justice. This way of thinking grounds the fiscal policy of all states on the assumption that taxes should depend on each citizen's "ability to pay." This principle has attained the rank of a condition of social justice.[115] Mises complains that in their political decisions governments in general do not devote attention to the neutral tax, which

---

[113] Mises, *Human Action*, 734.

[114] W. Giertych, ["Unused Capital"], 41.

[115] Social justice in Catholic social doctrine has nothing to do with its socialist understanding in which it is only an equivalent of class justice. This term appeared first in the teaching of the Church in Pius XI's encyclical *Quadragesimo Anno*, evidently derived from the Jesuit Oswald von Nell-Breuning. According to Michael Novak, social justice is a virtue that can only be attributed to persons' intentions, not a principle that may be attributed to social systems, as Nell-Breuning suggested (O. von Nell-Breuning, *Reorganization of Social Economy* [New York, 1935], 250–51). Social justice rightly understood is a species of justice, owing to which free citizens practice self-government by doing for themselves what they need without turning to government in these matters. It is designed to be concerned with the good of others, and not only the good of one acting subject. According to Novak, by introducing this term Pius XI had in mind the revival of civil society, at the time of the great economic crisis, through the principle of participation, which he linked with grassroots initiative; the state is only to provide appropriate conditions. M. Novak, ["Who Thirst for Righteousness … Defining Social Justice"], *Tygodnik Powszechny* 31 (2006): 11; M. Novak, *The Catholic Ethic and the Spirit of Capitalism* (New York: Free Press, 1993), 62–86.

would not enforce on the acting person behaviors other than those that would result from his struggles on the unhampered market.[116]

Benedict XVI teaches that we cannot build the kingdom of God on earth with our own effort.[117] Perfection cannot be attributed to human nature, for "the power of sin will continue to be a terrible presence."[118] This perspective helps us notice the danger hidden behind the concept *social justice*, which drives attempts to build the welfare state and introduce a tax system that would realize perfect justice. Hayek rightly notes that this term becomes equivalent to *distributive justice*.[119] The purported goal of social justice—the elimination of economic inequalities—neglects the simple fact that disproportions mainly result from individuals' choices and thus can be minimized only through the control of human choices.

The conception of justice that says that everyone must obtain from government whatever he deserves from the moral point of view, encourages people to abandon free enterprise and turn to the planned economy, and this may be accomplished only at the expense of the loss of personal freedom. Leo XIII reminds us of the old truth that total equality in society is not possible, for there are innumerable natural differences among people, giving rise to a variety of living conditions.[120] A world that by itself must create its own justice at the expense of limiting the freedom of its citizens is, according to Pope Benedict, a world without hope.[121]

The author of *Human Action* stresses that the basic assumption of the policy of interventionism is distribution of the incomes of the wealthier part of society, used as funds for the improvement of the living standards of the poorer strata of society. For this reason, in the sphere of public finance the most characteristic manifestation of this doctrine is progressive taxation on incomes.[122] Mises claims that high taxes for public expenditure are not compatible with a free market.

---

[116] Mises, *Human Action*, 738.

[117] Benedict XVI, *Spe Salvi*, no. 25.

[118] Benedict XVI, *Spe Salvi.*, no. 36.

[119] Hayek, *Fatal Conceit*, 117–19.

[120] Leo XIII, *Rerum Novarum*, no. 14.

[121] Benedict XVI, *Spe Salvi*, no. 42.

[122] Mises, *Human Action*, 857.

He stresses that the increase of taxes is not only unprofitable for the economy but also for the taxes themselves, because the whole tax system, which is built on the neutral tax, is of its nature self-defeating.[123] Money from the progressive tax, which could be used by entrepreneurs to accumulate additional capital, is by the treasury destined for current expenditures, a reality that impedes the pace of accumulation, technical progress, and the increase of marginal productivity of labor and its consequent increase of wages. Mises proves that progressive taxation checks economic progress and leads to the economy's ossification.[124] Betrand de Jouvenel, the French philosopher and economist, comes to the same conclusion. In *The Ethics of Redistribution*, he proves that the lower the tax—within a reasonable limit indispensable for the government to fulfill its functions—the more new investment will appear on the market.[125]

Jozef Majka thinks that the progression of income tax in the case of very high incomes is justified, but at the same time he adds that the state ought not increase its treasury beyond essential need, depriving its citizens of the right to save and accumulate wealth. Majka underlines that tax progression cannot be automatic and, in accord with the principles of commutative justice, it should not be based solely on the level of remuneration. John Paul II stresses that remuneration for work is the most important manner by which to make justice real in the relationship between worker and employer.[126]

Robert Gwiazdowski remarks that commentators on Catholic social teaching are ready to accept tax progression under certain conditions: if it does not weaken the interest in multiplying income, does not have any negative consequences for saving, does not evoke the sense of injustice in citizens (and in consequence does not create a tendency to hide incomes), and does not aim at incomes as remuneration for

---

[123] Mises, *Human Action*, 741.

[124] Mises, *Human Action*, 809.

[125] W. R. Luckey, "The Economics of Bertrand de Jouvenel," *Journal of Markets & Morality* 1, no. 2 (Fall 1998): 183.

[126] John Paul II, *Laborem Exercens*, no. 19. Gwiazdowski asks an important question: "It is worthwhile to ask whether the pope is thinking about gross remuneration, received by the worker from his employer, or net remuneration—after taxation." R. Gwiazdowski, ["Taxes as Theft"], in [*Theft and Economic Development*], 59.

work.[127] None of these conditions, however, is entirely fulfilled by tax progression; therefore, sympathy for such taxation among proponents of the social teaching is, in Gwiazdowski's opinion, incomprehensible. Bertrand de Jouvenel adds that this system is first of all a horizontal, not vertical, exchange of incomes and has only a psychological role, without playing any financial role.[128] The purchasing power distributed by the state actually derives from the same social stratum that receives it later on.[129] Contemporary classical liberals claim that only the system of proportional taxation is in accord with liberal requirements.[130]

Democracy

Our analysis so far has shown that Mises is far from saying that the state is not necessary, only that it cannot surpass a certain minimum that results from its tasks. He is also an advocate of democracy, which he understands above all as an indispensable tool of peaceful transition of power and a forum for the exchange of opinions in the socio-political space.[131] Mises' conception of democracy clearly corresponds with the social teaching of the Church. Patrycja Walter indicates that the axiological foundation to which Mises refers is primarily based on the principle of the individual's self-determination, which includes the arenas of the law and social peace.[132] For the same reason, the contemporary teaching of the Church values the democratic system. In *Centesimus Annus*, John Paul II stresses that democracy ensures the participation of citizens in making political choices and controlling its own governments through peaceful means. The pope emphasizes

---

[127] R. Gwiazdowski, ["Taxes"], 60.

[128] B. Jouvenel, *The Ethics of Redistribution* (Indianapolis: Liberty Fund, 1990), 91.

[129] The decisive majority of taxpayers is in the first sector of the tax scale (in Poland, 95 percent). R. Gwiazdowski, ["Taxes"], 60.

[130] J. Gray, *Liberalism* (Minneapolis: University of Minnesota Press, 1986), 78–79.

[131] Mises, *Memoirs*, 55; Mises, *Liberalism*, 41.

[132] P. Walter, ["Idea of Democracy"], Instytut Misesa, August 6, 2007, https://mises.pl/blog/2007/08/06/patrycja-walter-idea-demokracji-w-pracach-ludwiga-von-misesa/.

that the condition of a proper functioning of democracy is to assume a proper conception of man and establish structures of participation.[133]

Catholic social doctrine regards the recognition of the common good as an end and criterion of ordering political life as a condition of stability in democracy.[134] This postulate in Mises is realized through a duty to protect freedom, a duty regarded as one of the most important tasks of the rule of law. Equality under the law gives each citizen a real opportunity to generate his own goals, which may then be attained within the frameworks determined by the law. These frameworks, without which society cannot function, are defined by the state. Mises is well aware that those who hold power can give in to the temptation of abusing their rights;[135] therefore, in accord with the liberal tradition he devotes much space to the concept of individual liberties, which guarantee the individual freedom from self-willed and arbitrary actions of the government organs.[136] He thinks that only a system based on the rule of law can safeguard citizens' political liberty. Therefore, the law must in the same degree deal with the governing and the governed, and ensure a reasonable division of power.[137]

The magisterium of the Church acknowledges the principle of the division of power in the state.[138] The persons given authority within their specific legislative, executive, and judicial tasks should be committed to the service of the whole civil community.[139] According to

---

[133] John Paul II, *Centesimus Annus*, no. 46.

[134] *Compendium of the Social Doctrine*, no. 407.

[135] The most famous opinion on the corruptible character of power has been formulated by Lord Acton: (a) "Power tends to expand indefinitely, and will transcend all barriers, abroad and at home, until met by superior forces"; (b) "History is not a web woven with innocent hands. Among all the causes which degrade and demoralize men, power is the most constant and the most active"; and (c) "Power tends to corrupt and absolute power corrupts absolutely." Acton, *Lectures on Modern History, MSS*, quoted by G. Himmelfarb, *Lord Acton: A Study in Conscience and Politics* (San Francisco: ICS Studies, 1993), 220, 239; see also Lord Acton, *The History of Freedom* (Grand Rapids, MI: Acton Institute, 1993).

[136] Mises, *The Anti-Capitalistic Mentality*, 71–73.

[137] Walter, ["Idea of Democracy"].

[138] *Compendium of the Social Doctrine*, no. 408.

[139] *Catechism of the Catholic Church*, no. 2236.

Mises, a serious threat for such democratic governments is interventionism, which paralyzes the parliamentary system. In the parliaments of interventionist countries, no parliament member perceives his role as representing the nation as a whole and instead each represents only particular interests of some political parties or labor unions.[140] According to Mises, the dictatorial rule of the majority is a deformation of democracy and the antithesis of liberal doctrine.[141] The greatest failure of the parliamentary system is delegating the legislative power to the executive. Mises reminds us that Adolf Hitler, Benito Mussolini, and Philippe Petain ruled by virtue of such delegations of power, and through a formal relationship with democratic institutions their power took on the appearances of legality.[142] He makes the realization of democratic rule dependent on respect for the principle of checks and balances of power, for which Alexis de Tocqueville called in *Democracy in America*.[143]

Another danger that threatens democracy is excessive bureaucratization and corruption. According to Mises, bureaucratization itself is not bad, for the managing of state institutions requires such methods of administration. The harmful expansion of the sphere of bureaucratic management is a consequence of the limitation of individual freedom and "the substitution of government control for private initiative."[144] Bureaucrats who begin to decide about questions essential for each citizen are no longer servants but "arbitrary masters and tyrants."[145] John Paul II points to the same problem in *Christifideles Laici*, where he stresses that the growth of a complicated organizational structure, designed to control all available domains of life, leads to an overgrowth of bureaucracy and impersonal functionalism among those working in public administration.[146] Democratic processes are also deprived of their efficiency through the phenomenon of corruption and various

---

140 Mises, *Interventionism*, 47.

141 Mises, *Human Action*, 153.

142 Mises, *Interventionism*, 47–48.

143 A. de Tocqueville, *Democracy in America*, trans. H. Reeve (New York: Bantam Dell, 2002), 78–79.

144 Mises, *Bureaucracy*, 48.

145 Mises, *Bureaucracy*, 10.

146 John Paul II, *Christifideles Laici*, no. 41.

kinds of favoritism.[147] Mises notices the same problem and clearly proves that it is an inevitable effect of interventionism.[148]

The duty to protect freedom, recognized by Mises as one of the most important tasks of democratic governments, embraces also the guarantee of religious freedom. The principle of self-possession—in this case loyalty to one's own conscience—is the natural right of each person, and liberalism puts no obstacles in the way of choice of religion.[149] Mises speaks on behalf of the guarantee of religious freedom, for it is a condition for the harmonious coexistence of individuals within a given society.[150] In *Dignitatis Humanae,* the Second Vatican Council says that the very nature of the quest for God demands that all people be free from any coercion in matters concerning religion.[151] The Council Fathers also stress that the right to religious freedom is not unlimited and must be in accord with the demands of the common good and peaceful cooperation of all citizens.[152]

The State as a Free Organization

For Mises, the state is an entirely free organization.[153] It should be stressed that by the right to self-determination he does not mean the right of a definite national group but the right of the inhabitants of each territory to decide to which state they belong. In no case therefore is the point to detach and incorporate the territories belonging to another state into one's own state contrary to the wishes of its inhabitants.[154] Mises' thought corresponds here with the teaching of John Paul II, who firmly emphasizes the right of each nation to independence and freedom. This means the absolute right of each nation

---

[147] John Paul II, Message for the Celebration of the World Day of Peace (January 1, 1999), no. 6.

[148] Mises, *Human Action,* 734–35.

[149] Mises, *Human Action,* 157.

[150] Mises, *Liberalism,* 150–51.

[151] Second Vatican Council, Declaration on Religious Freedom *Dignitatis Humanae* (1965), no. 2.

[152] *Dignitatis Humanae,* no. 7.

[153] Mises, *Nation, State and Economy,* 27.

[154] Mises, *Liberalism,* 150–51.

to its own state, but the pope remarks that remaining in or leaving a multinational state must take place by way of peaceful dialogue.[155] The need for national independence based on cultural sovereignty leads sooner or later to political independence, which is manifested in the right to self-reliance, autonomy, and, ultimately, full independence.[156]

Mises' methodological anthropocentrism leads him to posit that the right to self-determination should be granted to each individual person, but—as he notes himself—it cannot be done for technical reasons. Liberalism forces no one to participate in the state's structures and one who wants can always emigrate.[157] It should be emphasized that John Paul II also recognizes the rights to leave one's native land for various motives in order to seek better conditions of life, and to return to the homeland.[158] The social teaching of the Church underlines that from the principle of subsidiarity follows the primacy of the family, which cherishes its own and primary right in relation to society.[159] The state must approve of and respect this superior role. It should not take away from the family the conditions by which it can fulfill its tasks on its own or within a free association.[160]

According to Mises, no nation or any part of it should be kept against its will in a political community with other nations. The liberal doctrine of freedom puts forward a postulate of the self-determinations of nations that stems directly from human rights.[161] The social teaching of the Church also resists the attempt to identify the nation with the state. The nation has a right to independence and cultural difference, to the preservation of cultural heritage and its development, and also to political independence and responsibility for its own fortunes.[162] John XXIII in *Pacem in Terris* writes that any activity against national minorities in order to limit their power and development is a serious

---

155 J. Czajkowski, [*Society, Nation, State in the Thought of John Paul II*] (Krakow, 1991), 129–36.

156 J. Majka, [*Social and Political Ethics*] (Warsaw, 1993), 137.

157 Mises, *Nation, State and Economy*, 32.

158 John Paul II, *Laborem Exercens*, no. 23.

159 *Dignitatis Humanae*, no. 5.

160 John Paul II, Apostolic Exhortation *Familiaris Consortio* (1981), no. 45.

161 Mises, *Nation, State and Economy*, 27.

162 Pius XII, *Summi Pontificatus*, no. 89; *Gaudium et Spes*, no. 79.

violation of justice.[163] Speaking at the United Nations in 1995, John Paul II laid stress on the necessity to codify and formally promulgate the rights of the nations in a manner analagous to human rights in the international convention.[164]

The social teaching of the Church sees in the respect for human rights the basis of state order. John Paul emphasizes that a nation is a cultural community in which the main stress falls on man as its subject.[165] Culture, understood as the material and spiritual heritage of the people of a nation, is an essential element in shaping national consciousness.[166] This is consistent with Mises, who speaks in favor of full economic freedom and elimination of obstacles in the development of trade, obstacles which result from the differences between political systems through the separation of the economy from the state. The author of *Human Action* thinks that for this purpose one does not need to create a universal empire; instead, the liberal economic system may function within a system of state borders. Particular nations themselves should decide to which degree they want to adjust their right to the right binding in other countries. The violation of their will is, Mises says, contrary to liberal principles,[167] and would also be a contradiction of the principle of participation. The latter, according to Catholic teaching, is always a free and noble commitment of the person to social exchange.[168]

Mises distinctly shows that free trade and other free economic activity directly affect the sociopolitical space. The Church proposes no ready-made models of social systems, for she is aware that such models can only be established by taking into account the concrete historical conditions of a given society.[169] One should stress, however, that although the Church has no need of democracy to live, she

---

163 John XXIII, *Pacem in Terris*, nos. 14 and 43.

164 John Paul II, Address to the Fiftieth General Assembly of the United Nations Organization (October 5, 1995), nos. 5–8.

165 John Paul II, "Address to UNESCO" (June 2, 1980), www.inters.org/John-Paul-II-UNESCO-Culture.

166 W. Piwowarski, ["Nation"], in [*Dictionary of Catholic Social Doctrine*], 112.

167 Mises, *Nation, State and Economy*, 30.

168 *Catechism of the Catholic Church*, no. 1913.

169 John Paul II, *Centesimus Annus*, no. 43.

appreciates it today as a system that ensures citizens' participation in political decisions and guarantees their opportunity to choose and control their own governments.[170] It is worth remembering here Mises' warning that democracy is not something given to man once for all, and that it needs our attention because there is always a possibility that someone may appear who will go beyond the laws and will start to shape anew the reality in which we are and act. Mises therefore calls us to concern about our own property and freedom, for they are superior values that protect us against enslavement. He agrees with John Paul II's contention that authentic democracy is possible only in a state where the law rules and does so on the foundation of a correct conception of the human person. The erection of a socioeconomic system therefore is not a task completed once for all. Benedict XVI stresses that it is the task of each generation to contribute to the establishment of a good and effective sociopolitical order.[171]

Morality and Economics

According to Mises, economics is an apolitical science. It is entirely neutral regarding value judgments, for it refers exclusively to means, never to the choice of the ultimate goal. The object of praxeology is the only visible manifestation of human life, which is action. If in summing up his research an economist states that *a* is a bad means, for not only does it fail to lead to *p*, but instead it leads to *g*—that is, to an effect which even the advocate of the means *a* regard as undesirable—he states merely that it is an improper means to accomplish the intended goal and does not declare a value judgment. In this sense, economists speak for instance about protectionism or prices or minimum wage rates. Economics is ruled by its own laws. In *Quadragesimo Anno,* Pius XI strongly affirms this, but at the same time adds that it would be a mistake to claim that the economic and moral orders are so far away and foreign to each other that the former does not rely on the latter at all.[172]

---

[170] M. Zieba, [*Democracy and Anti-evangelization*] (Poznan, 1997), 70–75.

[171] Benedict XVI, *Spe Salvi,* no. 25.

[172] Pius XI, *Quadragesimo Anno,* nos. 42–43.

Cultural Conditions of the Free Market

John Paul II rightly notes that decisions concerning production and consumption are always moral and cultural choices, because through them a definite culture is made manifest as a general conception of life.[173] In the context of Christian anthropology, man always appears as *homo ethicus* and can never act beyond morality.[174] The free market is only one aspect of society, and social relations are always based on moral values. The moral order refers not only to the system of relations between a person and the ultimate goal (i.e., God), and between a person and a system of values; it also embraces the system of interpersonal relations within the frames of society.[175] John Paul describes the threefold social structure composed not only of the free economy and the free political system but also the culture of freedom. The pope has no doubt that the great contemporary economic debate has been decided on behalf of the free market, and the great political debate has brought victory for democracy.[176] He is aware that we are now awaiting the struggle for a culture of freedom and ponders how it should be shaped. This aspect of the free economy is usually underappreciated and barely studied by Mises, but we cannot say that he altogether failed to notice it.

Mises is aware that each social order results from ideologies that precede it temporally and logically.[177] A permanent governmental system must be based on an ideology accepted by the majority. It has a moral and spiritual character, giving the government a real foundation for coercion toward resistant elements in society. The power of such ideology consists in the fact that people become subordinate to it without hesitation or scruples. Ideology for Mises[178] is what culture is for John Paul II. According to Maciej Zieba, for the pope it is a kind of metalevel that embraces all ethical, political, and economic

---

[173] John Paul II, *Centesimus Annus*, no. 36.

[174] J. Gocko, ["The Conceptions of Economic Morality"], *Roczniki Teologiczne* 48, no. 3 (2001): 171.

[175] Majka, ["Ethics"], 29.

[176] Novak, *The Catholic Ethic*, 115.

[177] Mises, *Human Action*, 187–91.

[178] Mises, *Human Action*, 188.

issues.[179] John Paul stresses that man is conditioned by the social structure in which he lives, by his upbringing and milieu.[180] These cultural conditions can affect him in a negative or positive manner. For this reason, John Paul adds that there is urgent work to do in the field of upbringing and culture, so that consumers are prepared for the use of the right to choose, producers for the acceptance of profound responsibility, and public authorities for the application of respective intervention.[181]

His support for the role of public authority does not mean that the pope opposes the free market. Michael Novak stresses that culture in the pope's view is characterized by special autonomy and primacy in relation to economics, politics, and other spheres of life. The pope distinguishes society from the state, and moral-cultural institutions of civil society from the political bodies of the government.[182] Culture should have a character that is open to other cultures and should seek the truth by way of dialogue.[183] Therefore it is not a static vision of culture, an ideal that should be accomplished, but an unending quest for values and truth, an ongoing attempt to distinguish between what is valuable in tradition and what is false, mistaken, or outdated.

Mises is also aware of moral imperatives that accompany economic activity and affect it. The system of the free economy is a social system of exchange, based on a free contract. The adjustment of the individual to the requirements of social cooperation demands sacrifices.[184] Mises claims that these are only transitory discomforts, because living in society ensures incomparably greater benefits. John Paul II reasons likewise in *Centesimus Annus*, where he states that disciplined human work and solidary cooperation are sources of the wealth of nations.[185] The pope also points to indispensable virtues that allow man to perform this task: diligence, industriousness, prudence, reliability and fidelity in interpersonal relationships, as well as courage

---

179 M. Zieba, [*The Popes and Capitalism*] (Krakow, 1998), 152.

180 John Paul II, *Centesimus Annus*, no. 38.

181 John Paul II, *Centesimus Annus*, no. 36.

182 Novak, *The Catholic Ethic*, 133.

183 Zieba, [*The Popes*], 157.

184 Mises, *Human Action*, 148.

185 John Paul II, *Centesimus Annus*, no. 32.

in carrying out decisions that are difficult and painful but necessary for the overall working of a business.[186]

Mises' Rational Utilitarianism

According to Mises, society and the state are the most important means for people to attain goals in conformity with their needs. Mises says that economics is a science about human action, and the only criterion by which to evaluate this action is whether it enables them to attain the goals at which they aim.[187] Mises' rational utilitarianism does not mean, however, that man aims only at the satisfaction of his material needs and is for himself the ultimate criterion of the evaluation of his action. Methodological individualism and subjectivist value theory do not reduce our thinking about man to the category of *homo oeconomicus,* and the concept of negative freedom does not reduce man merely to creative transcendence but permits him to develop receptive transcendence, open to the truth. Mises' anthropological assumptions, therefore, allow us to presume that each man's potential action in the context of freedom can be a morally good act. Man for Mises is free to aim at his goals, and morality, as John Paul states, consists in "the rational ordering of the human act to the good in its truth and the voluntary pursuit of that good, known by reason."[188]

Mises' rational utilitarianism should not be conflated with Jeremy Bentham's (1748–1832) utilitarianism either. The British philosopher claimed that the purpose of politics is to enable the attainment of the greatest happiness by the greatest number of people.[189] This is certainly a desirable goal, but according to Mises the social sciences must deal with the world as it is, not as it should be. Mises' utilitarianism is not a ready doctrine but a point of view that permits practical evaluation of the goal. The Austrian economist showed that utilitarianism appeared to be a useful method of finding common ground for a comparison between liberalism, socialism, and state interventionism.[190] Social

---

[186] John Paul II, *Centesimus Annus,* no. 32.

[187] Mises, *Human Action,* 193.

[188] John Paul II, *Veritatis Splendor,* no. 72.

[189] J. G. Hülsmann, *Mises: The Last Knight of Liberalism* (Auburn, AL: Mises Institute, 2007), 307.

[190] Mises, *Nation, State and Economy,* 176.

institutions can be justified only to the degree to which they improve the living conditions of members of society. For Mises, it is obvious that they can be improved only through productive efforts and division of labor, which is more productive than individual actions. These conditions presume the choice of political institutions that minimize violence, and democracy provides such a function.[191]

A Well-Conceived Egoism

Mises claims that people collaborate with one another in a system of the social division of labor, for this best serves their interests.[192] Each man's action is from the formal point of view egoistic because it always aims at improvement in his state of satisfaction. It is so even when he tends to directly improve the situation of others; the cause of acting (uneasiness) is his awareness of the fact that other people are in want and he can help them. The actor at such moments considers his activity on behalf of others as more satisfactory for himself. The system based on private ownership ensures that well-conceived egoism integrates man's actions with the overall system of production, and that giving in to one's own "greed" contributes to the organization of productive actions. Calling people to be governed by the public good instead of private profit does not lead to the creation of a satisfactory social order. Mises rightly notes that it does not suffice to say that people should not be governed by profit; one must make clear rules that govern conduct under concrete circumstances.[193]

In their economic activity, people are motivated by various forms of "profit"—above all economic, but also others, such as altruism. The market mechanism takes into consideration all these factors, and the society of negative freedom permits everyone to behave in accord with his own ends.[194] A special role in the free-market economy is played by prices, which, although they do not show all essential information, create a dynamic market space where the actions of many dispersed

---

[191] J. G. Hülsmann, *Last Knight*, 411. This appreciation of democracy is subject to the limitations mentioned earlier in this chapter.

[192] Mises, *Human Action*, 242.

[193] Mises, *Human Action*, 243.

[194] M. Dzielski, ["Liberalism and Christianity"], in Dzielski, [*The Restoration of the Spirit—the Construction of Freedom*], ed. G. Luczkiewicz (Krakow, 1995), 137.

individuals with different ends can be harmonized.[195] The mechanism of market prices is appropriate not only for a community of people concentrated on drawing their own profits but also for a genuinely altruistic society. One may be directed by altruism only when one knows human needs, values, and preferences, and in the free-market system they are conveyed by means of prices. The price mechanism permits altruists to effectively order competitive plans of helping people in need and effectively grant them with respective means. If there are no market prices, as in the socialist system, altruists have little opportunity to attain the disinterested ends they regard as most important.[196] They may respond to the needs of only a small group of individuals, and they are never sure whether the profits of their action exceed the costs. The market is therefore a social institution that allows people to take effective action.[197]

According to Mises, a well-conceived egoism cannot be identified with treating a neighbor on the free market as a means to the attainment of one's own ends and making oneself absolute in the immanent order.[198] The Austrian philosopher stresses that man living in isolation does not have moral norms and can do without remorse whatever he or she deems profitable. As a member of society, however, he must take into account not only his direct profit but also the preference of the group in which he lives, because his life is dependent on social cooperation. These are only temporal sacrifices, and for Mises the individual does not have to sacrifice himself for others, because the continuous existence of society as an association of cooperating persons is in the interest of each individual.

Mises rejects the criticism of utilitarianism that sees in it only a pursuit of material goods and the neglect of higher ends. The accomplishment of the highest productivity from labor is for utilitarianism the highest end, but this does not mean that human existence is limited

---

[195] R. Garrison, "Austrian Economics as the Middle Ground: Comment on Loasby," in *Method, Process*, 31–38.

[196] D. R. Steele, *From Marx to Mises* (La Salle, IL: Open Court, 1992), 205.

[197] J. Meadowcroft, "Altruism, Self-Interest, and the Morality of the Private Sector: An Austrian Approach," *Journal of Markets & Morality* 10, no. 2 (Spring 2007): 361–63.

[198] S. Witek, ["Egoism"], in [*The Catholic Encyclopedia*], vol. 4, ed. G. Lukaszyk, L. Bienkowski, and F. Gryglewicz (Lublin, 1985), 704–5.

to the security of material pleasure. People tend to welfare and wealth not because they see in them the highest value, but because a higher and inner culture presumes external welfare.[199] We can agree with Mises, for scarcity of goods that satisfy basic needs makes it difficult for persons to move beyond the quest "to have" and on to the more important effort "to be."[200] It was already St. Thomas Aquinas who stressed the necessity to safeguard material conditions for the sake of spiritual development. He claimed that scarcity is linked with the danger of isolating man from his proper calling and reducing him to a purely biological creature.[201] Industrial civilization has brought much good to the development of man and whole societies.[202] But John Paul II stresses that accumulation of goods and services does not suffice to achieve real human happiness. The multitude of resources and opportunities at the disposal of man should be governed by a moral sense and oriented at the true good, for otherwise it may easily turn against man and lead to enslavement.[203]

Consumerism as a Philosophical Error

According to Mises, the market is the only method by which to adjust production to changing conditions. By means of price changes it forces people to restrict the production of articles less asked for and to expand the production of those articles for which consumers' demand is more urgent.[204] A key question in the analysis of consumerism arises here, namely how to distinguish artificial needs from real needs.[205] The structure of production and supply should always refer to real human

---

[199] Mises, *Nation, State and Economy*, 179.

[200] F. Kampka, ["*Homo consumens* in the World of Moral and Social Values"], in [*John Paul II, Centesimus Annus: Text and Commentary*], ed. F. Kampka and C. Ritter (Lublin, 1998), 313.

[201] I. Tokarczuk, ["Economic Conditions and Man's Spiritual Development according to St. Thomas Aquinas"], *Roczniki Teologiczno-Kanoniczne* 12, no. 3 (1965): 53–78.

[202] P. Goralczyk, ["Ethics in Economics"], *Communio* 6 (1997): 90.

[203] John Paul II, *Sollicitudo Rei Socialis*, no. 28.

[204] Mises, *Human Action*, 728.

[205] H. Marcuse, *One-Dimensional Man: Studies in the Ideology of Advanced Society* (Boston: Beacon Press, 1968), 4–5.

needs.[206] John Paul II indicates that a definite culture as a general conception of life is manifested in defining and creating consumer needs.[207] He is well aware that economic mechanisms alone are incapable of stimulating such a process; there is need of great work in the field of education and culture, which would embrace the preparation of consumers for responsible usage of the rights of choice.[208] It should be stressed that John Paul II interpreted the phenomenon of consumerism as a spiritual malady that has no strict relation with a particular regime or political-economic system.[209]

Consumerism originates not in the sphere of economics but on the level of culture. John Paul stresses that in the economic system itself there are no criteria for correctly distinguishing new and higher forms of satisfying human needs from artificial new needs.[210] Therefore he concludes that the free-market economy is not responsible for contemporary consumerism. The essence of the problem is inherent in a culture which, isolated from ethics, is conducive to the absolutization of the sphere of economics and creates a quasi-culture of economism with a pragmatic-hedonistic system of values.[211] The economy is only one aspect of human activities. Placing production and consumption of commodities in the center of social life makes the whole sociocultural system weaker. The pope's criticism of consumerism is not directed against a particular economic system. Like Mises, John Paul thinks that moral principles cannot directly determine the norms of economic activity. Mises rightly fears that such a solution would involve unambiguous commands as to what should be done and which choices to make, and this would limit the individual's right to choose and act.

In *Centesimus Annus*, there are four subjects responsible for the shaping and creating of proper consumer needs: consumers, producers, the media, and public authorities.[212] John Paul calls on the

---

[206] Kampka, ["*Homo consumens*"], 314.

[207] John Paul II, *Centesimus Annus*, no. 36.

[208] John Paul II, *Centesimus Annus*, no. 36.

[209] J. Schasting, *Unterwegs mit den Menschen: Kommentar zur Enzyklika "Centesimus Annus" von Johannes Paulus II* (Vienna, 1991), 90.

[210] John Paul II, *Centesimus Annus*, no. 36.

[211] M. Zieba, [*The Popes*], 120.

[212] John Paul II, *Centesimus Annus*, no. 36.

participants of market exchange to discover anew their freedom and order economic liberties in accord with full personal freedom. In like manner Mises claims that this sphere of freedom is an indispensable condition of freedom within a system of social cooperation under the division of labor.[213] The task of the media and public authorities consists above all in maintaining a proper system of values and shaping desired "lifestyles." The pope sees a need for a conscious strategy by which to transform mass culture, for in it definite, most often consumer, lifestyles are shaped and promoted; therefore the renewal of the system of values must begin in culture.[214] The teaching of the Church does not eliminate the drive for ever more satisfactory living standards and greater wealth, but neither does it accept the lifestyle that elevates *having* above *being*.[215] The role of the Church in opposing consumerism is essential and consists in educating for proper choices through a building of the civilization of love, because in the economic system alone there are no criteria that dictate a proper distinction between authentic needs and artificial needs.[216]

Mises claims that moral reforms, just like any other form of interventionism, hamper the market process and inevitably lead to authoritative control of the economy.[217] Accepting in full Mises' statement on government interventionism and its negative impact on the economy, we cannot agree with his attempts to identify moral reforms with interventionism in the market process.[218] In his *magnum opus*, Mises defines the market process not as a place or thing but as a process that is entirely a result of human actions.[219] In this context, it is difficult to agree with him when he fears the advocates of social reforms because they recommend that people of good will be governed in their

---

[213] Mises, *Human Action*, 729.

[214] R. J. Neuhaus, *Doing Well and Doing Good*, 205ff.

[215] John Paul II, *Centesimus Annus*, no. 36.

[216] J. Gocko and P. Janowski, ["Consumerism"], in [*The Catholic Encyclopedia*], vol. 9, ed. A. Szostek et al. (Lublin, 2002), 242.

[217] Mises, *Human Action*, 724.

[218] S. A. Beaulier and D. L. Prychitko, "Does Morality Hamper the Market Process? A Reappraisal of the Mises Thesis," *Journal of Markets & Morality* 4, no. 1 (Spring 2001): 45.

[219] Mises, *Human Action*, 258.

action on the free market by the voice of conscience in accord with the principles of Christianity and rules of "true" morality. On the free market, assuming the mode of Mises' argumentation, their action is in no way different than advertising whose aim is to be clever enough to persuade consumers into buying everything the producer wishes to sell. One cannot deny that in many cases concrete moral reformers and religious institutions resort to coercion applied by the state, but this does not mean that their original motivation was to introduce regimentation. Market limitations that seek to foster economic personalism are only moral limitations and have nothing in common with the typical solutions offered by the advocates of government interventionism. In order to persuade and strengthen individual conduct on the market in accord with the truth of the human person, economic personalists seek means that do not entail coercion.[220] Mises therefore makes a mistake that he should avoid as a proponent of praxeology. All his fears are based on historical observations, one of which is the attempt to apply the doctrine of a just wage, but praxeology cannot elicit general laws from historical examples.[221]

Economism and Moralism

Mises has proved that man is not a creature acting merely out of economic stimuli, meaning one that is governed solely by the desire for maximum material and financial benefits. Economics based on subjective value theory is not limited to the formulation of theorems dealing with the actions of self-interested people, nor does it depend on the fictional *homo economicus.* The subject matter of praxeology is all real categories of human action. Theories formulated by praxeology concerning prices of commodities, wages, and interest rates describe all these phenomena but neglect the motivation that makes people buy and sell or restrains them from buying and selling. It thus excludes two extreme positions in the relationship between the

---

[220] G. Gronbacher, "The Need for Economic Personalism," *Journal of Markets & Morality* 1, no. 1 (Spring 1998): 15.

[221] Beaulier and Prychitko, "Does Morality Hamper the Market Process?," 52.

economy and morality: economism and moralism. Instead it assumes an indirect position.[222]

Economism is manifested by the absolutizing of economic finality and in action based on the conviction that material reality is superior and generates rational behavior. Aniela Dylus stresses that such a model of behavior, defined as *homo economicus*, has for the last century become an independent anthropological conception.[223] Economism means that decisive priority is given to economic rationality over moral demands; in case of a possible conflict moral reasons must yield to the appointed economic goal.[224] The subjective value theory proposed by Mises does not allow us, however, to fall for extreme economism. Mises has proved that man in action is governed by his own scale of values when making a decision, on the basis of which he can satisfy first his most valued need. Man's ultimate goals in economics do not fall under evaluation from the point of view of absolute standards. Praxeology remains neutral and is interested only in whether the means used by man in action are appropriate to accomplish his goal from the formal point of view.

Economics as a science based on the praxeological categories of human action also protects us against falling into the second extreme, which Mises defines as moralism. Man discovers the reality of the laws of praxeology by means of the same signs that permit him to discern the laws of nature. Failing to observe them is automatically punished.[225] The position of moralism is most often assumed by ethicists or theologians who are dealing with an evaluation of socioeconomic reality without a thorough knowledge of economics, and they put unrealistic

---

222 A. Dylus, [*Extreme Morality as a Problem for Catholic Social Doctrine*] (Warsaw, 1992), 163.

223 A. Dylus, [*Extreme Morality as a Problem for Catholic Social Doctrine*] (Warsaw, 1992), 163.

224 J. Gocko, ["Conceptions of Economic Morality"], *Roczniki Teologiczne* 48, no. 3 (2001): 173.

225 Mises wrote in *Human Action*: "Only the insane venture to disregard physical and biological laws. But it is quite common to disdain praxeological laws. Rulers do not like to admit that their power is restricted by any laws other than those of physics and biology. They never ascribe their failures and frustrations to the violation of economic law" (762).

demands and postulates on the practice of economic life.[226] Unlawful claims regarding the subjects of economic life or unjust protests and condemnations of concrete decisions are born in an atmosphere of belief in a lawful subordination of the economy to morality.

According to Mises, placing economics within a broader perspective of the general principles of human action means that in theoretical reflection and practical activity we no longer have to be doomed to a choice between economism and moralism, between the economy and morality. The Second Vatican Council speaks on behalf of the recognition of a certain autonomy in the area of economics, which does not mean separating it from moral principles.[227] A proper relationship between economics and ethics, however, cannot be established by simplifications of reality. Giannino Piana, an Italian moral theologian, proposes a new model of the relationship between ethics and economics, which he defines as a "hermeneutic bond."[228] In this model, the antinomy between ethics and economics loses its anthropological foundations, for man is not so much an opposition of matter and nature as their extension in the area of culture. On the one hand he experiences a profound relationship with the world of things, recognizing its regularities, and on the other transforms it under the influence of his reference to the ethical order. Economic institutions are historical man's artifacts and belong to the area of culture. The market economy bears no action against economic rationality but itself is more than an automatic market mechanism.

Liberalism as a Political Doctrine

Murray N. Rothbard, in *The Ethics of Liberty*, asks if one can combine the libertarianism of Mises, for which Rothbard was an ardent advocate, with the principle of abstinence from value judgment in economics and do so without reference to the principles of objective ethics.[229] Mises claims that as an economist and praxeologist he can-

---

[226] Gocko, ["Conceptions"], 174.

[227] *Gaudium et Spes*, no. 36.

[228] G. Piana, "Razionalità etica e razionalità economica. Quale rapporto?," *Credere oggi* 46, no. 4 (1998): 59–61, quoted in Gocko, ["Conceptions"], 175–76.

[229] M. N. Rothbard, *The Ethics of Liberty* (New York: New York University Press, 1998), 206ff.

not promote libertarianism, but he can do it as a "citizen" who lives in a concrete cultural reality. He assumes that people prefer to live in welfare and health rather than poverty and hunger. The difference between praxeology and liberalism therefore consists in using differently the concepts of "happiness" and "removal of uneasiness." Praxeology uses them in a purely formal sense, claiming that man, while making decisions, is always directed by his own scale of values, and liberalism attaches to them a concrete meaning in practice from the point of view of a general political doctrine.[230]

Rothbard therefore is right that Misesian praxeology and utilitarianism do not suffice to promote libertarianism. One cannot agree, however, with his argument that in economics one should assume a kind of objective ethics, which will confirm the superior value of freedom and will condemn all forms of statism from the moral point of view.[231] Mises is right: praxeology and economics are neutral with respect to moral principles, and those who disagree with the laws of economics can refute them only by way of discursive reasoning, not by adhering to arbitrary if seemingly ethical standards.[232] Criticizing the policy of government interventionism as economist, Mises does not claim that government interference in the prices of commodities is bad, but he only proves that such interference leads to worse conditions, not to their improvement, which was the government's primary intention. Rothbard asks, however, how Mises knows that the advocates of price control have no such intentions and, as socialists, do not want to use this method for a gradual transformation of society into a collectivist economy. Mises himself answers this question. As a liberal, he grounds his claim on a belief that the decisive majority of people prefer welfare to poverty, and life to death. The author of *Human Action* does not have to refer to any principles of objective ethics, for it is not only that human action is based on the imperative of natural law—that good should be done—but also that the very laws of economics are based on the inclinations of human nature;

---

[230] Mises, *Human Action*, 154.

[231] Rothbard, *Ethics of Liberty*, 214.

[232] L. von Mises, "Epistemological Relativism in the Sciences of Human Action," in *Relativism and the Study of Man*, ed. H. Schoeck and J. W. Wiggins (Princeton: Princeton University Press, 1961), 133.

and the first of them—according to St. Thomas—is the preservation of one's own life.

Mises is an economist with a utilitarian bias and, as he himself says in his *magnum opus,* the economist cannot demand that man renounce his welfare for the good of society. His task is to show what the person's rightly understood interest consists in.[233] Social cooperation is for Mises the most important means for people to attain ends in accord with their needs. He thinks that social cooperation is more productive and effective, and wherever there are conflicts and the use of force, there can be no discussion of cooperation or social bonds. Debates and conflicts of interests in liberalism are solved through the division of labor, and biological and Hobbesian competition is replaced by free competition. Social cooperation, peace, and stability are conditions of human success and happiness. Misesian utilitarianism therefore concentrates on external outcomes and results.[234] On this basis, the Austrian economist rejects all concepts of society, state, or nation for which such social organization is an end in itself and that treat citizens like slaves.

Therefore he rejects the philosophies of universalism, collectivism, and totalitarianism, and, as he himself stresses, only in this sense can utilitarianism be called a philosophy of individualism.[235] Critics of liberalism present individualism as a drawback of the liberal conception of ethics and stress that it has an asocial character and lacks classical moral rules, including neighborly love.[236] One cannot agree with the statement that egoism automatically undermines a sense of moral rules, which of its nature should have an altruistic profile. On this understanding of altruism, whatever is done in the name of the good of others is something useful, and everything that is done in the name of self-interest is reprehensible.[237] Assuming such a conception would force man to live in a constant chasm between morality and practicality. A full altruism is unreachable, for it would be an annihila-

---

[233] Mises, *Human Action,* 146.

[234] E. W. Younkins, "Mises's Utilitarianism as Social Cooperation," *Le Quebecois Libre,* July 6, 2002, no. 165, www.quebecoislibre.org/020706-19.html.

[235] Mises, *Theory and History,* 39.

[236] S. Kowalczyk, [*Liberalism and Its Philosophy*] (Katowice, 1995), 164.

[237] Kwasnicki, [*History of Liberal Thought*], 207.

tion of itself. According to Mises, the only reasonable outcome that eliminates this conflict is the concern for self-interest, and thereby also concern about others in the system of social division of labor.

For Mises, as for other utilitarian thinkers, the basic value judgment is approval of happiness and disapproval of unhappiness. It should be stressed that for Mises the concepts of pleasure and pain, usefulness and uselessness, are applied in praxeology only in their formal sense and they are deprived of material content.[238] They refer to what man wishes to accomplish or to avoid. Therefore, one cannot agree with the criticism of liberalism that claims it is economism and concentrates on material-measurable values.[239] Mises agrees that the end of some individuals is only to improve their own situation; others, however, feel so uneasy about the troubles of their fellow men that they treat their worries as their own.[240]

Mises stresses that what counts for utilitarianism is only the question of social usefulness. Democratic rule, protection of private property, tolerance, and freedom do not result from the just nature of such institutions but from the utility that they bring to society. Methodological individualism, however, does not allow Mises to assume the presuppositions of utilitarians, for whom the ultimate end is the greatest possible happiness for the greatest number of people. Happiness supported by social institutions is not, according to Mises, happiness in general, nor does it refer to concrete persons.[241] The task of economics, therefore, is not to determine how to provide the maximum satisfaction for the greatest number of people.[242] Mises thus rejects the numerical conception of utilitarianism for which he has been unjustly attacked.

At the end of his work on socialism, Mises concludes that everyone who wants society to endure and develop must accept without reservations and limitations the private ownership of the means of production. The starting point for such reasoning is his vision of man and society

---

[238] L. von Mises, *Epistemological Problems of Economics*, trans. George Reisman (New York: New York University Press, 1976), 53–54.

[239] S. Kowalczyk, [*Liberalism*], 163.

[240] Mises, *Human Action*, 14.

[241] L. B. Yeager, "Mises and His Critics on Ethics, Rights, and Law," in *The Meaning of Ludwig von Mises*, 327.

[242] Mises, *Human Action*, 242.

based on freedom. In line with this vision, man can choose the way in which he wants to join a social life that consists in the fact that each serves his fellow citizens, and they in turn serve him.[243] In this way of understanding freedom, the government's task is only to ensure a peaceful and effective functioning of the market and to protect it against fraud or coercion.[244] The Misesian conception of the social order corresponds with the conception of the polycentric order,[245] in which social balance is accomplished spontaneously through "natural laws" of interaction in the form of individual decisions and respect for the norms of social cooperation. The social order therefore is not a static, determined-once-for-all state of affairs but is continuously constructed and maintained by the participants of social life.[246]

The form of government preferred by Mises, as we have seen, is democracy, for it gives the greatest guarantee to preserve internal peace. In her social teaching, the Church respects the legitimate autonomy of the democratic order but does not indicate any concrete institutional or constitutional solution.[247] She only points to objective and everlasting values of a categorical character, which have basic importance for personal and social life. In *Evangelium Vitae*, John Paul II stresses that democracy calls for a new discovery of moral values that belong to the essence and nature of man and result from the truth about man and protect his dignity. These values are prior to society, and no individual, the majority, or the state can create, change, or destroy them.[248] No legislation, however, is capable of removing anxieties, prejudices, or attitudes of egoism and pride, which stand

---

[243] Mises, *Economic Policy*, 19.

[244] Mises, *Economic Policy*, 55.

[245] In addition to the polycentric order, Stanislaw Ossowski distinguishes an order of collective representations and a monocentric order. S. Ossowski, ["Conceptions of the Social Order and Types of Representations"], in [*Peculiarities of the Social Sciences*], ed. S. Ossowski (Warsaw, 1983), 86.

[246] J. Marianski, ["Moral Order"], in [*The Catholic Encyclopedia*], vol. 11, ed. E. Zieman (Lublin, 2006), 348.

[247] John Paul II, *Centesimus Annus*, no. 47.

[248] John Paul II, Encyclical Letter *Evangelium Vitae* (1995), no. 71.

in the way of establishing truly brotherly communities.[249] Some problems that arise in a free society can be overcome only by the principle of solidarity, a firm and stable commitment to the common good.[250]

Mises is also aware that the striving for better conditions is never an inevitable process. A return to unsatisfactory conditions can occur at any moment as a result of abandoning economic calculation on which social cooperation on the basis of the division of labor depends. According to Mises, people must therefore choose between the market economy and socialism. The choice of a "third way" is impossible, for it inevitably leads to government interventionism. According to Mises, man is free only inasmuch as he can choose between various modes of action. The social teaching of the Church indicates, however, that true freedom calls for order in the sphere of values.[251]

In the end, we may firmly claim that morality is not limited to the correcting or integrating functions in relation to economic knowledge but that it has a fully constitutive function, for in fact it is on this function that man's further life and his civilization depend.[252] Completing *Human Action*, Mises wrote: "Capitalism gave the world what it needed, a higher standard of living for a steadily increasing number of people. But the liberals, the pioneers and supporters of capitalism, overlooked one essential point. A social system, however beneficial, cannot work if it is not supported by public opinion."[253]

---

[249] *Catechism of the Catholic Church*, no. 1931.

[250] John Paul II, *Sollicitudo Rei Socialis*, no. 38.

[251] ["John Paul II's Fifth Pilgrimage to his Homeland"], Sandomierz, 1997, in J. Poniewierski, ed., [*John Paul II, Pilgrimages to Homeland 1979, 1983, 1987, 1991, 1995, 1997, 1999, 2002: Addresses and Homilies*] (Krakow, 2005), 26.

[252] Goralczyk, ["Ethics"].

[253] Mises, *Human Action*, 864–65.

CONCLUSION

It is not easy to evaluate Misesian man acting in the economic sphere from the point of view of theology. The author of *Human Action* never used the term *person* in his description and analysis of human action. An analysis of his economic system, however, allows us to state that he does not understand the free-market economy as an abstract entity composed of mechanic elements to which society must adjust itself, but as an institution that remains in accord with human nature. Contemporary theology, which is more interested in the problem of the human person, due to the teaching of Wojtyła and his synthesis of personalism and free-market economics, permits us to grasp a potent relationship between Christianity and the principles of the free market based on subjective value theory.

The concept of the person is important both in theology and in economics. It refers to those characteristic traits of man that are important for his relationship with God and other people. Now the introduction of this concept in the history of thought has brought about two revolutionary changes that were essential for the development of economic thought. The first consists in the statement that there is a real and interpersonal relationship between autonomic persons, a key feature of the free-market exchange. The second, however, consists in implementing the concept of the person as a dynamic subject called to work on behalf of a better world. This subject is the main factor of economic growth. Without these basic Christian concepts, which present the person in interpersonal relations as a real being, the development of the market system and economics would not be possible.

Mises and the Austrian school of economics should be credited with the fact that today we can have a theological interpretation of the market system as a practical means by which to realize the history of salvation. According to Mises, the acting and thinking person can accomplish a broadly understood welfare only at the cost of effort and toil, or what we commonly call economic conduct. Struggling against the limitations of the world, which nature and the challenge of scarcity impose on man, is man's most important task. Scarcity, Mises says, is not a historical category but a constant element of the created world. This mystery of the "primary scarcity" that has existed from the beginning of the world and its continuous overcoming has been written into the history of the salvation of each person.

Each person, as Mises says, is always striving to increase the degree of his satisfaction and fulfillment. This seemingly egoistic and individualistic mode of thinking and acting corresponds with the truth of the sinful and imperfect nature of man who is constantly striving for perfection but is incapable of accomplishing it on his own. He must cooperate with others on the free market. The profits coming from the division of labor are always reciprocal. The free-market economy is an imperfect but effective means, making possible not only a dynamic and free exchange of goods and services on a great scale, but also the drawing of man out of the isolation typical of totalitarian governments and the overcoming of inertia typical of systems based on central planning. Human history is a history of people striving for perfection. The market system—and the economic growth that is its fruit—is an indispensable means for its attainment.

The most important implication of Christianity's introduction of the concept of person is that it provides an opportunity for a more profound understanding of the essence of social life, which for the Christian is always a reflection of an intimate relationship between the three distinct and loving Persons of the Holy Trinity. Mises shows that the market system, taken in its legal framework and controlled by a limited government within the confines determined by the laws of praxeology, is able to place entirely different and free subjects in the market in the position of creative cooperation. The faith in the Triune God gives Christians an additional and supernatural pattern for the market system and can make them capable of further development of a fruitful exchange and more effective allocation of resources with respect for the dignity of the other person.

Mises' analysis of man in action in the socioeconomic sphere allows us to understand how important economic knowledge is for proper moral judgment. Mises shows that the economic sciences' task is to describe a factual state of affairs, not determine how man should act. A detailed description of the laws governing human action in the economic sphere has enabled us to notice that acquaintance with the laws of economics is indispensable for a proper moral analysis. Moral judgment that is not supported by appropriate knowledge in this area has often led moralists astray; most frequently they have seen the solution for all crises in appealing to state intervention.

Mises claims that no ethical judgment can make an economic law invalid. This does not mean, however, that these principles should not be subjected to a theological-moral analysis and judged as to whether they fulfill the presuppositions of the personalist norm, which says that each person deserves affirmation on account of his or her intrinsic dignity. According to Mises, economics is knowledge about man in action. The task of theological analysis is to test whether it takes into account the special position of man as person and his respective identity and transcendence. Moral theology helps economics turn attention to the fact that this dependence between person and act has its ethical potentiality already in the ontic dimension. Mises' description of man in action in the economic sphere therefore satisfies basic requirements of the Christian concept of person as a rational, free, and transcendent being.

The causal-realistic approach to economics that Mises assumes coheres with Catholic social doctrine. This way of perceiving reality allows us to comprehend the world and its nature as an order of interdependence created by God out of nothing in time and governed by natural laws established by him. The laws of economics are also based on these laws. Rejecting mathematization of economics and artificial neoclassical models that reduce man to an impersonal atom, Mises has proved that economics is knowledge about man endowed with reason and free will. This is the principal reason economics has an exceptional character, and the reason its method differs from the mode of examining the world of animals and inanimate objects. Mises' statement that people endowed with reason and free will occupy an exceptional place in the world has enormous importance as a starting point for theological analysis, for it allows us to speak about the unusual dignity of man that he receives from God in the act of creation. Despite his sinful nature, from the ontological point of view man is always placed higher than the rest of created reality. The value of the person comes from the ontological significance of his or her being, not only from individual effort, talent, or personal accomplishments.

Analysis of Misesian man's action in the socioeconomic sphere is mainly based on the personalist defense of the free market and the evidence that free-market structures create social conditions for the affirmation of human dignity. The free market enhances many values and customs, which together create just social structures through respect for human nature. We find here above all respect for private ownership and its unconditional protection. Christian anthropology from the very beginning has approved of private ownership as a justified right of the person and natural extension of the sphere of human freedom. Now we owe it to Mises that we can see more clearly that not only does private ownership allow man to better manage material goods, but on the free market it is linked with the common destination of material wealth. The free usage of one's own property takes place only in the free-market system, and in this sense we may say that it respects human autonomy. Private ownership guarantees the indispensable space of negative freedom for the realization of a life-calling. It also furnishes an opportunity to practice neighborly love.

Mises has proved that only the free market is effective in producing and distributing economics goods. The accumulation of goods, however, is not an end in itself, and man does not think only in the categories of *homo economicus.* Not all forms of the good remain in harmony with human dignity, but it should be admitted that accumulated goods raise the general standard of life and contribute to the enhancement of its quality. Our analysis has shown that genuine economic development cannot be accomplished without referring to moral values. The market can contribute to the development of specific virtues in man, such as confidence, courage, frugality, and creativity, but the market itself at the same time needs them to function properly. They are indispensable because the first and most important form of economic wealth is the human person. Water, cultivated land, and natural resources in themselves have enormous value for people, but they require human intelligence and labor to be used effectively. Together with the development of technology and civilization, human intelligence and creativity become the most valuable assets of the human person.

The goal of this book was an analysis of man in action in the economic sphere that we find in the Austrian economist and philosopher Ludwig von Mises, from the point of view of Christian personalism, which explains a seeming contradiction between objective moral values and the subjective process of economic valuation. Mises persuades us that the promotion of the free market can contribute to the development of the economic order that draws its benefit from the market exchange and does not reduce the human person to a mechanical element in the social system of the division of labor. The personalist norm was already used as the basic principle of thinking in ethics, political philosophy, and social policy. Mises has shown us that it can also be successfully employed in economics. The analysis of his thought allows us to better understand from the theological point of view the theoretical bases of a true economics. In recent times, the collapse of the banking system teaches us again that there is a sphere of justified autonomy of the economy in which the state should not interfere. Loyalty to the social doctrine of the Church obliges us to reject the current, dominant system of state interventionism and to build the economy based on an economics that approves of the principal and positive role of the market.

Freedom, including economic freedom, must be based on solid moral foundations that emphasize the innate value and dignity of the human person. In his papal social teaching, John Paul II reminds us that the free market is only one of the elements of a free society. Market exchange is a powerful source of social transformations, but it would be a mistake to reduce all aspects of life to the market dimension. Mises is aware that many aspects of human life are not subject to the market game. He is also aware that free economics has its natural limitations, including human imperfection and weakness. Free economics therefore must always remain open to the influence of cultural institutions, because without their moral support the economy cannot properly function and develop in a free society.

Bibliography

Titles in brackets indicate English translations of the sources' original Polish titles.

Church Documents

All documents available at www.vatican.va unless otherwise noted.

The Catechism of the Catholic Church. 1993.

Second Vatican Council. Declaration on Religious Freedom *Dignitatis Humanae.* December 7, 1965.

Second Vatican Council. Pastoral Constitution on the Church in the Modern World *Gaudium et Spes.* December 7, 1965.

Second Vatican Council. Declaration on Christian Education *Gravissimum Educationis.* October 28, 1965.

Second Vatican Council. Dogmatic Constitution on the Church *Lumen Gentium.* November 21, 1964.

First Vatican Council. Dogmatic Constitution on the Catholic Faith *Dei Filius.* April 24, 1870, http://www.catholicplanet.org/councils/20-Dei-Filius.htm.

Congregation for the Doctrine of the Faith. Doctrinal Note on Some Questions Regarding the Participation of Catholics in Political Life. November 24, 2002.

Congregation for the Doctrine of the Faith. Instruction on Christian Freedom and Liberation *Libertatis Conscientia.* March 22, 1986.

Pontifical Council for Justice and Peace. *Compendium of the Social Doctrine of the Church.* 2004.

Benedict XVI. Address of His Holiness Benedict XVI to the Participants in the 14th Session of the Pontifical Academy Social Sciences, May 3, 2008.

Benedict XVI. Encyclical Letter *Spe Salvi,* November 30, 2007.

Benedict XVI. Encyclical Letter *Deus Caritas Est.* December 25, 2005.

Paul VI. Encyclical Letter *Populorum Progressio.* March 26, 1967.

Paul VI. Address to the United Nations Organization. October 4, 1965.

John XXIII. Encyclical Letter *Pacem in Terris.* April 11, 1963.

John XXIII. Encyclical Letter *Mater et Magistra.* May 15, 1961.

Pius XII. Encyclical Letter *Humani Generis.* August 12, 1950

Pius XII. Encyclical Letter *Summi Pontificatus.* October 20, 1939.

Pius XII. Christmas Message of 1942, www.papalencyclicals.net/Pius12/P12CH42.HTM.

Pius XI. Encyclical Letter *Quadrogesimo Anno.* May 15, 1931.

Leo XIII. Encyclical Letter *Rerum Novarum.* May 15, 1891.

Writings of Pope John Paul II/Karol Wojtyła

All documents available at www.vatican.va unless otherwise noted.

Message for the Celebration of the World Day of Peace. January 1, 2000

Address to the Participants in the Fifth General Assembly of the Pontifical Academy of Social Sciences. March 6, 1999.

Encyclical Letter *Fides et Ratio.* September 14, 1998.

Message for the Celebration of the World Day of Peace. January 1, 1999.

Message for the Celebration of the World Day of Peace. January 1, 1998.

Address to the Academy of Social Sciences. April 25, 1997.

["John Paul II's Fifth Pilgrimage to his Homeland"]. Sandomierz, 1997. In [*John Paul II, Pilgrimages to Homeland 1979, 1983, 1987, 1991, 1995, 1997, 1999, 2002. Addresses and Homilies*]. Edited by J. Poniewierski. Krakow, 2005.

Address to an International Conference for Representatives of Trade Unions. December 2, 1996.

Address to the Fiftieth General Assembly of the United Nations Organization. October 5, 1995.

Encyclical Letter *Evangelium Vitae.* March 25, 1995.

Letter to Families *Gratissimam Sane.* February 2, 1994.

Message for the XXVII World Day of Peace. January 1, 1994.

Encyclical Letter *Veritatis Splendor.* August 6, 1993.

Encyclical Letter *Centesimus Annus.* May 1, 1991.

Apostolic Exhortation *Christifideles Laici.* December 30, 1988.

Address to workers in Melo, Uruguay. May 8, 1988. *Origins,* May 26, 1988.

Encyclical Letter *Sollicitudo Rei Socialis.* December 30, 1987.

Apostolic Exhortation *Familiaris Consortio.* November 22, 1981.

Encyclical Letter *Laborem Exercens.* September 14, 1981.

Address to UNESCO. June 2, 1980, www.inters.org/John-Paul-II-UNESCO-Culture.

Encyclical Letter *Redemptor Hominis.* March 4, 1979.

Wojtyła, K. *The Acting Person.* Translated by A. Potocki. Dordrecht: R. Reidel, 1979.

Wojtyła, K. ["The Problem of Constituting Culture Through Human Praxis"] *Roczniki Filozoficzne* (no. 1, 1979).

Writings of Ludwig von Mises

Most titles available online at Mises.org.

Memoirs. Translated by A. Oost-Zinner. Auburn, AL: Mises Institute, 2009.

"The Individual in Society." In *Economic Freedom and Interventionism: An Anthology of Articles and Essays.* Edited by B. Bien-Greaves. Indianapolis: Liberty Fund, 2007.

Economic Policy: Thoughts for Today and Tomorrow. Auburn, AL: Ludwig von Mises Institute, 2006.

Nation, State and Economy: Contribution to the Politics and History of our Time. Translated by L. B. Yeager. Indianapolis: Liberty Fund, 2006.

The Ultimate Foundation of Economic Science: An Essay on Method. 1962; repr., Indianapolis: Liberty Fund, 2006.

Theory and History: An Interpretation of Social and Economic Evolution. 1957; repr., Indianapolis: Liberty Fund, 2005.

Liberalism in the Classical Tradition. Translated by R. Raico. Irvington-on-Hudson, NY: Foundation for Economic Education, 2002.

"The Equations of Mathematical Economics and the Problem of Economic Calculation in a Socialist State." *Quarterly Journal of Austrian Economics* 3, no. 1 (Spring 2000).

Interventionism: An Economic Analysis. Irvington-on-Hudson, NY: Foundation for Economic Education, 1998.

"The Austrian Theory of the Trade Cycle." In *Theory of the Trade Cycle and Other Essays.* Edited by R.M. Ebeling. Auburn, AL: Mises Institute, 1996.

The Anti-Capitalistic Mentality. Grove City, PA: Libertarian Press, 1994.

"Observation on the Russian Reform Movement." In *Money, Method, and the Market Process: Essays by Ludwig von Mises.* Edited by R. M. Ebeling. Auburn, AL: Mises Institute; and Norwell, MA: Kluwer Academic, 1990.

"On Equality and Inequality." In *Money, Method, and the Market Process: Essays by Ludwig von Mises.* Edited by R. M. Ebeling. Auburn, AL: Mises Institute; and Norwell, MA: Kluwer Academic, 1990.

"Social Science and Natural Science." In *Money, Method, and the Market Process: Essays by Ludwig von Mises.* Edited by R. M. Ebeling. Auburn, AL: Mises Institute; and Norwell, MA: Kluwer Academic, 1990.

"The Non-Neutrality of Money." In *Money, Method, and the Market Process: Essays by Ludwig von Mises.* Edited by R. M. Ebeling. Auburn, AL: Mises Institute; and Norwell, MA: Kluwer Academic, 1990.

"The Treatment of 'Irrationality' in the Social Sciences." In *Money, Method, and the Market Process: Essays by Ludwig von Mises.* Edited by R. M. Ebeling. Auburn, AL: Mises Institute; and Norwell, MA: Kluwer Academic, 1990.

Bureaucracy, Grove City, PA: Libertarian Press, 1983.

The Theory of Money and Credit. Translated by H. E. Batson. 1934; repr., Indianapolis: Liberty Fund, 1981.

Planned Chaos. Irvington-on-Hudson, NY: Foundation for Economic Education, 1977.

Epistemological Problems of Economics. Translated by George Reisman. New York: New York University Press, 1976.

Omnipotent Government: The Rise of the Total State and Total War. 1944; repr., New Rochelle, NY: Arlington House, 1969.

The Historical Setting of the Austrian School of Economics. New Rochelle, NY: Arlington House, 1969.

Human Action: A Treatise on Economics. Chicago: Contemporary Books, 1966.

"Epistemological Relativism in the Sciences of Human Action." In *Relativism and the Study of Man.* Edited by H. Schoeck, and J. W. Wiggins. Princeton: Princeton University Press, 1961.

Socialism: An Economic and Sociological Analysis. Translated by J. Kahane. New Haven, CT: Yale University Press, 1951.

Secondary Literature

Acton, Lord John. *The History of Freedom.* Grand Rapids, MI: Acton Institute, 1993.

Baeck, L. "Spanish Economic Thought: The Social School of Salamanca and the Arbitristas." *History of Political Economy* 20, no. 3 (Spring 1988).

Bartnik, C. ["Agatic-Telematic Structure of Reality"]. *Philosophical Annals* 41 (1994).

Bartnik, C. ["Nature, Person, and Freedom"]. *Bobolanum* 4 (1993).

Bartnik, C. [*Personalism*]. Lublin 1995.

Bastiat, F. "What Is Seen and What Is Not Seen." In Bastiat, *Selected Essays on Political Economy.* Translated by S. Cain. Irvington-on-Hudson, NY: Foundation for Economic Education, 1995.

Beabout, Gregory R., et al. *Beyond Self-Interest: A Personalist Approach to Human Action.* Lanham, MD: Lexington Books, 2002.

Beaulier, S. A., and D. L. Prychitko. "Does Morality Hamper the Market Process? A Reappraisal of the Mises Thesis." *Journal of Markets & Morality* 4, no. 1 (Spring 2001): 43–54.

Berlin, I. *Four Essays on Liberty.* London: Oxford University Press, 1969.

Biesaga, T. ["K. Rahner's Personalism and K. Wojtyła's Personalism in the Debate on Moral Theology"]. *Analekta Cracoviensia* 32 (2000).

Blaug, M. *Economic Theory in Retrospect.* Cambridge: Cambridge University Press, 1990.

Buttiglione, R. *Karol Wojtyła: The Thought of the Man Who Became Pope John Paul II.* Translated by Paolo Guietti and Francesca Murphy. Grand Rapids, MI: Eerdmans, 1997.

Callahan, G. *Economics for Real People: An Introduction to the Austrian School.* Auburn, AL: Mises Institute, 2004.

Chafuen, A. A. *Faith and Liberty: The Economic Thought of the Late Scholastics.* Lanham, MD: Lexington Books, 2003.

Chafuen, A. A, and L. P. Liggio. "Cultural and Religious Foundations of Private Property." Unpublished typescript.

Cleveland, P. A. "Connections between the Austrian School of Economics and Christian Faith: A Personalist Approach." *Journal of Markets & Morality* 6, no 2 (Spring 2003).

Crosby, J. F. *The Selfhood of the Human Person.* Washington, DC: Catholic University of America Press, 1996.

Cross, D. E. "Wojtyła's Thought, John Paul II's Pontificate." *Religion & Liberty* (January/February 1988).

Curran, C. E. "The Common Good and Official Catholic Social Teaching." In *The Common Good and U.S. Capitalism.* Edited by O. F. Williams and J. Houck. Lanham, MD: University Press of America, 1987.

Czajkowski, J. [*Society, Nation, State in the Thought of John Paul II*]. Krakow, 1991.

Dec, I. ["Realistic Philosophy versus Man's Self-Fulfillment"]. In [*Towards the Revival of Man and Society*]. Edited by I. Dec. Wroclaw, 1996.

Dylus, A. [*Extreme Morality as a Problem for Catholic Social Doctrine*]. Warsaw, 1992.

Dzielski, M. ["Liberalism and Christianity"]. In Dzielski, [*The Restoration of the Spirit—the Construction of Freedom*]. Edited by G. Luczkiewicz. Krakow, 1995.

Ebeling, R. M. *The Age of Economists: From Adam Smith to Milton Friedman.* Hillsdale, MI: Hillsdale College Press, 1999.

Egger, W. H. "The Contributions of W. H. Hutt." *Review of Austrian Economics* 7, no. 1 (1993).

Engels, F. *Origin of the Family, Private Property, and the State.* 1884. http://www.marxists.org/archive/marx/works/download/pdf/origin_family.pdf.

Finn, D. R. "The Economic Personalism of John Paul II: Neither Right Nor Left." *Journal of Markets & Morality* 1, no. 1 (Spring 1999).

Galkowski, J. ["Labor According to Cardinal K. Wojtyła"]. *Philosophical Annals* 2 (1979).

Galkowski, J. ["Labor and the World"]. *W drodze* 5 (1977).

Galkowski, J. ["The Problem of Labor in Papal Encyclicals"]. *Annals of the Social Sciences* 1 (1991/1992).

Giertych, W. ["Unused Capital"]. *W drodze* 2 (2008).

Gniadek, J., SVD. ["Christian Hospitality for the Stranger as a Challenge for the Restrictive Policy of Immigration of the States of the European Commonwealth"]. *Nurt SVD* (no. 3/4, 2007).

Gniadek, J., SVD. ["The Social Dimension of Private Ownership in the Free-Market Economy according to Ludwig von Mises"]. *Forum Teologiczne* 11 (2010): 51–66.

Gocko, J. ["Conceptions of Economic Morality"]. *Roczniki Teologiczne* 48, no. 3 (2001).

Gocko, J. ["The Moral Problem of the Principle of the Autonomy of Earthly Realities"]. *Roczniki Teologiczne* 3 (2004).

Gocko, J., and P. Janowski. ["Consumerism"]. In [*The Catholic Encyclopedia*], vol. 9. Edited by A. Szostek et al. Lublin 2002.

Goralczyk, P. ["Ethics in Economics"]. *Communio* 6 (1997).

Gordon, D. "Justice and Redistributive Taxation: James Buchanan versus Ludwig von Mises." *Review of Austrian Economics* 8 (1994): 117–131.

Granat, W. [*Christian Personalism: The Theology of the Human Person*]. Poznan 1985.

Gray, J. *Liberalism.* Minneapolis: University of Minnesota Press, 1986.

Gronbacher, G. M. A. *Economic Personalism: A New Paradigm for a Humane Economy.* Grand Rapids, MI: Acton Institute, 1998.

Gronbacher, G. M. A. "The Need for Economic Personalism." *Journal of Markets & Morality* 1, no. 1 (Spring 1998).

Gruszecki, T. ["The Enterprise (Firm) and the Market in Contemporary Economics and in the Social Doctrine of the Church"]. In [*Centesimus Annus: The Text and Commentaries*]. Edited by F. Kampka and C. Ritter. Lublin, 1998.

Gwiazdowski, R. ["Taxes as Theft"]. In [*Theft and Economic Development*]. Edited by A. A. Chafuen et al. Warsaw, 2006.

Hayek, F. A. von. *Individualism and Economic Order.* Chicago: University of Chicago Press, 1948.

Hayek, F. A. von. *Law, Legislation and Liberty*, vol. 1: *Rules of Order.* Chicago: University of Chicago Press, 1978.

Hayek, F. A. von. *The Fatal Conceit: The Errors of Socialism.* Chicago: University of Chicago Press, 1989.

Hengel, M. *Property and Riches in the Early Church: Aspects of a Social History of Early Christianity.* Translated by J. Bowden. Philadelphia: Fortress Press, 1974.

Hilaire, Y. M. ["Catholics Did Not Always Abhor Money"]. *Communio* 6 (1997).

Himmelfarb, G. *Lord Acton: A Study in Conscience and Politics.* San Francisco: ICS Studies, 1993.

Hoppe, H.-H. *The Misesian Case against Keynes.* Mises Institute, January 28, 2009. mises.org/daily/2492.

Hoppe, H.– H. *Democracy—The God That Failed: The Economics and Politics of Monarchy, Democracy, and Natural Order.* New Brunswick: Transaction, 2001.

Hoppe, H.–H. "How is Fiat Money Possible?—or, The Devaluation of Money and Credit." *Review of Austrian Economics* 7, no. 2, 1994.

Hülsmann, J. G. "Facts and Counterfactuals in Economic Law." *Journal of Libertarian Studies* 17 (Winter 2003).

Hülsmann, J. G. *The Ethics of Money Production.* Auburn, AL: Mises Institute, 2008.

Jankowski, A. ["St. Paul's Letters from Prison"]. In [*The Holy Scripture of the New Testament. An Introduction—Translation from the Original—Commentary*], vol. 8. Edited by E. Dabrowski. Poznan, 2006.

Jaruzelska, I. [*Property in the Biblical Law*]. Warsaw, 1992.

Jaworski, M. ["The Endangered Man and the Merciful God: An Anthropological Method in the Encyclical *Dives in misericordia*"]. *W drodze* 4 (1981).

Kaminski, S. ["Autonomy"]. In [*The Catholic Encyclopedia*], vol. 1, 1160. Edited by F. Gryglewicz, R. Lukaszyk, and Z. Sulowski. Lublin, 1973.

Kampka, F. ["*Homo consumens* in the World of Moral and Social Values"]. In [*John Paul II, Centesimus annus: Text and Commentary*]. Edited by F. Kampka and C. Ritter. Lublin, 1998.

Karkowski, A. ["Usury"]. In [*A Dictionary of Catholic Social Doctrine*]. Edited by A. Piwowarski. Warsaw, 1993.

Kirzner, I. M. "Mises and his Understanding of the Capitalist System." *Cato Journal* 19, no. 2 (Spring 1999).

Kowalczyk, S. [*Liberalism and its Philosophy*]. Katowice, 1995.

Krapiec, M. A. M. ["The Common Good and the Threat of Alienation"]. In [*At the Sources of the Identity of European Culture*]. Edited by T. Rakowski. Lublin, 1994.

Krapiec, M. A. M. [*Human Freedom and its Limits*]. Lublin, 2000.

Krapiec, M. A. M. [*Man and the Natural Law*]. Lublin, 1999.

Krapiec, M. A. M. [*Man as Person*]. Lublin, 2005.

Krucina, J. ["The Common Good"] In [*The Catholic Encyclopedia*], vol. 3. Edited by R. Lukaszyk, L. Bienkowski, and F. Gryglewicz. Lublin, 1979.

Krzysztofowicz, J., OP. ["Liberalism versus the Social Teaching of the Church on the Common Good—On the Basis of Ludwig von Mises' Thought"] *Teofil* 2 (1998).

Kwasnicki, W. [*History of Liberal Thought*]. Warsaw, 2000.

Landreth, H., and D. C. Colander. *History of Economic Thought.* Boston: Houghton Mifflin, 2002.

Lesniak, M. ["Natural Law"]. In [*The Encyclopedia of John Paul II's Social Teaching*]. Edited by A. Zwolinski. Radom, 2003.

Lindenberg, A. *The Free Market in a Christian Society.* Translated by D. H. Sandin. Washington, DC: St. Antoninus Institute, 1999.

Locke, J. *Second Treatise of Government.* 1689. Some Texts from Early Modern History, http://www.earlymoderntexts.com/authors/locke.

Luckey, W. R. "The Economics of Bertrand de Jouvenel." *Journal of Markets & Morality* 1, no. 2 (October 1998): 169–91.

Majka, J. [*Considerations on the Ethics of Labor*]. Wroclaw, 1986.

Majka, J. [*Social and Political Ethics*]. Warsaw, 1993.

Majka, J. [*Social Philosophy*]. Wroclaw, 1982.

Majka, J. [*The Ethics of Economic Life*]. Warsaw, 1982.

Makowski, T. ["The Present Understanding of Natural Law in the Light of the Official Teaching of the Church"]. *Ateneum Kaplanskie* 81, no. 2 (1973).

Marcuse, H. *One-Dimensional Man: Studies in the Ideology of Advanced Society.* Boston: Beacon Press, 1968.

Marianski, J. ["Moral Order"]. In [*The Catholic Encyclopedia*], vol. 11, 348. Edited by E. Zieman. Lublin, 2006.

Maritain, J. [*Man and the State*]. Translated by A. Grobler. Krakow, 1988.

Maritain, J. [*Philosophical Writings*]. Translated by J. Fenrychowej. Krakow, 1988.

Marx, K. and Engels F. *The Communist Manifesto.* Arlington Heights, IL: Harlan Davidson, 1955.

Marx, K. *Theses on Feuerbach.* https://www.marxists.org/archive/marx/works/1845/theses/theses.htm.

Mazurek, F. ["Property"]. In [*A Dictionary of Catholic Social Doctrine*]. Edited by A. Piwowarski. Warsaw, 1993.

Meadowcroft, J. "Altruism, Self-Interest, and the Morality of the Private Sector: An Austrian Approach." *Journal of Markets & Morality* 10, no. 2 (Spring 2007): 357–73.

Menger, C. *Principles of Economics.* Translated by J. Dingwall and B. F. Hoselitz. Grove City, PA: Libertarian Press, 1994.

Menger, C. *Problems of Economics and Sociology.* Edited by Louis Schneider. Translated by Francis J. Nock. Urbana: University of Illinois Press, 1963.

Mill, J. S. *Utilitarianism.* Indianapolis: Bobbs-Merrill, 1957.

Murphy, R. P. "Consumer Sovereignty: What Mises Meant." Mises Institute, April 4, 2018. http://mises.org/library/consumer-sovereignty-what-mises-meant.

Murphy, R. P. "The Rothbardian Critique of Consumer Sovereignty." Mises Institute, April 13, 2018. http://direct.mises.org/library/rothbardian-critique-consumer-sovereignty.

Nell-Breuning, O. von. *Reorganization of Social Economy: The Social Encyclical Developed and Explained.* New York: Bruce Publishing, 1936.

Neuhaus, R. J. *Doing Well and Doing Good: The Challenge to the Christian Capitalist.* New York: Doubleday, 1992.

Novak, M. *Freedom with Justice: Catholic Social Thought and Liberal Institutions.* New York: Harper & Row, 1984.

Novak, M. *Free Persons and the Common Good.* Lanham, MD: Madison Books, 1989.

Novak, M. *The Catholic Ethic and the Spirit of Capitalism.* New York: Free Press, 1993.

Novak, M. ["Who Thirst for Righteousness ... Defining Social Justice"] *Tygodnik Powszechny* 31 (2006).

Nowak, S. ["The Bond with God Through Work"]. In [*Laborem exercens: Text and Commentary*]. Edited by J.W. Gałkowski. Lublin, 1986.

Olejnik, S. [*Moral Theology: The Gift, Calling, Response*], vol. 2. [*Man and His Action*]. Warsaw, 1988.

Olejnik, S. [*Moral Theology: The Gift, Calling, Response*], vol. 5. [*Service to God and Openness to the World*]. Warsaw, 1991.

Olejnik, S. [*Moral Theology: The Gift, Calling, Response*], vol. 7. [*Morality of Social Life*]. Warsaw, 1993.

Ossowski, S., ed. ["Conceptions of the Social Order and Types of Representations"]. In [*Peculiarities of the Social Sciences*]. Warsaw, 1983.

Pegis, A. C., ed. *Introduction to St. Thomas Aquinas, The Summa Theologica, The Summa Contra Gentiles.* New York: The Modern Library, 1948.

Persky, J. "The Ethnology of Homo Oeconomicus." *Journal of Economic Perspectives* 9, no. 2 (1995).

Piana, G. "Razionalità etica e razionalità economica. Quale rapporto?," *Credere oggi* 46, no. 4 (1998).

Pipes, R. [*Property and Freedom*]. Translated from the original English by L. Niedzielski. Warsaw, 2000.

Piwowarski, W. ["Nation"]. In [*A Dictionary of Catholic Social Doctrine*]. Edited by A. Piwowarski. Warsaw, 1993.

Piwowarski, W. ["The Principle of Subsidiarity"]. In [*A Dictionary of Catholic Social Doctrine*]. Edited by A. Piwowarski. Warsaw, 1993.

Piwowarski, W. ["The Subsidiary State in Catholic Social Doctrine"]. *Chrzescijanin w Swiecie* 2 (1993).

Piwowarski, W. ["Unemployment"]. In [*A Dictionary of Catholic Social Doctrine*]. Edited by A. Piwowarski. Warsaw, 1993.

Pokrywka, M. ["The Primacy of the Human Person in Social Life"]. *Roczniki Teologiczne* 47, no. 3 (2000).

Raico, R. "The Austrian School and Classical Liberalism." In *Advances in Austrian Economics*, vol. 2. Edited by P. Boetker, I. M. Kirzner, and M. J. Rizzo. Greenwich, CT: JAI Press, 1995.

Rauscher, A., SJ. ["Private Ownership in the Service of Man"]. In M. Novak, A Rauscher, SJ, and M. Zięba, OP. [*Christianity, Democracy, and Capitalism*]. Poznań, 1993.

Riber, M. [*Labor in the Bible*]. Translated by Z. Zwolska. Warsaw, 1979.

Robbins, L. C. *An Essay on the Nature and Significance of Economic Science.* London: Macmillan, 1932.

Rothbard, M. N. *An Austrian Perspective on the History of Economic Thought*, vol. 1. *Economic Thought before Adam Smith.* Auburn, AL: Mises Institute, 2006.

Rothbard, M. N. *Classical Economics: An Austrian Perspective on the History of Economic Thought*, vol. 2. Auburn, AL: Mises Institute, 2006.

Rothbard, M. N. *For a New Liberty: The Libertarian Manifesto.* New York: Libertarian Review Foundation, 1989.

Rothbard, M. N. "In Defense of Extreme Apriorism." *Southern Economic Journal* (January 1957).

Rothbard, M. N. *Man, Economy and State: A Treatise on Economic Principles; with Power and Market: Government and the Economy*, Scholar's Edition. Auburn, AL: Mises Institute, 2004.

Rothbard, M. N. "Praxeology: The Methodology of Austrian Economics." In *Economic Controversies.* Auburn, AL: Mises Institute, 2011.

Rothbard, M. N. *What Has Government Done to Our Money?* Auburn, AL: Mises Institute, 1990.

Rybka, R., OP. ["The Common Good: A Relict of the Past or a Concrete Task for Today and for Tomorrow?"]. *Teofil* 2 (1998).

Sadovsky, J. *The Christian Response to Poverty.* London: Social Affairs Unit, 1985.

Santelli, A. J., et al. *The Free Person and the Free Economy: A Personalist View of Market Economics.* Lanham, MD: Lexington Books, 2002.

Schasting, J. *Unterwegs mit den Menschen: Kommentar zur Enzyklika "Centesimus annus" von Johannes Paulus II.* Vienna, 1991.

Selgin, G. A. "Praxeology and Understanding: An Analysis of the Controversy in Austrian Economics." *Review of Austrian Economics* 2 (1988): 19–58.

Sennholz, H. F. *Age of Inflation.* Belmont, MA: Western Islands, 1979.

Skobel, S. "Real Theft and Apparent Theft." *Communio* 1 (1999).

Slipko, T. [*An Outline of Applied Ethics*], vol. 1. Krakow, 1982.

Smith, J. "Natural Law and Personalism in *Veritatis Splendor.*" In *Veritatis Splendor: American Responses.* Edited by E. Allsopp and J. J. O'Keefe. Kansas City, MO: Sheed and Ward, 1995.

Soto, H. de. *The Mystery of Capital: Why Capitalism Triumphs in the West and Fails Everywhere Else.* New York: Basic Books, 2000.

Soto, J. H. de. *Money, Bank Credit and Economic* Cycles. Auburn, AL: Mises Institute, 2006.

Soto, J. H. de. "The Ongoing Methodenstreit of the Austrian School," *Journal des Économistes et des Études Humaines* 8, no. 1 (March 1998): 1–40.

Steele, D. R. *From Marx to Mises: Post-Capitalist Society and the Challenge of Economic Calculation.* La Salle, IL: Open Court, 1992.

Styczen, T. [*An Outline of Ethics: Metaethics*]. Lublin, 1974.

Styczen, T. ["The Personal Dignity of the Subject of Labor as a Source of its Sense and Value"]. In [*John Paul II, Laborem exercens: Text and Commentary*]. Edited by J. Chmiel and S. Ryłko. Lublin, 1986.

Szostek, A. ["Alienation: The Ever-Current Problem"] In [*John Paul II, Centesimus annus: Text and Commantary*]. Edited by F. Kampka and C. Ritter. Lublin, 1998.

Szostek, A. [*Nature—Reason—Freedom. A Philosophical Analysis of the Conception of Creative Reason in Contemporary Moral Theology*]. Rome, 1990.

Szostek, A. [*On the Dignity of Truth and Love*]. Lublin, 1995.

Szymczek, J. ["What State: Welfare or Subsidiary?"] *Chrzescijanin w swiecie* 2 (1993).

Terpilowski, W. [*The Problem of Labor in the Church's Post-Conciliar Teaching: The Moral-Social Aspect*]. Swidnica, 2006.

Thomas Aquinas. *Commentary on the Letter of Saint Paul to the Romans.* Translated by F. R. Larcher, OP. Lander: Aquinas Institute for the Study of Sacred Doctrine, 2012.

Thomas Aquinas. *Summa Contra Gentiles.* http://www.catholicprimer.org/aquinas/aquinas_summa_contra_gentiles.pdf.

Tocqueville, A. de. *Democracy in America.* Translated by H. Reeve. New York: Bantam Dell, 2002.

Tokarczuk, I. ["Economic Conditions and Man's Spiritual Development according to St. Thomas Aquinas"] *Roczniki Teologiczno-Kanoniczne* 12, no. 3 (1965).

Troska, J. ["The Christian View of Work"]. *Poznanskie Studia Teologiczne* 4 (1983).

Tucker, J. A., and L. H. Rockwell. "The Cultural Thought of Ludwig von Mises." In *The Meaning of Ludwig von Mises.* Edited by J. H. Herbener. Norwell, MA: Kluwer Academic, 1993.

Waldstein, M. "The Common Good in St. Thomas and John Paul II." *Nova et Vetera* (English edition) 3 (2005): 569–78.

Walter, P. ["Idea of Democracy"]. Mises Institute (Polish). http://mises.pl/blog/2007/08/06/patrycja-walter-idea-demokracji-w-pracach-ludwiga-von-misesa/.

Walter, P. ["Property, Freedom, and Cooperation"]. Mises Institute (Polish). http://www.mises.pl/wp-content/uploads/2007/08/pwalter-mises-wlasnosc.pdf.

Waskiewicz, H. ["Natural Law in the Encyclical *Pacem in terris*"]. [*Learned Fascicles of the Catholic University of Lublin*] 1 (1964).

Witczak, H. ["The Image of God in Man—the Source and Aim of Moral Action"]. In [*Theological-Moral Anthropology. Conceptions—Controversies—Inspirations*] Edited by I. Mroczkowski and J. A. Sobkowiak. Warsaw 2008.

Witek, S. ["Egoism"]. In [*The Catholic Encyclopedia*], vol. 4. Edited by G. Lukaszyk, L. Bienkowski, and F. Gryglewicz. Lublin, 1985.

Wojciechowski, M. ["Private Ownership in the Bible"]. In A. A. Chafuen et al., [*Theft and Economic Development*]. Warsaw, 2006.

Wojtkiewicz, K. [*St. Thomas Aquinas' Personalism in "Tract on Man"*]. Olsztyn, 1999.

Woods, T. E. *How the Catholic Church Built Western Civilization.* Washington, DC: Regnery, 2005.

Woods, T. E. *The Church and the Market: A Catholic Defense of the Free Economy.* Lanham, MD: Lexington Books, 2005.

Wyszynski, S. [*The Spirit of Human Labor: A Thought on the Value of Labor*]. Warsaw, 2001.

Younkins, E. W. "Mises' Utilitarianism as Social Cooperation." *Le Quebecois Libre.* July 6, 2002, no. 106, http://www.quebecoislibre.org/020706-19.hml.

Zabielski, J. ["Building a City Worthy of Man: An Inspiring Role for the Social Teaching of the Church in the Creation of Stable Foundations of Social Life"]. *Lomzynskie Wiadomosci Koscielne* 1 (2005).

Zannotii, G. J. "Misesian Praxeology and Christian Philosophy." *Journal of Markets & Morality* 1, no. 1 (Spring 1998): 60–66.

Zeleznik, T. ["Freedom"]. In [*A Dictionary of Catholic Social Doctrine*]. Edited by A. Piwowarski. Warsaw, 1993.

Zieba, M. [*Democracy and Anti-evangelization*]. Poznan, 1997.

Zieba, M. [*The Popes and Capitalism*]. Krakow, 1998.

Zwolinski, A. [*Ethics of Growing Rich*]. Krakow, 2002.

About the Author

Jacek Gniadek SVD (b. 1963) is a Catholic missionary priest and moral theologian. Currently he lives and works in Warsaw, Poland. Previously he worked in Africa (Congo, Botswana, Liberia, and Zambia). He writes on missions and economics, trying to connect the economic and the theological, *homo economicus* and *homo religiosus.*

His second book, *Divine and Human Economy: Free Market Sermons* (Polish, 2015), analyzes Jesus's economic parables from the perspective of the Austrian School of Economics. It proceeds from the belief that there is a strong relationship between Christianity and the principles of the free market, based on a subjective theory of value. The subject of deliberation in the free-market sermons is not the *homo economicus* invented by mainstream economists but a real man who wants to pursue his life vocation within the space of freedom assigned to him by God, within the limits of private property. The free-market sermons are aimed at anyone who knows that he himself is the "basic capital" that must be well invested to achieve his goal, which is eternal life.

www.ingramcontent.com/pod-product-compliance
Ingram Content Group UK Ltd.
Pitfield, Milton Keynes, MK11 3LW, UK
UKHW022025190726
13853UKWH00005B/2118